POLITICS
A Complete Introduction

To my wife, Ju[illegible] and my daughters,
Emmeline and Eleanor

Teach®
Yourself

POLITICS
A Complete Introduction

Peter Joyce

First published in Great Britain in 2015 by Hodder and Stoughton. An Hachette UK company.

British Library Cataloguing in Publication Data: a catalogue record for this title is available from the British Library.

Library of Congress Catalog Card Number: on file.

ISBN: 9781473601529

eISBN: 9781471804519

1

Typeset by Cenveo® Publisher Services.

Printed and bound in Great Britain by CPI Group (UK) Ltd., Croydon, CR0 4YY.

John Murray Learning policy is to use papers that are natural, renewable and recyclable products and made from wood grown in sustainable forests. The logging and manufacturing processes are expected to conform to the environmental regulations of the country of origin.

Hodder & Stoughton Ltd
338 Euston Road
London NW1 3BH
www.hodder.co.uk

Contents

How to use this book

This Complete Introduction from Teach Yourself® includes a number of special boxed features that have been developed to help you understand the subject more quickly and remember it more effectively. Throughout the book, you will find these indicated by the following icons.

 The book includes concise **quotes** from other key sources. These will be useful for helping you understand different viewpoints on the subject, and they are fully referenced so that you can include them in essays if you are unable to get your hands on the source.

 The **case study** is a more in-depth introduction to a particular example. There is at least one in most chapters, and hopefully they will provide good material for essays and class discussions.

 The **key ideas** are highlighted throughout the book. If you only have half an hour to go before your exam, scanning through these would be a very good way of spending your time.

 The **spotlight** boxes give you some light-hearted additional information which will liven up your learning.

 The **fact-check** questions at the end of each chapter are designed to help you ensure you have taken in the most important concepts from the chapter. If you find you are consistently getting several answers wrong, it may be worth trying to read more slowly, or taking notes as you go.

 The **dig deeper** boxes give you ways to explore topics in greater depth than we are able to go to in this introductory level book.

1

Key issues in the study of politics

Human relationships are crucial to the study of politics. Human beings do not live in isolation; we live in communities. These may be small (such as a family) or large (such as a country). Politics embraces the study of the behaviour of individuals within a group context. The focus of its study is broad and includes issues such as inter-group relationships, the management of groups, the operations of collective decision-making processes (especially the activities and operations of the state), and the implementation and enforcement of decisions. The regulation of conflict between individuals and groups is central to the study of the concept of power and the manner in which it is exercised and is a key focus of political analysis. In this chapter we discuss a number of key issues that relate to the study of politics. These are referred to as 'concepts' and provide us with an underpinning of themes and ideas that are considered in more detail throughout this book.

Political culture

Key idea (1)

The term political culture refers to an underlying set of values held by most people living in a particular country concerning political behaviour, one important aspect of which is the degree of trust which citizens have in their political leaders.

We expect to see a number of common features shared by liberal democratic political systems. These include institutions such as a chief executive, legislatures and courts, organizations such as political parties and pressure groups, processes such as elections, and a range of personal freedoms that are guaranteed to every citizen. However, the composition, conduct, powers, relationships, and operations of these common features differ from one country to another so that the workings of the political system in each liberal democracy are subject to wide variation. In France, for example, there is a high degree of tolerance for conflict as a means of settling political disputes, whereas in Sweden the spirit of compromise tends to guide the actions of key participants to the political process. In the United Kingdom there is a tradition of evolutionary rather than revolutionary change.

These differing attitudes influence the conduct of political activity by both politicians and the general public. When we refer to a country's political culture, we are emphasizing the similarity of views held within any particular country. We are suggesting that within any one country there is a tendency for the majority of people to think, feel and act in a similar manner concerning the conduct of political affairs. However, these sentiments may be quite different from the core values espoused by citizens in other liberal democracies.

Nevertheless, the extent of a common political culture can be overstated. Within any country, differences are likely to exist concerning fundamental values related to political behaviour. The term 'homogeneity' denotes a wide level of similarity in these attitudes, but universal agreement is not accorded to them. Factors such as deindustrialization (which has resulted in the emergence of an 'underclass' in many liberal democracies) or immigration (which has led to the development of multi-ethnic societies) have fundamental significance for the existence of universally agreed sentiments underpinning political behaviour. These may give rise to a heterogeneous society (in which dominant attitudes are challenged by sub-cultural values) or result in a looser attachment to mainstream values by some sections of society.

Political Culture

This key political concept has been defined as *'the set of attitudes, beliefs and sentiments that give order and meaning to a political process and which provide the underlying assumptions and rules that govern behaviour in the political system'* (Pye, 1968: 218). A further definition views political culture as *'the political system as internalised in the cognitions, feelings and evaluations of its population'* (Almond and Verba, 1965: 13–14).

Almond, G. and Verba, S. (1965) *The Civic Culture: Political Attitudes in Five Nations.* Boston: Little, Brown and Company.

Pye, L. (1968) Political Culture in D. Sills, R. Merton, (1968) *International Encyclopaedia of the Social Sciences.* New York: Macmillan, Volume 12.

There is debate concerning the development of political cultures and their ability to inform the conduct of political affairs.

Liberal theorists suggest that a country's political culture is fashioned by its unique historical development and is transmitted across the generations by a process termed 'political socialization'. Agencies such as the family, schools, the media, and political parties are responsible for instructing citizens in such beliefs and values.

Marxists, however, tend to view political culture as an artificial creation rather than the product of history. They view political culture as an ideological weapon through which society is indoctrinated to accept the views that are in the interests of its dominant classes (defined as those who own the means of production).

States and governments

Key idea (2)

States and governments are key terms related to the conduct of politics: they may be used interchangeably but have precise definitions that we need to be aware of. These are considered below.

A state consists of a wide range of permanent official institutions (such as the bureaucracy, police, courts, military, parliament, and local government) which are responsible for the organization of communal life within specific geographic boundaries. These entities are usually referred to as a 'country' or 'nation' and the state exercises sovereignty within them. Decisions that are taken in the name of the state are binding on all members of that society and may, if necessary, be enforced by the legitimate use of power to prevent, restrain or punish breaches of the law.

There are a wide range of views concerning the operations of the state, in particular as to whether it displays bias towards certain sections of society. Liberal analysis suggests that the state is neutral and independent of any class interests. It arises out of the voluntary agreement of its members and serves impartially to mediate the conflicts which arise within society, seeking to promote the national interest above sectional concerns. Elite theorists, however, suggest political power is wielded by a ruling elite whose interests are maintained and advanced by the state. Marxism identifies this ruling elite as the economically powerful, the bourgeoisie, and views the state as a mechanism that will mediate between the conflict between capital and labour (which they assert to be inevitable) in order to sustain class exploitation and profit accumulation.

The term 'state' is often substituted for the term 'government'. They are, however, different concepts. 'Government' refers to the institutions concerned with making, implementing and enforcing political decisions. In a narrower sense, government is often associated with those who wield executive power within a state who give direction to its activities. In liberal democracies, political parties compete for control of the state and, in this sense, governments have a limited and temporary existence dependent on the choices made by the public at national election contests, whereas states are permanent entities.

The role of the state

Key idea (3)

When we discuss the role of the state we are referring to the services that the state provides for its citizens. These functions are subject to variation between states, and also within one state across historical time periods, which raises the issue as to what the legitimate scope of state activity is.

There are widely differing views concerning the desirable scope of state activity. Historically the role of the state was confined to a few key areas, which usually included defence and foreign affairs. The development of social policy added to these responsibilities in some countries during the nineteenth century. Many states were subject to pressures during and following the Second World

War, which drastically increased the role of state activity. In the UK, for example, this period witnessed the development of the welfare state. The concept of a welfare state implies that the state plays a major role in promoting the economic and social well-being of its citizens. In the UK, this concept was considerably advanced by the Beveridge Report, which urged the government to tackle the 'five giants' of Want, Disease, Ignorance, Squalor and Idleness. This gave rise to measures that included the 1948 National Insurance Act, the 1948 National Assistance Act and the 1948 National Health Service Act, an acceptance that the maintenance of full employment should be a state responsibility, and the placing of several key industries under state control and direction through the policy termed 'nationalisation'.

Political ideology (an issue that is explored in Chapter 3) is important in influencing the level of state activity. In the UK, liberalism in the nineteenth century was sceptical of increasing the role of the state, whereas socialism sought to expand it during the twentieth century.

During the 1980s, governments influenced by New Right ideology, especially that of Margaret Thatcher in the UK and Ronald Reagan in America, succeeded in reversing the trend towards increased state activity by 'rolling back' the frontiers of the state in both economic and social areas of responsibility. In the economic sphere, the free market and private enterprise were seen as superior to state control or involvement, which was depicted as both wasteful and inefficient. It was further alleged that the role played by the state in people's lives undermined their capacity for personal responsibility and created a culture of dependency. This culture was said to enhance the power of the bureaucracies that administered state-provided services. Those who received state aid (for example, in the form of welfare payments) were depicted as being dependent on the state and thus relinquished their ability to take decisions affecting the conduct of their everyday lives. The thinking, active citizen had therefore been transformed into a passive recipient of handouts while those in employment were adversely affected by the high level of taxation needed to finance the existing activities performed by the state.

Power, authority and legitimacy

Key idea (4)

A major concern of politics is to provide an understanding as to why we obey those who rule over us. The terms 'power', 'authority' and 'legitimacy' are important concepts that help to explain why as citizens we do what our governments tell us to do.

A major concern of a government is to secure the obedience of its citizens to its decisions.

Political obligation is the concept that seeks to explain why, and under what circumstances, citizens are required to obey their governments. There are various explanations for this, although an important one is the idea that the existence of government and the powers which it exercises are based on the consent of the governed. This is a central belief put forward in social contract political philosophies. Should a government undermine the rights and liberties of the citizen it was established to protect, it is morally acceptable to disobey the state's laws and, in extreme circumstances, to institute a new government which does possess the consent of its people.

There are two further concepts that are related to explaining why a government is able to secure popular compliance to its objectives or policies. These are power and authority.

POWER

Power consists of a relationship between two parties in which one has the ability to compel the other to undertake a course of action that would not necessarily have been carried out voluntarily. The preferences of one party become binding on the other because the former has the ability to compel compliance by the threat or the use of penalties. The desire to avoid the penalty thus ensures the obedience of one party to another. Governments may exercise power over their citizens by compelling them to either obey the law or suffer some form of punishment administered by the law enforcement agencies if they fail to do so. However, in liberal democratic political structures, coercion is often coupled with resources at the government's disposal, enabling it to offer rewards in addition to or as well as coercive means to secure obedience. Social security benefits, for example, may be paid to poor people to encourage them to lead law-abiding, crime-free lives.

The nature of power is a fundamental issue for the study of politics. Three dimensions to power have been identified. The one-dimensional view of power refers to the ability of individuals to alter the behaviour of others who are involved in the decision-making process, and thus ensure that their wishes prevail. This often involves getting others to do something that they would not otherwise agree to undertake. The second dimension of power focuses on the ability of individuals to achieve their ends through manipulating the political agenda to produce an outcome that they wish. An important aspect of this is the ability to keep items off of the agenda, or exclude those with a legitimate interest in participating in the decision-making process. Both of these dimensions suggest that some form of conflict was a necessary component of attaining power.

However, the third dimension is a means of power that may be secured by methods that avoid the use of conflict and through the use of non-coercive means. These include such methods as ideological control, which succeeds in manipulating people's needs and preferences to endorse a position that might be prejudicial to their own needs or concerns – *'A exercises power over B when A affects B in a manner contrary to B's interests'* (Lukes, 1974: 34).

This view was summarized by arguing that *'A may exercise power over B by getting him to do what he does not want to do, but he also exercises power over him by influencing, shaping or determining his very wants'* (Lukes, 1974: 23). This may happen *'in the absence of observable conflict, which may have been successfully averted'* (Lukes, 1974: 25). It was asserted that *'the most effective and insidious use of power is to prevent such conflict from arising in the first place'* (Lukes, 2004: 27 and 28–9).

Lukes, S. (1974) *Power: A Radical View.* Basingstoke: Macmillan.

Lukes, S. (2004) *Power: A Radical View.* Basingstoke: Palgrave / Macmillan, 2nd ed.

The exercise of power by a government is closely entwined with a consideration of the source of the power that it wields. There is, however, disagreement concerning the manner in which power is distributed within society.

Pluralists argue that power is widely distributed throughout society and that the role of the state is to adjudicate in the constant competition that exists between competing groups and interests. Decisions thus reflect the process of bargaining between such diverse bodies which is dispassionately presided over by the government.

Elitist theories, however, contend that power is concentrated in the hands of a relatively small, organized group of people, and that this minority is able to force its will on the majority of citizens. Marxists identify the ruling elite as those who possess economic power within society and who are able to use the political system and the actions undertaken by the government to further their own interests.

Power is different from influence, which entails the ability of governments (and also of those who are not participants to the formal policy-making process) to be able to affect the content and nature of public policy. Their ability to secure subsequent compliance to these decisions may be based upon factors that include the intellectual weight of arguments which are put forward rather than the ability to enforce penalties.

AUTHORITY

The second explanation to account for governments being able to exert control over their citizens is the authority possessed by such institutions. Authority is based on moral force. An individual or institution that possesses authority secures compliance to its suggestions primarily when there is general agreement that those who put forward such ideas have the right to propose and implement them. Citizens thus obey governments because there is a general consensus that it has the right to take decisions, even if the content of them may not always be generally popular.

The sociologist Max Weber suggested that authority could be derived from one of three sources. The first of these was **traditional authority,** where acceptance of the right to rule is based on custom. Popular consent is accorded to decisions made by those from a background that traditionally exercises the functions of government within a state. Hereditary monarchs (who rule by virtue of birth) enjoy this form of authority. Second was **charismatic authority**, which is derived from characteristics that are personal to a political leader. The main criterion for obedience is that the public stand in awe of the person taking decisions. Charisma is particularly associated with dictators, including Adolf Hitler in Germany and Juan Péron who served as President of Argentina between 1946–55 and 1973–74. The final source was **legal-bureaucratic** or **legal-rational** authority. In this case, compliance to decisions made by rulers is based on the office that an individual holds within a state and not his or her personal characteristics. It is thus the prestige accorded by the public to an office that influences the ability of an official to secure acceptance to his or her wishes.

In liberal democratic political systems the political office occupied by those who give orders forms the main basis of their authority. We accept that presidents or prime ministers have the right to give orders by virtue of the public positions they occupy. However, political leaders frequently derive their authority from more than one source: in Britain the association of the prime minister with a government carried out in the name of the monarch gives this office holder authority derived from both traditional and legal-bureaucratic sources.

In liberal democracies, governments possess both power and authority. They are obeyed partly because there is general consent that they have the right to govern, but also because the police, courts and penal system may be used as a sanction to force compliance to their laws. Power that is divorced from authority is likely to produce an unstable political structure in which violence, disorder and revolution threaten the existence of the government.

LEGITIMACY

Legitimacy entails popular acceptance of the exercise of power. It is closely linked to the concept of authority that underpins our acceptance of a ruler's right to govern. The term is commonly applied to political systems, whereas authority is generally related to specific public officials.

In liberal democratic political systems, legitimacy is founded on the notion of popular consent derived from elections in which all citizens are entitled to participate (and are required to if voting is compulsory, which is the case in some countries). Securing victory at an election is the basis of a government's legitimacy. This legitimacy permits the government to claim the obedience of its citizens to the actions which are subsequently undertaken, provided they are in accordance with the established rules of political conduct. Marxists, however, emphasize that legitimacy entails public acceptance of the distribution of power within society. This view asserts that legitimacy is not derived from genuine popular approval but, rather, is the product of ideological control exerted in the interests of the ruling class over the masses and is designed to secure their acceptance of political, social and economic inequality.

Legitimacy, whether it is based upon manipulation or genuine popular approval, is important in establishing a stable government that is able to draw upon the obedience of its citizens. However, legitimacy may be undermined by a range of political, social or economic factors, such as repeated failures by governments to act in accordance with the wishes of their citizens or by perceptions that those who occupy political office seek to use their position to bring them personal benefits. Factors such as these may result in what is termed a 'legitimation crisis' in which citizens question the right of the government to remain in office and take decisions.

The rule of law

Key idea (5)

The rule of law suggests that the power wielded by the state over its citizens is based upon clearly laid-down procedures embodied in law which are subject to universal application – it applies to all of us. The rule of law also regulates the conduct of individual citizens towards each other.

The rule of law suggests that when citizens have broken the law, they can only be punished by the state using formalized procedures, and that all citizens will be treated in the same way when they commit wrongdoings. Nobody is 'above the law': penalties cannot be handed out in an arbitrary manner and the punishments meted out for similar crimes should be the same regardless of who has committed them. This suggests that the law is applied dispassionately and is not subject to the biases and prejudices of those who enforce it. Additionally, all citizens should be aware of the contents of the law. The rule of law, therefore, provides a powerful safeguard to the citizen against arbitrary actions committed by the state and its officials, and is best guaranteed by a judiciary that is independent of the other branches of government.

This principle may be grounded in common law, which was historically the situation in Britain, or it may be incorporated into a codified constitution, as is the case in America.

In America, the freedom of citizens from arbitrary actions undertaken by government is incorporated into the Constitution. This insists that punitive actions can arise only as the result of formal legal procedures in which the right of the accused is protected through provisions that include double jeopardy (not being tried twice for the same criminal offence) and which prohibit self-incrimination (not being required to testify against yourself).

The fifth amendment (ratified in 1791) states that no person should *be subject for the same offence to be twice put in jeopardy of life or limb; nor shall be compelled in any criminal case to be a witness against himself, nor be deprived of life, liberty or property, without due process of law.'* The term 'pleading the fifth' is used by defendants who wish to not answer questions put to them in a court of law if they fear the answers may be prejudicial to their defence.

The fourteenth amendment (ratified in 1868 following the Civil War) states that *'No state shall make or enforce any law which shall abridge the privileges or immunities of citizens of the United States; nor shall any state deprive any person of life, liberty, or property, without due process of law.'*

Source: *The Constitution of the United States*,
Amendment 5 and Amendment 14.

Although many of the requirements embodied in the principle of the rule of law constitute practices that are widely adhered to in liberal democracies, most liberal democratic states deviate from the strict application of the rule of law. Factors, which include social background, financial means, class, race or gender, may play an influential part in determining whether a citizen who transgresses the law is proceeded against by the state and may also have a major bearing on the outcome of any trial. Additionally, governments may deviate from strict application of the rule of law when emergencies occur. Marxists equate the rule of law with the protection of private property rights, which they view as underpinning the social inequalities and class exploitation found in capitalist societies.

Equality

Key idea (6)

Equality refers to the ideal of citizens being equal. There are, however, several dimensions to the concept of equality, and a diverse range of measures through this ideal can be achieved.

Initially, equality sought to remove the privileges enjoyed by certain groups within society so that all of its members were able to lead their lives without impediments derived from factors such as birth, race, gender or religion being placed upon them. This is termed *formal equality* and is based on views such as the assertion in the American Declaration of Independence (1776) that 'all men are created equal'. This perception of a shared common humanity underpinned the extension of civic rights to all members of society. These included the rule of law (which emphasized equality of all citizens before the law) and reforms such as the abolition of slavery and the removal of restrictions to voting, thus providing for universal male and female enfranchisement.

Although formal equality removed the unfair disadvantages operating against some citizens, it did not tackle the underlying social or economic factors that might enable some members of society to achieve more than others. Other forms of equality have addressed this issue. *Social equality* is especially concerned with improving the status and self-esteem of traditionally disadvantaged groups in society. Equality of opportunity has underpinned reforms to aid materially the poorer and weaker members of society, often achieved by some measure of redistribution of wealth. From 1945 onwards, this concept gave rise to the welfare state in the United Kingdom.

In more recent years, the goal of formal equality has underpinned efforts by government to tackle discrimination based on factors such as race, gender or disability. In the UK, this has taken the form of legislation that has included the 1970 Equal Pay Act, the 1975 Sex Discrimination Act and the 2006 and 2010 Equality Acts as well as a range of measures seeking to combat aspects of racial discrimination, commencing with the 1965 Race Relations Act.

The UK Equalities and Human Rights Commission (EHRC)

Some governments have set up organizations to advance equality and combat discrimination suffered by groups within society. Here we consider the role performed by the UK's Equalities and Human Rights Commission (EHRC).

The EHRC was set up under the provisions of the 2006 Equality Act. It was formed from three existing commissions that had responsibility for combating discrete forms of discrimination – the Commission for Racial Equality, Disability Rights Commission and the Equal Opportunities Commission. The EHRC's remit does not extend to Northern Ireland where a separate Equality Commission for Northern Ireland was set up by the Northern Ireland Act 1998.

The EHRC has the status of an executive Non-Departmental Public Body, sponsored by the Department of Culture, Media and Sport. It reports to the Government's Equality Office. Its mission is to act as a catalyst for change and improvement on issues related to equality and human rights in order to promote a fairer and more equal society. In doing so, it is subject to the Public Sector Equality Duty.

The EHRC monitors human rights and combats discrimination, protecting equality across nine specified areas – age, disability, gender, race, religion and belief, pregnancy and maternity, marriage and civil partnership, sexual orientation and gender reassignment. It performs this role in a number of ways, giving information to individuals regarding their rights and providing information to a range of organizations including businesses, public authorities and schools relating to their responsibilities under equality law. In cases where an individual's rights have been breached, the EHRC may provide legal advice and, in some circumstances, take cases to court (especially if the case seems to raise legal issues that have not previously been tested in a court). The EHRC also funds organizations that provide aid and advice in relation to discrimination and human rights and seeks to influence government policy in the areas of equality and discrimination.

Of special significance is the ability of the EHRC to conduct a formal inquiry into organizations where it seems that equality, diversity, human rights or good relations between groups have been breached in contravention of the 2010 Equality Act. One example of this was its decision in September 2014 to carry out an investigation into unlawful discrimination, harassment and victimization of persons employed by London's Metropolitan Police Service (MPS).

Some socialists favour *equality of outcome*, which seeks a common level of attainment regardless of an individual's background, personal circumstances or the position in society which they occupy. This may entail a levelling-out process, whereby some members of society are penalized in order to ensure social equality. The abolition of wage differentials (so that all persons were paid the same wage regardless of the job they performed) would be one way to secure equality of outcome.

Spotlight

Social prejudices make it difficult for groups that have historically suffered discrimination to secure a position of equality in society. At the 1997 UK general election, 101 female Labour MPs were elected who supported the government headed by Tony Blair. These were insultingly referred to in some sections of the media as 'Blair's Babes'.

AFFIRMATIVE ACTION

Affirmative action (or 'positive discrimination') refers to a programme of measures designed to give preferential treatment to certain groups who have historically been disadvantaged as the result of discrimination encountered within a society. Such groups may include racial minorities, who suffer from such problems as social and economic deprivation and political marginalization, but may also embrace other minorities such as persons with physical handicaps and those who have been the victims of popular prejudice by virtue of their sexuality.

Affirmative action is a more radical approach than equal opportunity programmes. The latter seeks to ensure that members of disadvantaged groups do not experience discrimination in areas such as job applications or interviews, and will be treated on a par with applicants not drawn from minority groups. Affirmative action, however, seeks to ensure that positive steps are taken to guarantee that members of disadvantaged groups can gain access to facilities such as jobs, housing and education. One means of securing this is through the use of quotas, this would ensure, for example, that in an area in which 25 per cent of the population were from an African–Caribbean background, employment opportunities in the public and private sectors would reflect this ratio.

Affirmative action programmes were initiated in America by the 1964 Civil Rights Act. Title VI of that Act prohibited discrimination under any programme that received any form of federal financial assistance and Title VII made it illegal to discriminate in employment matters.

To be effective, affirmative action needs to be underpinned by strong sanctions which may be applied against those who continue to discriminate against disadvantaged groups. American courts are empowered to hear class actions (that is, an application on behalf of an entire group which alleges discrimination and which, if successful, will result in all members being compensated). However, critics of this approach believe that failing to treat all members of society equally can result in injustices.

In America, for example, unhappiness with the application of affirmative action to university admissions (which could mean that qualified candidates were overlooked in favour of less qualified ones for whom a set number of places had been set aside) resulted in the Supreme Court case of Regents of the University of California v. Bakke (1978), prohibiting the use of rigid racial quotas for medical school admissions (although it did not prevent race being considered a factor when determining admissions, a situation which was latterly confirmed by the Supreme Court in 2003 in a decision affecting the admissions policy of Michigan State University's law school). New Right politicians were sceptical of affirmative action, believing that the position of disadvantaged minorities would be enhanced through the expanding economy rather than as the result of affirmative action programmes.

Dig Deeper

Bingham, T. (2010) *The Rule of Law*. London: Allen Lane.

Budge, I. et al. (2007) *The New British Politics*. London: Routledge, 4th ed.

Jones, B. and Norton, P. (2010) *Politics UK*. Harlow: Longman, 7th ed.

Moran, M. (2011) *Politics and Governance in the UK*. Basingstoke: Palgrave/Macmillan, 2nd ed.

Garnett, M. and Lynch, P. (2009) *Exploring British Politics*. Harlow: London, 2nd ed.

Fact-check

1 A body that exercises power may secure obedience to its decisions by:
   a Persuasion
   b The use of sanctions
   c Authority
   d Bribery

2 The concept that seeks to explain why and under what circumstances citizens are required to obey the government is termed:
   a The rule of law
   b Political obligation
   c Political culture
   d Legitimacy

3 In America, a citizen who 'pleads the Fifth' is:
   a Refusing to answer questions because they may be self-incriminatory
   b Refusing to acknowledge the authority of the Fifth amendment of the American Constitution
   c Pleading guilty to the fifth charge s/he is accused of
   d Asking the fifth witness to withdraw his/her testimony

4 Social equality seeks to:
   a Make all citizens equal before the law
   b Introduce quota systems to guarantee equal opportunities in the job market
   c Enable more women to be elected to public office
   d Improve the status and self-esteem of traditionally disadvantaged groups in society

5 In liberal democratic political systems, legitimacy is founded on:
   a Popular consent
   b Election to public office
   c Power
   d Authority

6 Liberal analysis argues that the state:
   a Has the same meaning as 'government'
   b Is neutral of class interests
   c Is controlled by an economically powerful elite
   d Is too powerful and its role should be reduced

2

Liberal democracy

In this chapter we will consider the liberal democratic political system. This is the system mostly used in the Western World and the one we are most familiar with. We will identify the key features of the system and, in particular, will consider the mechanisms through which the wishes of the majority of the population are able to influence the operations of government and the conduct of the legislature.

Political systems

Key idea (1)

There are a wide variety of political systems throughout the world. These consist of 'liberal democratic', 'communist', 'totalitarian' and 'oligarchic' political systems. These systems are distinguished from one another by a process of differentiation termed classification.

A political system is the constitutional framework through which demands are put forward and decisions are made. It has no physical dimension or formal existence, but consists of the institutions, processes and relationships involved in the process of agenda setting, policy formulation and decision making. These include the formal institutions of government and informal agencies such as the media.

Political systems are distinguished from each other in a number of ways. The process of differentiation is termed 'classification'. There are four broad types of political systems – liberal democratic, communist, totalitarian and oligarchic. The extent of civil rights in liberal democratic systems facilitates a wider degree of public participation in political affairs than is permitted in the other two systems.

In liberal democratic political systems, members of the general public may secure involvement in policy making through mechanisms that allow them to express their views to the policy makers on particular issues. Consultation implies the right to be heard. Citizens may be invited to express their opinions on particular matters to which the policy makers listen, but are not required to act on. Participation, however, involves a shift in the power relationship between policy makers and the public. Policy making is transformed into a joint exercise involving governors and the governed.

Political participation is a key feature of liberal democracy. American political scientists described it as follows: *'Political participation affords citizens in a democracy an opportunity to communicate information to government officials about their concerns and preferences and to put pressure on them to respond ... They may express their views directly by communicating with public officials or indirectly by attempting to influence electoral outcomes; they may give time and effort or contribute dollars; they may work alone or in concert with others; they may be active at the national, state or local level'* (Verba et al., 1995: 37).

Participation differs from consultation, which is also a feature of the operations of liberal democratic political systems.
Verba, S., Schlozman, K. and Brady, H. (1995) *Voice and Equality: Civic Voluntarism in American Politics.* Cambridge, Massachusetts: Harvard University Press.

Consultation and participation might be regarded as beneficial to liberal democracies as they permit the policy preferences of the public to be considered or acted on by public officials. However, the lack of information in the hands of the general public might make meaningful discussion impossible and may result in the public being manipulated into giving their backing to contentious proposals put forward by the policy makers.

Communist political systems (sometimes referred to as socialist democracies) are political systems based on the ideas of Karl Marx. The most notable feature of communist states is the paramount position of an official socialist ideology and the domination or total monopolization of political affairs by the official Communist Party, whose leading members exert control over institutions such as trade unions, the media and the military, and over key state-provided services such as education. Considerable differences exist between communist states although, in general, these countries are characterized by the existence of little or no private property ownership, a planned economy (which is viewed as essential to achieving equality and classlessness) and a comprehensive welfare state.

Communist states included the former Soviet Union and its East European satellite neighbours, but following the 'collapse of communism' in Eastern Europe between 1989 and 1991, it is now confined to a smaller number of countries which include the People's Republic of China, Vietnam, Cuba and North Korea.

Totalitarian political systems are those in which the state controls every aspect of the political, social, cultural and economic life of its citizens. It is governed by a ruling elite whose power is based upon ideological control exerted over the masses and underpinned by the use of coercive methods for control. Civil liberties, human rights and the ability of citizens to participate in decision making are very limited, if not totally absent in such societies. The term 'authoritarian' applies to societies that are also governed by an elite with considerable power, although this is not always exerted over every aspect of civil life as is the case with totalitarianism.

The ideology that is found in totalitarian societies is subject to wide variation. Communist political systems exhibit totalitarian characteristics as they are totally under the control of the Communist Party. Other totalitarian regimes may be dominated by the ideology of fascism, in which only one political party is permitted to exist and representative institutions such as directly elected legislatures are typically absent.

Regimes of this nature may also be based upon a religious ideology. These are termed 'theocracies', a word that literally means 'rule by God'. A main feature of theocratic government is its intolerance of viewpoints other than those of the dominant religious sect. Religion or faith plays a dominant role in those countries with this form of government: for example, in Iran the president and legislature (which are elected) are subject to the supervision and direction of the clerics. Similarly, the operations of government in Saudi Arabia (which is technically a monarchy) are controlled by a version of the Shari'a (a term which denotes traditional Islamic law) and the Koran that effectively constitutes that country's constitution.

Totalitarian regimes differ from oligarchic ones. An oligarchy is a political system in which power is held by a small group of persons who govern in their own interests rather than seeking to advance a political ideology. These interests may be economic or may consist of the desire to wield power. As with totalitarian regimes, few political freedoms exist in oligarchic regimes. The general public is not allowed to play any part in politics and these regimes are frequently characterized by brutality and coercion meted out by the police or military who exercise a prominent role in civil affairs. Oligarchies embrace a wide variety of political arrangements, including military dictatorships and one-party states, and are typically found in less-developed countries.

Democracy and liberal democracy?

Key idea (2)

A democratic society is one in which political power resides with the people who live there: it is they who are sovereign. A democratic political system is one whose actions reflect the will of the people (or at least the majority of them).

Democratic government was initiated in the Greek city state of Athens in the fifth century BC. The word 'democracy' is derived from two Greek words, *demos* (meaning 'people') and *kratos* (meaning 'power'). The term literally means 'government by the people'. Initially, major decisions were taken by meetings at which all free males attended. It was possible for government to function in this way when the population was small and when the activity of the state was limited. Today, however, ancient city states have been replaced by bigger units of government with a greater range of responsibilities delivered to larger numbers of people. It was necessary, therefore, to invent a political system through which the notion of popular sovereignty could be reconciled with an effective decision-making process. We term such a political system 'liberal democracy'. It has two fundamental characteristics. Government is 'liberal' in terms of the core values which underpin it and 'democratic' concerning the political arrangements that exist within it.

There are many definitions of democracy. It has been asserted that *'Democracy is direct self-government over all the people, for all the people, by all the people'* (Parker, 1858). These words were subsequently repeated by President Lincoln in a speech delivered following the Civil War Battle of Gettysburg in 1863.

Parker, T. (1858) sermon delivered in Boston, Massachusetts July 4 entitled 'The Effect of Slavery on the American People'. Cited in *Quote / Counter Quote*. [Online] *http://www.quotecounterquote.com/2010/11/ government-of-people-by-people-for.html* [Accessed 11 May 2014].

LIBERAL DEMOCRATIC POLITICAL SYSTEMS

Key idea (3)

In a liberal democratic political system, governments function in the name of the people and are ultimately accountable to them for the actions that they undertake.

A political system consists of the formal and informal processes through which demands are put forward and decisions are made. The term 'system' implies that the component parts that shape decision making form part of an integrated structure. The stability of this structure is secured by the actions undertaken by governments broadly matching the demands placed upon it by public opinion, however this is articulated. If this fails to be the case, disequilibrium may occur in which demands outstrip a government's willingness or ability to match them. This may result in revolution.

As we argued above, several forms of political systems exist throughout the world, a key distinction concerning the allocation of power. In liberal democratic political systems, the public possesses the ability to make demands through a number of channels, which include political parties, pressure groups, the media, elections, and extra-parliamentary political action. The suggestions put forward in this manner are key aspects of the agenda for the consideration of the formal institutions of government (the legislature, judiciary, executive and bureaucracy), who may also put forward policy proposals of their own. These institutions determine whether to act on demands which are presented to them and, if so, through what means. Their actions may involve repealing contentious legislation, enacting new laws or taking policy or budgetary decisions.

Popular consent in liberal democratic political systems is secured through representation: liberal (or, as it is sometimes referred to, representative) democracy entails a small group of people making political decisions on behalf of all citizens who live in a particular country. Those who exercise this responsibility do so with the consent of the citizens and govern in their name. However, their right to take decisions depends on popular approval, and may be withdrawn should they lose the support of the population to whom they are accountable for their actions. In these cases, citizens reclaim the political power they have ceded and reallocate the responsibility for government elsewhere. Elections, which provide a genuine opportunity to exert popular choice over the actions and personnel of government, are thus an essential aspect of liberal democracies. This requires all adults having the right to vote, the regular holding of elections, and political parties being able to compete openly for power.

There are wide variations in the political structures that exist within liberal democratic political systems. A major distinction is between those that have presidential systems of government (such as America) and those that have parliamentary systems (such as the United Kingdom). In some cases, the executive branch of government tends to be derived from one political party, but in others it is drawn from a coalition of parties, perhaps making for a more consensual style of government.

Liberal democratic political systems are associated with the capitalist economies of first world countries. Marxists allege that an incompatibility exists between the political equality and social inequality found in such countries. They dismiss liberal democracy as 'bourgeois democracy' whose values and operations are underpinned by the defence of private property ownership and whose legitimacy is secured through the ideological control exercised by the ruling class.

ACCOUNTABILITY

Accountability (which is often referred to as responsibility) is a key aspect of a liberal democratic political system. This term denotes that an individual or organization to whom power has been delegated is required to submit to the scrutiny of another body or bodies to answer for the actions which have been undertaken. Additionally, the body or bodies to whom the organization or individual is answerable possesses sanctions which can be used in the event of actions being undertaken which are deemed to be unacceptable.

There are two forms of accountability. The individual or organization may have to seek prior permission before taking actions. Alternatively, accountability may entail an individual or organization being free to take actions but are required to report what has been done to another body. This is termed *ex post facto* accountability.

In liberal democratic political systems, governments are accountable to the electorate. While in office they may take decisions, but the electorate has the ultimate ability to remove them from power at a national election if they disapprove of what has been performed. Elections are thus an essential aspect of liberal democracy that enables the public to exert influence over the legislative and executive branches of government and hold them accountable for their actions. Effective accountability also requires that citizens are in possession of information by which to judge the activities undertaken by public officials. Many liberal democracies provide for this through freedom of information legislation, enabling public access to official documents.

Additionally, governments in liberal democratic political systems are accountable to legislatures. They may be required to submit their policies to the scrutiny of legislative bodies, and in parliamentary forms of government, such as that in the United Kingdom, legislatures possess the ability to remove the government by passing a vote of 'no confidence' in it.

ELECTORAL PROCEDURES AND LIBERAL DEMOCRACIES

Key idea (4)

Elections are an essential aspect of the liberal democratic political process. However, they require the existence of a range of procedures to ensure that they are fairly conducted and that the result genuinely reflects popular opinion.

Citizens in liberal democracies enjoy a wide range of civil and political liberties. These include entitlements such as the freedoms of expression, movement and association, the existence of an impartial judicial system, and freedom from arbitrary arrest. Of particular importance, however, are the procedures that determine how we choose our representatives.

Liberal democracies require mechanisms whereby the general public can exercise choice over who will represent them, and also to dismiss such persons if they feel that policies lacking popular support are being pursued. This suggests that elections are essential to the operations of liberal democratic political systems. However, elections are not confined to liberal democracies. Countries with alternative political systems may also utilize them. An essential characteristic of elections in liberal democracies is that these contests should provide a genuine opportunity to exert popular choice over the personnel and policies of government. Below we consider some of the mechanisms to ensure that the outcome of elections represent public opinion.

FREEDOM OF POLITICAL EXPRESSION

Elections will only provide the public with meaningful political choice if a diverse range of opinions can be articulated. Measures which impose censorship on the media, or which place restrictions or bans on political parties, trade unions or other forms of political activity must be pursued extremely cautiously by liberal democratic governments. The freedom of speech, thought and action are essential features of liberal democracies, distinguishing them from more totalitarian systems in which the ability to dissent is limited.

Nonetheless, a line needs to be drawn between what is acceptable political behaviour and what the state is justified in wishing to prohibit. This affects issues such as what political parties are allowed to say and the means they use to put their case across to the electorate. We refer to this as political toleration.

One justification for imposing restrictions on the freedom of political expression is where parties fail to support the basic principles underlying liberal democracy. For example, a party might achieve power through the ballot box, but once installed in power will transform a country's political system into a totalitarian one. The 1947 Italian Constitution banned the re-formation of the Fascist Party on these grounds, while the 1958 French Constitution stipulated that political parties must respect the principles of national sovereignty and democracy. A similar provision applies in the 1949 German Constitution.

The doctrines put forward by a political party may, further, be viewed as threatening, not merely to a country's political system but to the very existence of the state itself, and therefore limits on political activity can be deemed to be justified. Fear of the Soviet Union and communism (which was believed to be embarking upon a quest for world domination) was prominent in America during the 1950s. The American Communist Party was banned by the 1954 Communist Control Act, and perceived sympathy for communism led to discriminatory actions against individuals such as dismissal from employment.

The methods used by political organizations may also justify curbs on political expression. Organizations whose views, opinions or statements offend other citizens (and may possibly provoke violence against them) may be subject to restrictions in order to maintain public order. Groups which actually carry out acts of violence to further their political objectives are also likely to be the subject of state constraints. In the United Kingdom, for example, groups which utilize violence to further their political ends are banned (or 'proscribed') by the 2000 Terrorism Act.

A WIDE ELECTORATE

The exercise of popular control over government necessitates a broad electorate in which the vast majority of the population possesses the right to vote. We refer to this as 'the franchise'. In the nineteenth century, the franchise in many countries was based on property ownership: those who owned little or no property were not regarded as citizens and thus were unable to play any part in conventional political activities. The enfranchisement of adults, regardless of wealth, gender or race, is necessary to ensure that government accurately reflects the wishes of their populations, and progress towards universal adult suffrage is a major measurement by which progress towards establishing liberal democracy can be judged.

THE TIMING OF ELECTIONS

Elections facilitate popular control over the activities of government only if they are held regularly and if their timing is not totally determined by the incumbent office holders. In some countries, legislators or executives hold office for a fixed period of time, at the end of which fresh elections must be held. In America, for example, the president is elected for a four-year term, while members of the House of Representatives and the Senate serve for two and six years respectively. Other countries do not hold elections at predetermined intervals. In the United Kingdom, for example, the executive has the ability to determine when general elections are held, subject to the proviso that fresh elections to the House of Commons must take place at least every five years.

ELIGIBILITY TO BE A CANDIDATE FOR NATIONAL OFFICE

There are a wide variety of regulations in liberal democracies governing eligibility to stand as a candidate for national office. In the United Kingdom, these rules are very broad. Any citizen over the age of 18 (subject to disqualifications laid down in legislation enacted in 1975) may seek election to parliament. A candidate merely requires endorsement from ten registered voters in the constituency he or she wishes to contest and a deposit of £500 (which is returned if the candidate secures over 5 per cent of the votes cast in the election).

In other countries the rules are more complex. Candidates may be required to be nominees of political parties, which in turn may be subject to controls governing their ability to contest elections. These may require a party to demonstrate a stipulated level of support in order to be entered on the ballot paper. In Germany, candidates must be nominated by a party with at least five representatives in the *Bundestag* or a state parliament or (in the case of a new party) have given formal notice to the Federal Election Committee of their intention to contest the election. Additionally, candidates must be nominated by 200 persons who are eligible to vote.

THE CONDUCT OF ELECTIONS

Public involvement in political activities occurs only when elections are conducted fairly. Factors, which include the secret ballot and freedom from intimidation, are required to ensure that the outcome of election contests reflects genuine public sentiments. Electoral districts should also be constructed fairly to prevent candidates benefitting from the way in which they are composed and each should contain approximately the same number of electors to ensure that all votes are of equal value in an election contest.

Spotlight

Attempts to rig the construction of electoral districts to benefit one candidate over another are referred to as 'gerrymandering'. *'The term "gerrymander" comes from the original manipulation of district lines in Massachusetts in 1811, when Governor Elbridge Gerry signed a bill that created a district* [in which the majority of the voters were sympathetic to his Democratic-Republican party] *in the shape of a salamander to promote his party's interests'* (Canon, 2002: 150). 'Gerrymander' is an amalgam of 'Gerry' and 'salamander'.

Canon, D. (2002) Electoral Systems and the Representation of Minority Interests in Legislatures in G. Loewenberg, P. Squire and D. Kiewiet (eds) *Legislatures: Comparative Perspectives in Representative Assemblies.* Michigan: University of Michigan Press, pp 149–177.

Liberal democracy also requires incumbent office holders to accept the verdict delivered by the electorate and not to oppose it by methods which have sometimes been utilized by non-democratic systems of government. These include setting election results aside by declaring them null and void, or supporting a military take-over to preserve the political status quo when an election has demonstrated popular support for fundamental change.

Legislators and public opinion

Key idea (5)

Those elected to legislatures in a liberal democratic political system should represent public opinion. There are a number of dimensions involved in achieving this ideal.

We have argued that liberal democracy involves a small group of people taking political decisions on behalf of the entire population. This typically takes the form of what we term 'territorial representation' whereby legislators represent a specific geographic area and those who live there. There is, however, an alternative form of representation termed 'functional representation'. This entails legislators representing specific sectional or vocational interests rather than being directly elected by the general public. The Irish *Seanad* is partly constituted on this basis.

In the sections that follow we will consider whether persons elected to legislatures (who are termed 'legislators') adequately reflect public opinion.

THE PARTY SYSTEM

Parties may enhance public involvement in policy making, although the extent to which they achieve this is dependent on factors such as the size of their membership. Further, the development of party systems may distort the relationship between an elected official and his or her electorate. Voters may support candidates for public office on the basis of their party label rather than their perceived ability to put forward the needs of local electors. While in office, party discipline may force legislators to sacrifice locality to party if these interests do not coincide. The extent to which this happens depends on the strength of party discipline, which is stronger in some liberal democracies, such as the United Kingdom, Australia and New Zealand, than in others, such as America, where local influences (termed 'parochialism') play a significant part in determining a voter's choice of candidate for public office.

THE ELECTORAL SYSTEM

Electoral systems vary in the extent to which those who are elected to legislatures accurately reflect the voting preferences of members of the general public. A fundamental division exists between the first-past-the-post electoral system and proportional representation. In the United Kingdom, for example, the former has been charged with distorting the wishes of the electorate and producing a legislative body that does not accord with popular opinion as expressed at a general election. We will consider these issues more fully in Chapter 4.

THE STATUS OF LEGISLATORS

Those who are elected to legislatures (termed 'legislators') may fulfill the role of either a delegate or a representative. A delegate is an elected official who follows the instructions of the electorate as and when these are given. A delegate has little freedom of action and is effectively mandated by voters to act in a particular manner. A representative claims the right to exercise his or her judgement on matters which arise. Once elected to office a representative's actions are determined by that person's conscience and not by instructions delivered by voters. A representative can, however, be held accountable by the public at the next election for actions undertaken while occupying public office.

In the UK, Members of Parliament are regarded as representatives. This derived from the views of an eighteenth-century statesman, Edmund Burke, who put forward the trustee model of representation, which argued that an MP should apply his judgement to serve the interests of the nation as a whole rather than having to obey the wishes of a local electorate.

> The trustee model of representation, which argued an MP was a representative and not a delegate, stemmed from the arguments of Edmund Burke, whose address to his local electors in Bristol in 1774 argued *'it ought to be the happiness and glory of a representative to live in the strictest union, the closest correspondence, and the most unreserved communication with his constituents. Their wishes ought to have great weight with him; their opinion, high respect; their business, unremitted attention ... But his unbiased opinion, his mature judgment, his enlightened conscience, he ought not to sacrifice to you, to any man, or to any set of men living ... Your representative owes you, not his industry only, but his judgment; and he betrays, instead of serving you, if he sacrifices it to your opinion'* (Burke, 1774).
>
> Burke, E. (1774) Speech to the Electors of Bristol. 3 November. Cited in "Representation". The Founders Constitution. [Online] http://press-pubs.uchicago.edu/founders/documents/v1ch13s7.html [Accessed 10 May 2014].

A Member of Parliament is subject to no formal restraints on his or her actions once elected. The system of recall, which is practiced in some American states, has never applied in the United Kingdom. A Member of Parliament cannot be forced to resign by local electors: their only power is their ultimate ability to select an alternative representative when the next election occurs.

However, there are informal pressures that may influence the behaviour of United Kingdom Members of Parliament, for example the discipline exerted by the party system or criticism voiced by the media. But even this may prove an ineffective restraint on their behaviour.

The composition of the legislatures in America and the UK

At the 2010 UK general election 650 members of parliament were elected. Of these,

- ▶ 143 (22.0 per cent) were women
- ▶ 27 (4.2 per cent) were from minority ethnic communities
- ▶ 480 (73.8 per cent) were white males

If the House of Commons were socially representative, around half of its members would be women and 7.9 per cent (or 51 MPs) would be drawn from minority ethnic communities. The 2002 Sex Discrimination (Election Candidates) Act (which enabled political parties to use positive discrimination to select election candidates if they wish to do so) has served to slightly increase the number of women MPs in the longer term, although in 2010, 262 constituencies had no female candidates.

In America, the 113th Congress (which first met in January 2013) consists of 100 Senators and 435 members of the House of Representatives. It was composed of:

- ▶ 44 African Americans (42 in the House and 2 in the Senate)
- ▶ 102 women (82 in the House and 20 in the Senate)
- ▶ 37 Hispanic/Latino members (33 in the House and 4 in the Senate)
- ▶ 13 Asian / Pacific Islanders (12 in the House and 1 in the Senate)
- ▶ 2 native Americans (Indians) (both in the House)

Representatives from minority ethnic backgrounds are organized into caucuses – the Congressional Black Caucus (formed in 1971, based on an earlier organization set up in 1969), the Congressional Hispanic Caucus (set up in 1976) and the Congressional Asian Pacific American Caucus (established in 1994). The aim of caucuses is to represent the interests of the communities from which they derive, although they are not limited to promoting minority ethnic concerns – for example, some Republican members of Congress are aligned to the Congressional Tea Party Caucus which was first launched in 2010.

THE SOCIAL COMPOSITION OF LEGISLATORS

The term 'characteristic representation' suggests that the institutions of representative government can only validly represent public opinion when they constitute a microcosm of society, containing members from diverse social groups in proportion to their strength. However, in many liberal democracies key divisions in society (such as its occupational make-up or its class, ethnic or religious divisions) are not reflected in this manner. Many liberal democracies were slow in according women the right to vote. New Zealand granted this in 1893 and the United Kingdom (on a restricted basis) in 1918. However, white, male, middle-class persons of above average education continue to dominate the composition of legislatures, making them thus socially unrepresentative of those they represent, although possibly reflective of the characteristics required to achieve success in all aspects of social activity.

The lack of social representativeness may result in the institutions of government becoming out of tune with public opinion and being seen as an anachronistic defender of the status quo when the national mood demands reform and innovation. This problem may be accentuated by the procedures adopted by legislative bodies: the seniority system used by the American Congress tended to entrench the conservative influence over post-war American domestic affairs and persisted until changes to these procedures were introduced during the 1960s and 1970s. Groups who perceive that their needs are being inadequately catered for by the institutions of government (such as women, youth or racial minorities) may resort to alternative means of political expression that may have long-term consequences for the authority of such bodies.

PUBLIC INVOLVEMENT IN POLICY MAKING

Elections play a major role in liberal democratic political systems. However, the ability to elect representatives and (at a subsequent election) to deliver a verdict on their performance in public office does not give the general public a significant role in political affairs. In many liberal democracies, therefore, other mechanisms exist which seek to provide citizens with a more constant role in policy making. These consist of pressure groups (whose operations we will consider in Chapter 6), and various forms of protest (sometimes referred to as extra-parliamentary political activities, which we will discuss in Chapter 7).

Referendums

Key idea (6)

A referendum gives the general public the opportunity to vote on specific policy issues. They are utilized widely in some liberal democracies such as Switzerland and the Scandinavian countries, but more sparingly in others such as the United Kingdom.

ADVANTAGES OF A REFERENDUM

A referendum possesses many advantages to the operations of liberal democratic political systems. The main ones are discussed below.

▶ Direct democracy

A referendum permits mass public involvement in public policy making. We term this 'direct democracy'. There are various forms of referendums. They may entail the public being given the opportunity to approve a proposed course of action before it is implemented, or to express their views on actions previously undertaken by a government. In America, the referendum is frequently used in State Government. A widely used version is the petition referendum. This enables a predetermined number of signatories to suspend the operation of a law passed by the state legislature, which is then placed before the public at a future state election.

A referendum avoids the dangers of public office holders not accurately reflecting public opinion by enabling the citizens themselves to express their approval or disapproval of the issues that affect their everyday lives. The power exercised by policy makers over the content of public policy is reduced, and they are required to pursue actions that are truly reflective of the views of the public.

It is important, however, that the initiative to hold a referendum should not solely rest with those who discharge the functions of government. A referendum will only provide a mechanism to secure public involvement in policy making if the public themselves have the right both to call one and to exercise some control over its content. In New Zealand, for example, the 1993 Citizens Initiated Referenda Act gave 10 per cent of registered electors the opportunity to initiate a non-binding referendum on any subject. This must be held within one year of the initial call for a referendum, unless 75 per cent of members of parliament vote to defer it. A related measure is the initiative petition, which is used in approximately half of the American states. This enables a set number of a state's voters to put a proposed law on a ballot paper, which becomes law if approved by a majority of voters regardless of whether the state legislature chooses to enact it.

▶ Determination of constitutional issues

It is not feasible to suggest that referendums should be held to ascertain the views of the public on every item of public policy. However, they do provide a means whereby major issues (perhaps of considerable constitutional importance) can be resolved. In many European countries, referendums were held on membership of the European Union (EU) or treaties (such as Maastricht) which were associated with it because of their implications for fundamental matters such as national sovereignty. Of particular significance was the Constitutional Treaty that was designed to provide the EU with a written constitution. The 25 member states were required to ratify it within two years, and some countries did this by holding a referendum. The rejection of this constitution by French and Dutch voters in 2005 effectively made it a 'dead duck'. This resulted in the constitution (which would have replaced all earlier EU treaties) being replaced by a treaty (the Treaty of Lisbon) which merely amended the existing Treaties of Rome and Maastricht.

In the United Kingdom, there is no legal requirement to hold a referendum to settle any political issue and they are held sparingly. In 1997, referendums were used to enable people living in Scotland and Wales to give their views on the government's devolution proposals for these two countries.

In 1998, referendums were held in Northern Ireland to assess the public mood on the Good Friday Peace Agreement and in the Irish Republic to approve the amendment of its Constitution which laid claim to the six counties of Northern Ireland.

2011 Referendum

In the UK, the 2010 Parliamentary Voting and Constituencies Act provided for a referendum on the question 'at present, the UK uses the "first-past-the-post" system to elect MPs to the House of Commons. Should the "alternative vote" be used instead?'

This was the first UK-wide referendum to be held since 1975, and was put forward at the insistence of the Liberal Democrats who made the referendum a condition of their involvement in the 2010 Coalition government.

The referendum was held on 5 May 2011:

▶ 42.2% of the electorate voted
▶ 32% of those who voted supported this proposal
▶ 68% of those who voted opposed it

Accordingly, the first-past-the-post electoral system remained in place for future elections to the UK House of Commons.

DISADVANTAGES

There are, however, a number of problems associated with a referendum, which we will now consider.

▶ Devalue the role of the legislature

A referendum may devalue the role performed by legislative bodies. In some countries (such as France) they were deliberately introduced to weaken the power of parliament. Although they can be reconciled with the concept of parliamentary sovereignty when they are consultative and do not require the legislature to undertake a particular course of action, it is difficult to ignore the outcome of a popular vote even when it does not theoretically tie the hands of public policy makers. Thus the Norwegian Parliament announced in advance of the 1972 consultative referendum on entry into the European Economic Community that its outcome would determine the country's stance on this issue.

▶ Unequal competition

Competing groups in a referendum do not necessarily possess equality in the resources which they have at their disposal, and this may give one side an unfair advantage over the other in putting its case across to the electorate. This problem is accentuated if the government contributes to the financing of one side's campaign, as occurred in the early stages of the 1995 Irish referendum on divorce.

▶ Complexity of issues

The general public may be unable to understand the complexities of the issues that are the subject of a referendum. This may mean that the level of public participation is low, or that the result is swayed by factors other than the issue that is placed before the voters for their consideration. For example, the September 2000 referendum in Denmark to reject entry into the single European currency, the Euro, was determined more by arguments about the erosion of national identity and independence rather than the economic arguments related to joining the Euro.

▶ Underlying motives may not be progressive

We should also observe that a referendum is not always a progressive measure designed to enhance the ability of the public to play a meaningful role in policy making. Dictators may use them instead of representative institutions such as a parliament, asserting that these bodies are unnecessary since the public are directly consulted on government policy. The use of the referendum by Germany's Nazi government (1933–45) resulted in the 1949 West German Constitution prohibiting their future use.

A referendum may also be proposed by governments to preserve party unity on an issue which is extremely divisive. The British referendum in 1975 on the Labour government's renegotiated terms for membership of the European Economic Community was primarily put forward for such partisan reasons. This avoided the government having to take a decision which might have split the party.

▶ 'Mob rule'

A referendum may facilitate the tyranny of the majority with minority interests being sacrificed at the behest of mob rule. This may mean that political issues are resolved by orchestrated hysteria rather than through a calm reflection of the issues which are involved.

▶ Low turnout

Public interest in a referendum is not always high, and is affected by factors which include the extent to which established political parties are able to agree on a stance to be adopted and campaign for this. Some countries that utilize the referendum have a requirement that turnout should reach a stipulated figure in order for reforms to be initiated. This seeks to prevent minorities securing control of the political agenda. In Portugal, for example, a turnout of 50 per cent of the electorate is required for a referendum to have binding authority.

Dig Deeper

Holden, B. (1993) *Understanding Liberal Democracy*. New York: Harvester Wheatsheaf, 2nd ed.

Crepaz, M. and Steiner, J. (2012) *European Democracies*. Harlow: Pearson Education, 8th ed.

Fact-check

1 The process whereby political systems are differentiated from each other is known as:
   a Government
   b Political culture
   c Classification
   d Homogeneity

2 In liberal democratic political systems, governments are accountable to:
   a Themselves
   b The electorate
   c The President
   d The United Nations

3 In the UK, a Member of Parliament has the status of:
   a A representative
   b A delegate
   c A public official
   d An office holder under the Crown

4 In the UK, a referendum has to be held:
   a In connection with a matter of constitutional importance
   b To determine the timing of a general election
   c To give approval to a coalition government taking office
   d Never – there is no requirement to hold a referendum on any political issue

5 In the UK, women were first given the right to vote in:
   a 1832
   b 1867
   c 1918
   d 1928

6 In America, an election to choose the President of the United States has to be held every:
   a 2 years
   b 4 years
   c 6 years
   d 8 years

3

Political ideologies

Political ideology underpins the policy that is promoted by political parties. Thus politicians, when elected to public office, do not make things up as they go along but, rather, their actions are shaped by a fundamental set of values that will underpin their policies. There are several competing political ideologies, and in this chapter we will examine some of the key ideas (both historic and contemporary) that influence political conduct.

What is political ideology?

Key idea (1)

Political ideology defines the core values of political parties and provides them with ideals that underpin the society they wish to establish.

Ideology is commonly defined as the principles that motivate political parties, in particular providing a vision of the society they wish to create. Ideology thus serves as a unifying force between party leaders and supporters: all are spiritually united in the promotion of a common cause.

Ideology is not, however, always the guiding force in party politics. American political parties appear far less ideological than their Western European counterparts. Even in these countries, parties (especially when in power) are often forced to respond to events rather than to fashion them. Parties on the left of the political spectrum have sometimes been accused of abandoning ideology in favour of pragmatism (that is, responding to events as they occur without referring to any preconceived ideology) or of redefining their ideology to improve their chances of election.

There is a danger that politicians are perceived as seeking office for the power it gives them as individuals when political ideology is not prominent as a driving force motivating a political party. This may influence the level of popular involvement in political affairs. The absence of pronounced ideology may also result in a situation in which electors find it difficult to differentiate between the political parties. The term 'consensus' is used to describe a situation where similar goals and policies are put forward by competing political parties.

Marxists adopt a more precise definition of ideology. They refer to a coherent set of ideas, beliefs and values through which an individual can make sense of the social world they inhabit which ought to derive from a person's social class. However, Marxists contend that liberal democracies are dominated by the ideology of the ruling class (or bourgeoisie) that secures the acquiescence of the working class (proletariat) to exploitation and social inequality. The dominance accorded to bourgeois ideas in such societies (arising from the control they exert over agencies such as the education system and the media) results in the proletariat suffering from what Friedrich Engels referred to as a 'false consciousness'. This is where they fail to appreciate the fact that they are exploited and thus consent to the operations of the existing social system, which is thus accorded legitimacy by this intellectual form of control.

The political spectrum

Key idea (2)

The term political spectrum is used to place different political ideologies in relationship to one another, thereby enabling the similarities and differences that exist between them to be identified.

The various political ideologies are grouped under the broad headings of 'Left', 'Right' and 'Centre'. The Right consists of fascism and conservatism, the Centre consists of liberalism and social democracy and the Left comprises socialism, communism and anarchism. Anarchism is located on the far left of the political spectrum and fascism is on the far right. This terminology was derived from the French Revolution in the late eighteenth century: the Left was associated with revolution while the right was identified with reaction.

The terms 'Right', 'Left' and 'Centre' lack precise definition but are used broadly to indicate the stances that the different ideologies adopt towards political, economic and social change. Historically, the Right opposed this, preferring tradition and the established order of the past. The Left endorsed change as a necessary development designed to improve the human condition. The Centre was also associated with change, but wished to introduce this gradually within the existing economic and political framework, which the Left sought to abolish as a prerequisite to establishing an improved society.

The political spectrum is concerned with ideologies, not with the political systems or practices with which they may be associated. Communism and fascism (which are on the opposite ends of the political spectrum) are both associated with totalitarian political systems in which citizens are deprived of a wide range of civil and political liberties and personal freedom is sacrificed to the common interests which are defined by the state. However, the nature of the society with which these two ideologies is associated is entirely different.

INDIVIDUALISM AND COLLECTIVISM

Key idea (3)

Individualism and collectivism are fundamental principles which help to distinguish different political ideologies.

Individualism places the interests of individual citizens at the forefront of its concerns and is the opposite of collectivism. As a political doctrine, individualism suggests that the sphere of government should be limited so as to not unduly encroach on the ability of individuals to pursue their own interests and thereby achieve self-fulfillment. As an economic principle, it opposes government intervention in the workings of the economy in preference to support for the free market and laissez-faire capitalism (which sees no place for government imposing restrictions affecting matters such as wages and conditions of work). Individualism is a core value of American society.

Individualism is historically linked to liberalism, where the classical notion of limited government (derived from natural rights) held that individuals should be as free as possible from state interference, since this would deprive them of their ability to exercise responsibility for the conduct of their lives.

It could, however, be justified in order to prevent actions by some which would impede the ability of others to advance their own interests. This belief would, for example, justify legislation against monopolists, since these prejudiced the position of individual entrepreneurs. By the same token, state involvement in social policy (especially to protect the poorer and weaker members of society) was rejected by liberals for much of the nineteenth century on the grounds that individuals should be responsible for their own welfare.

Individualism was thus historically viewed as the opposite of collectivism. However, some strands of liberal thought have suggested their compatibility by arguing that individual enterprise is hindered by circumstances, such as the operations of the economy, which are not of the individual's own making. State action directed at those who are placed in such circumstances can thus be justified in the belief that it would remove impediments preventing people from being able to assert control over their own destinies.

The 'New Right' enthusiastically adopted many of the ideas associated with classical liberalism in the 1980s, in particular support for the free market and opposition to social welfare policies. In America individualism underpins the opposition voiced by militia movements against government involvement in people's lives.

Collectivism entails the sacrifice of self-interest to commonly agreed goals. These are often asserted by a central political authority, and results in the state taking an active role in directing the resources at its command to achieve these objectives.

Collectivism is usually depicted as the opposite of individualism, since group needs are placed above the pursuit of individual interests. However, some aspects of liberal thought argue that these ideas are not incompatible since the sense of co-operation and fraternity that is developed through collective endeavour enables individuals to develop their personalities to a greater extent than would be possible if they existed in isolation.

Collectivism emerged in the United Kingdom towards the end of the nineteenth century when various socialist organizations advocated a more vigorous response by the state to social problems, especially poverty, which would entail an enhanced level of government intervention in the economy and some redistribution of resources from the more affluent members of society. Some within the Liberal Party (the 'new Liberals') also moved towards advocating activity by both central and local government to improve social conditions. This resulted in legislation in the early twentieth century to benefit the poorer and weaker members of society and ultimately developed into the welfare state.

Collectivism is traditionally closely identified with socialism, especially those who view state ownership of the means of production (achieved through policies such as nationalization) as the way to achieve a more just society. However, collective action can be organized through social units other than the state (such as communities that possess a wide degree of political autonomy) and may underpin economic ventures such as co-operatives in which people can work together and pursue common aims within a capitalist economic system.

Left-wing political ideologies

Key idea (4)

The left of the political spectrum embraces a wide range of political ideologies, including anarchism, communism and socialism. All seek to promote fundamental social change based upon the redistribution of wealth and resources which typically entails the destruction of the existing social order through revolution.

A number of political ideologies are identified as being on the left of the political spectrum. These seek the destruction of capitalism and the establishment of a new social order based upon a fundamental redistribution of wealth, resources and power.

ANARCHISM
Anarchism literally means 'no rule' and is a form of socialism which rejects conventional forms of government on the basis

that it imposes restraints on individuals without their express consent having been given. Accordingly, anarchists urge the abolition of the state and all forms of political authority, especially the machinery of law and order (which they view as the basis of oppression, providing for the exercise of power by some members of society over others). Most anarchists deem violence as the necessary means to tear down the state.

Anarchists assert that government is an unnecessary evil since social order will develop naturally. Co-operation will be founded upon the self-interest of individuals and regulated by their common sense and willingness to resolve problems rationally. They assert that traditional forms of government, far from promoting harmony, are the root cause of social conflict. Private ownership of property, which is a key aspect of capitalist society, is regarded as a major source of this friction.

Some aspects of Marxism (especially the view that under communism the state would 'wither away') are compatible with anarchist views. Anarchist thought has been concerned with developing social structures outside conventional forms of government in the belief that the elimination of the state would eradicate exploitation, and that co-operation, fraternity and a fair division of goods and labour would be facilitated in smaller forms of social organization. These have included syndicalism (which sought worker control of industry to be achieved by strike action), communes, and a wide range of co-operative endeavours (which were characterized by relatively small groups of individuals owning and operating a productive enterprise which is managed for their mutual economic benefit).

COMMUNISM

Communism (sometimes referred to as socialist democracy) is a political system based on the ideas of Karl Marx. According to Marxist theory, communism occurs following the overthrow of capitalism and after an intermediary phase (referred to as socialism) in which the Communist Party functions as the vanguard of the proletariat, ruling on their behalf and paving the way for the eventual establishment of communism. This is characterized by the abolition of private property and class divisions and the creation of equality in which citizens live in co-operation and harmony. In this situation the state becomes unnecessary and will 'wither away'.

States which have called themselves 'communist' have not achieved the ideal situation referred to by Marx. Considerable differences existed between them (especially the former USSR and China, whose approach to issues such as social equality was dissimilar) although in general, these countries were characterized by the existence of little or no private property ownership, a planned economy (which was viewed as essential to achieving equality and classlessness) and a comprehensive welfare state.

The most notable feature of communist states is the paramount position of an official socialist ideology and the domination or total monopolization of political affairs by the official Communist Party. As the massacre of protesters at Tiananmen Square in Beijing in 1989 evidenced, dissent is not encouraged in communist states. The control which the Communist Party exerts over government means that the judiciary is less able to defend civil and political liberties than in liberal democratic political systems.

The Manifesto of the Communist Party put forward the view that communism required the revolutionary overthrow of capitalist society. Society was viewed as being composed of *'two great hostile camps'* (Marx and Engels, 1848: 40) – those who owned the means of production (the bourgeoisie) and those who formed the working class (the proletariat). The former exploited the latter in order to make profits. However, awareness of exploitation would give rise to class consciousness, which would generate class conflict and, ultimately, a class revolution. Marx and Engels wrote *'The Communists ... openly declare that their ends can be attained only by the forcible overthrow of all existing social conditions ... The proletarians have nothing to lose but their chains. They have a world to win'* (Marx and Engels, 1848: 94).

Mark, K. and Engels, R. (1848) *Manifesto of the Communist Party*. The version quoted here was published in 1966. Moscow: Free Press. The first English translation was published in 1888.

Communist states included the former Soviet Union and its East European satellite neighbours, but is now confined to a smaller number of countries. The communist heritage of the former states has resulted in weak party systems and limited levels of public participation in political affairs. Civil liberties are relatively poorly protected. A considerable degree of state ownership remains, although vigorous attempts are being made to move towards a capitalist economy.

▶ Marxism–Leninism

Marxism–Leninism combines the ideas of Karl Marx and Vladimir Ilyich Lenin. Marx asserted that actions and human institutions were economically determined and that the class struggle was the key instrument of historical change. Lenin was especially concerned with the organization of a post-capitalist society. Marxism–Leninism formed the basis of the political system that was established in Russia following the 1917 Revolution.

Marxist theory, like elitism, questioned the pluralist nature of society. It held that in industrialized societies the elite consisted of the economically dominant class, the bourgeoisie. Their wealth was the underpinning for their political power in which the state was used as an instrument to dominate and exploit the working class (or proletariat). Although those who owned and controlled capital were not necessarily the same as those who exercised political power, the economic interests and cultural values of the former determined the actions undertaken by the latter. Popular consent to such decisions is especially reliant on the ideological control exerted over the population by this economically powerful elite.

Marx stressed that social classes were in an inevitable state of competition with one another and that the exploitative nature of capitalism made a proletarian or working-class revolution inevitable. Exploitation would result in increased class consciousness. This would develop into class conflict, resulting in a revolution involving the overthrow of the ruling class and the emergence of a new society based on what he termed 'the dictatorship of the proletariat'. The new socialist society would be characterized by the abolition of private property ownership, which was viewed as the basis of the inequalities of the class system.

Marx said little concerning how a socialist society should be organized. This was a major concern of Lenin's, who argued that it was the role of the Communist Party to act as the vanguard (that is, leader) of the proletariat which would direct the revolution and control society while true socialism was being constructed. A key objective of this period would be to rescue the masses from the false consciousness which had been cultivated by the previous regime. This meant that a one-party state operated in countries controlled by Marxist–Leninist ideology.

Most Eastern European communist parties subscribed to Marxist–Leninist doctrines. These were, however, challenged elsewhere. Maoism, named after the Chinese leader Mao Tse-Tung, viewed the peasantry as the revolutionary class rather than the industrial proletariat and, in common with Leon Trotsky's ideas, Maoism also rejected the centralized power exerted by the Communist Party in favour of the popular involvement of the masses in the revolutionary transformation of society.

SOCIALISM
Socialism arose in reaction to the exploitative nature of capitalism. It rejects a society in which inequalities in the distribution of wealth and political power result in social injustice, and is committed to the ideal of equality. Socialists seek a society in which co-operation and fraternity replace the divisions based on the class lines that characterize capitalist societies. There is, however, considerable disagreement concerning both the nature of an egalitarian society and how it would be created. These stem from the diverse traditions embraced by socialism.

Labour Party and 'Clause IV Socialism'

In the UK, the Labour Party was traditionally associated with embracing a socialist ideology. This ideological commitment was enshrined in Clause IV, Part 4 of the Labour Party's Constitution, adopted in 1918, which committed the Labour Party *'to secure for the workers by hand or by brain the full fruits of their industry and the most equitable distribution thereof that may be possible, upon the basis of the common ownership of the means of production, distribution and exchange and the best obtainable system of popular administration and control of each industry or service'* (Labour Party 1918). However, although it was argued that this statement committed the party to socialism, others saw the adoption of socialism as largely an illusion. It was argued that Clause IV and the 1918 Programme *'Labour and the New Social Order were cast at such a level of generality that it committed the party to virtually nothing'* (Barker, 1972: 85).

Barker, R. (1972) *Education and Politics 1900–1951: A Study of the Labour Party*. Oxford: Clarendon Press.

Labour Party (1918) Annual Conference Report. January and February 1918, *Appendix 1, Constitution of the Labour Party*. London: Labour Party.

The roots of socialism include the economic theories of David Ricardo (who suggested that the interests of capital and labour were opposed), the reforming activities of Robert Owen (who advocated the ownership of the means of production by small groups of producers organized into societies based upon the spirit of co-operation), the Christian impulse (which was relevant to socialism through its concern for the poor and the early experiences of Christians living in a society in which property was held in common), and the writings of Karl Marx and Friedrich Engels who asserted that inequality was rooted in private property ownership and the class system which derived from this.

The varied impulses that influenced socialism explain the differences within it. A key division is between fundamentalist and reformist socialism (or social democracy). Fundamentalist socialists believe that state control of all means of production is indispensable to the creation of an egalitarian society, and is thus viewed as their main political objective. They reject the free market and instead have historically endorsed the centralized planning of the economy and the nationalization (or 'socialization' as it is termed in America) of key industries to achieve this goal. Reformist (or revisionist) socialists, however, believe that an egalitarian society can be created by reforming the capitalist system rather than abolishing it. This version of socialism is commonly referred to as social democracy. This has resulted in nationalization being applied to selected industries on a piecemeal basis and an acceptance of the coexistence of state-owned and privately-owned industry within what is termed a mixed economy. Central economic planning has typically been used to supplement the workings of the free market rather than seeking to replace it.

Feminism

Feminism is not a coherent political ideology. However, the desire of some aspects of feminist thinking to fundamentally change the power relationships in society make it compatible with ideologies on the left of the political spectrum.

Feminism refers to a wide range of theories which assert that the power relationship between the sexes is unequal, and which view this problem as a social construction rather than a natural situation arising from biological differences between male and females. Feminist ideas inspired campaigns waged from the late nineteenth century onwards seeking equal legal and political rights for women, but the modern feminist movement derived from North America in the 1960s.

There are a number of strands to feminist thought. Liberal feminism seeks to combat discrimination experienced by women in the public sphere and seeks equality of treatment. Measures to secure formal equality embodied in equal rights legislation (such as the United Kingdom's 1970 Equal Pay Act, the 1975 Sex Discrimination Act, and the 2006 and 2010 Equality Act) derive from this perspective.

Radical feminism seeks the liberation of women. It focuses not on inequality but, rather, on the system of sexual oppression which was termed 'patriarchy' (or 'rule by men'). Radical feminists believe that patriarchy is the key power relationship in society and is reproduced in each generation by the family. They believe that sexual equality requires a revolution in cultural and social values, and cannot be attained by providing additional legal rights for women within the existing social structure. Marxist feminism attributes the oppression of women to the operations of capitalism. This is said to give rise to economic dependency, which is viewed as the basis of women's oppression. They assert that only in a communist society would this situation be remedied. Socialist feminism concentrates on the way in which the twin forces of patriarchy and class oppression interact in a capitalist society and place women in a socially subordinate position. Unlike radical feminists, however, they do not view the interests of men and women as being permanently opposed. Post-modernist feminism rejects the certainty and objectivity which underlay the Marxist view of class interests. It does not see all women as being subject to the same processes and believes that different groups encounter different experiences.

Feminist politics are especially associated with extra-parliamentary political action, although in some countries they are advanced by women's political parties. One example of this is Iceland's Women's Alliance, which was formed in 1983 to promote women's and children's issues.

The centre and centre-left of the political spectrum

Key idea (5)

Social democracy and liberalism are associated with the centre / centre-left of the political spectrum. These ideologies seek to promote political, economic and social reforms within the basis of society as it is currently constituted.

This section outlines the key aspects of liberalism and social democracy which are identified with the centre-left and centre of the political spectrum. The parties based on these ideologies promote social, economic and political change, which they wish to achieve through the ballot box rather than through revolution.

SOCIAL DEMOCRACY

Social democracy rests within the reformist (or revisionist) tradition of socialism. It suggests that social inequalities can be addressed by an enhanced level of state intervention within the existing structure of the capitalist economic system. The influence of social democracy was increased after 1945 when capitalism was seen to be bringing many benefits to working-class people (such as a rising standard of living and social mobility) in a number of countries, which in turn tended to reduce the hostility between the social classes.

Lord John Maynard Keynes was especially influential in the development of social democratic politics. He argued that a market economy subject to an enhanced degree of state intervention to manage demand could provide an effective solution to the problem of unemployment. His policy of demand management was adopted by a number of socialist parties as an alternative to state control of the economy.

Social democracy also sought to remove social problems affecting the poorer members of society through the establishment of a welfare state. This was a mechanism to provide for the redistribution of wealth within society since the welfare state would be financed by public money obtained through the taxation of income, so that the rich would contribute towards addressing the health and welfare needs of the poor. Social democracy was also associated with other policies designed to improve the access of poorer members of society to a range of services such as housing and education.

There are a number of key differences between Fundamentalists and Social Democrats. The latter have a negative view towards nationalization, viewing it as one means among many that may be used to secure state influence over the workings of the economy. This view is to some extent flavoured by a perception that state ownership of industry (where this occurred in countries such as the United Kingdom) resulted in bureaucracy and inefficiency without substantially improving the position of the working class. Fundamentalists assert that social democratic policies such as the welfare state serve not to create a socialist society but, rather, to hinder the development of class consciousness, thereby perpetuating capitalism and its essentially exploitative nature.

The third way

The 'third way' embraces the goals of opportunity and social inclusion within the framework of a capitalist economic system. It is especially associated with the UK sociologist, Anthony Giddens, who wrote *The Third Way: The Renewal of Social Democracy* in 1998. Many social democratic parties in Europe (such as the United Kingdom Labour Party and the German Social Democratic Party) shifted towards the 'third way' during the late 1990s, and its approach also influenced the policies pursued by President Bill Clinton in America (1993–2001).

The first way was the approach of New Right (or neo-liberal) governments of the 1980s, in particular those in America and the UK, headed by President Reagan (1981–9) and Margaret Thatcher (1979–90) respectively. The emphasis they placed on the free market intensified social divisions and enhanced social exclusion. Much of the wealth that had been created was not invested, which meant that it failed to percolate throughout society and instead had created an 'underclass' who felt themselves to be permanently excluded from society, deprived of work, power and prospects.

The second way consisted of that form of socialism that placed considerable importance on the nationalization of key industries and public utilities. Third-way theorists regarded this approach as an 'exhausted project'. Alternatively, third way theorists endorsed private ownership (further developing the New Right privatization and deregulation agendas) and the profit motive within the framework of a competitive market, but attempted to reshape the way private enterprise worked by advocating that a company's responsibilities to its shareholders should be combined with responsibility to the wider community, which included their customers, the workers they employed and the localities where they operated. The third way is also associated with policies seeking to promote sound money, fiscal stability and lower taxes.

The third way is associated with the centre-left of the political spectrum, and is underpinned by stakeholding directed towards the pursuit of social justice and the provision of wider opportunities for all within a market economy. It sought to equip individuals with the skills and capacities necessary to succeed in the highly flexible and constantly changing labour markets of modern capitalism, but could also be depicted as a reform which was essential to the smooth operations of a market economy. A dynamic market required flexibility, which was hindered by a permanently excluded underclass. The stakeholder economy was thus an approach that would provide for economic efficiency at the same time as dispensing a measure of social justice. In addition to these objectives, stakeholding has also been associated with political reforms, covering issues that include the empowerment of citizens (secured by policies that include the decentralization of power) and the insistence that the government should be both accountable and responsive to its citizens.

The third way has, however, been criticized for the importance it has attached to wooing business leaders, and for failing to exert adequate controls on the operations of multinational companies. It has also been asserted that insufficient progress in eliminating social and economic inequality has been made by governments endorsing the third way.

LIBERALISM

Modern liberalism emerged from the fight for religious freedom waged in late sixteenth- and seventeenth-century Western Europe. The close link that existed between Church and State ensured that the objective of religious freedom was associated with political dissent. Liberal theorists argued that the social order was a compact (or contract) voluntarily entered into by those who were party to it rather than being a structure handed down by God. Social contract theory was developed by liberal theorists such as Thomas Hobbes and John Locke. The belief that government emerged as the result of rational choice made by those who subsequently accorded their consent to its operations ensured that the rights of the individual were prominent concerns of liberal philosophers. The people were viewed as the ultimate source of political power and the government was legitimate only while it operated with their consent.

As a political doctrine, liberalism emphasized individualism and asserted that human beings should exercise the maximum possible freedom consistent with others being able to enjoy similar liberty. They sought to advance this belief through their support for limited government and their opposition to the intervention of the state in the everyday lives of its citizens. They argued that this intervention would dehumanize individuals since they were not required to take responsibility for their own welfare, but would instead become reliant on others whom they could blame if personal misfortunes befell them. As an economic doctrine, liberalism was additionally associated with the free market, laissez-faire capitalism and free trade.

The American Declaration of Independence gave practical form to the ideas of social contract theorists regarding governments being founded on the consent of those over whom they ruled. This document (which was used to justify the decision of Britain's American Colonies from the rule of the UK Crown) stated:

'We hold these truths to be self-evident, that all men are created equal, that they are endowed by their Creator with certain unalienable Rights, that among these are Life, Liberty and the pursuit of Happiness. That to secure these rights, Governments are instituted among Men, deriving their just powers from the consent of the governed, That whenever any Form of Government becomes destructive of these ends, it is the Right of the People to alter or to abolish it, and to institute new Government, laying its foundation on such principles and organizing its powers in such form, as to them shall seem most likely to affect their Safety and Happiness'.

Source: The Declaration of Independence 1776, being the unanimous Declaration of the thirteen united states of America.

The perception that social problems such as unemployment and poverty were not the fault of the individual but, rather, were dependent on factors such as the workings of the economy over which the individual had no control resulted in significant changes to liberal ideology. In many countries, liberals advocated state intervention in welfare provision and economic management. In the United Kingdom, this approach was especially associated with Lord William Beveridge and Lord John Maynard Keynes, and in America with the 'New Deal Liberalism' pursued by President Franklin Delano Roosevelt. Traditional liberal principles, however, subsequently influenced the New Right in the 1980s.

▶ Freedom

Freedom suggests that individuals are able to live their lives as they see fit with no impediments being placed on their actions. However, this assertion would find little support outside anarchist thought: other ideologies suggest that some form of regulation needs to be applied since unrestrained freedom would enable some members of society to harm others. A key issue affecting freedom, therefore, is the relationship between the individual and the state, and under what circumstances it is acceptable for the state to undertake interventions that intrude on some or all of its members.

Liberal thought saw a close distinction between freedom and rights. Freedom was especially associated with civil liberties and was defined in a negative sense, whereby individuals were deemed free to undertake actions unless the interests of others required that constraints should be placed upon them. Freedom was equated with privacy and minimal state activity, seeking to enhance an individual's freedom of action.

The concept of freedom was later developed in liberal thought into that of positive freedom, which viewed a more vigorous form of state activity as essential to enable individuals to exercise freedom defined in terms of self-fulfillment. Industrial capitalism had created conditions whereby large numbers of individuals lived in poverty and distress, and were thus not able to exercise freedom. Socially and economically deprived individuals therefore needed state action (typically in the form of a welfare state and intervention in the management of the economy) to create conditions in which they regained autonomy over the conduct of their lives.

A reaction against state intervention occurred in a number of liberal democratic countries in the later decades of the twentieth century. Neo-liberals focused on an economic definition of freedom which was equated with the advocacy of free market capitalism and the reduction of state interference in social and economic affairs. It was asserted that state intervention had eroded freedom by constraining consumer choice, by transforming recipients of state aid into a position of dependency whereby they lost the freedom to exercise control over their everyday lives, and by sacrificing individual autonomy to the power wielded by large-scale bureaucracies.

PROGRESSIVISM

Progressivism is generally identified with the centre-left of the political spectrum and seeks social and political reform deemed to be beneficial to the majority of the population. These reforms are put forward within the existing framework of capitalist society and thus exclude those groups that seek revolutionary change or upheaval. Constitutional reform is a particular concern of progressive movements, whose objective is to bring government closer to the people.

In America, the progressive movement initiated a number of political reforms between 1890 and 1920, many of which affected state government. These included the use of the referendum, which typically took the form of the petition referendum enabling a predetermined number of signatories to suspend the operation of a law passed by the state legislature which would be placed before the public at a future state election. A further reform was the petition referendum which has been discussed on pages 38–9. Most states have adopted some form of referendum and around half utilize the initiative petition.

Other reforms associated with American progressivism included enabling a set number of electors to re-call an elected representative at either state or federal level (which has the effect of 'de-electing' this person), the introduction of the direct election of senators, civil service examinations (a method to enable popular choice to determine the selection of candidates put forward by political parties, termed 'primary elections'), and the long ballot. In Congress, progressive pressure succeeded in drastically reducing the power of the Speaker of the House of Representatives to control its actions. Progressive parties have also stood in presidential elections in 1912, 1924 and 1948, the most successful of which was the 'Bull Moose Party', led by former President Theodore Roosevelt. This was a splinter from the Republican Party and obtained 88 Electoral College votes in 1912.

In the United Kingdom progressive opinion is not located in one political movement but has historically been spread across the major parties. It is currently identified with the Liberal Democrats, the Labour Party, and Left-wing Conservatives.

Right-wing political ideologies

Key idea (6)

Conservative and fascist ideologies are located on the right wing of the political spectrum. They oppose fundamental changes to society and its institutions advocated by left, centre-left and centre political ideologies.

This section discusses the main aspects of ideologies on the right of the political spectrum.

CONSERVATISM

The essence of conservative ideology is scepticism towards change and a disinclination to support reform unless this prevents more radical ones from being implemented. The desire to 'retain things as they are' is especially concerned with what are deemed to be the key institutions and values on which society is based. These include support for private property ownership. This results in opposition to any form of social (including moral) upheaval, support for firm (but not despotic) government and a belief that political institutions should evolve naturally rather than being artificially constructed from an abstract theory or blueprint. Conservatism rejects the goal of equality achieved by social engineering, believing that the differences that exist between people are natural and should not be tampered with. Conservatism is often equated with nationalistic sentiments, seeking to safeguard domestic values and the way of life against foreign incursions.

Conservative thought developed in the eighteenth century and was especially influenced by the events of the French Revolution. Conservatism in the United Kingdom was considerably influenced by *Reflexions on the Revolution in France*, written by Edmund Burke in 1792. Although he had initially been sympathetic to the French Revolution, he subsequently turned against it when the scale of the destruction of the established order became apparent. He explained this alteration in the direction of his thought by providing a summary of the 'British way', which constituted a classic statement of conservatism. He argued that an Englishman's freedom was a national inheritance that was most effectively secured by a government which balanced democracy, aristocracy and monarchy. His defence of traditions and institutions was coupled with the advocacy of evolutionary change. He accepted that change would sometimes be necessary, but advocated that this should be minimal and should seek to preserve as much of the old as was possible. In France, Joseph de Maistre contributed to conservative thought by providing a defence of established authority against revolutionary ideas and emphasizing the need for order.

In practice, conservative parties are often pragmatic; that is, they show a willingness to fashion policies in order to respond to pressing problems rather than seeking to advance a specific ideology.

> In England, the party traditionally known as the Tories stood opposed to any significant degree of social, political or constitutional change. However, in 1834, Sir Robert Peel (in a letter to his electors in the Borough of Tamworth) issued a declaration that is widely regarded as establishing the principles of modern Conservatism – a willingness to embrace moderate reforms in order to preserve the bedrock interests that the party wished to defend (in particular the established position of the Church of England and the power of the landed aristocracy). In this declaration he sought to appeal to the newly established middle class electorate by accepting the reform of the franchise that had been enacted in the 1832 Reform Act, viewing it as a *'final and irrevocable settlement of a great constitutional question.'* He further stated that *'if the spirit of the Reform Bill implies merely a careful review of institutions, civil and ecclesiastical, undertaken in a friendly temper combining, with the firm maintenance of established rights, the correction of proved abuses and the redress of real grievances, – in that case, I can for myself and colleagues undertake to act in such a spirit and with such intentions.'*
>
> Peel, R. (1834) To The Electors of the Borough of Tamworth.
> Cited in D. Hurd (2007) Sir Robert Peel: The Making of a Party.
> *History Today* 57(7) pp 11–17.

NEW RIGHT

The term 'New Right' refers to a body of ideas that underpinned the policies pursued by a number of conservative parties in the 1980s, most notably in governments led by Margaret Thatcher in the United Kingdom and Ronald Reagan in America.

New Right policies were based on two specific traditions. The first of these was termed '**neo-liberalism**'. This version of economic liberalism was rooted in classical liberal ideas and sought to reduce the activities of the state whose frontiers would be 'rolled back' by the application of policies such as privatization and reduced levels of government spending on functions such as welfare provision. This aspect of New Right thinking voiced support for private enterprise and the free market, and led to Keynesian economics (which regarded unemployment as the key problem to be addressed by economic policy) being replaced by alternative economic methods such as monetarism, which identified inflation as the main social evil. This resulted in policies that included controlling the money supply and keeping a tight rein on interest rates. It was argued that government intervention in the economy led to inefficiency, but that economic growth, employment, productivity and widespread prosperity would be secured if the government ceased its attempts to regulate wages and prices.

Privatization was a key aspect of neo-liberalism. One aspect of privatization entailed transferring an industry from the public sector to the private sector. In the United Kingdom this was referred to as 'denationalization'. This policy was pursued by a number of New Right governments, although their motives for embarking on it differed. In the United Kingdom, a key concern was to extend a 'shareholding democracy' by selling shares in former nationalized industries to ordinary members of the general public. In New Zealand, however, shares were mainly sold to large multinational companies. Here, the aim of privatization was to benefit the tax payer both by ensuring that shares were purchased for high prices and as a consequence of economic efficiency, which was presumed to be due to the transfer of a state-owned industry to an existing major company.

The second basis of New Right thinking was termed '**neo-conservatism**'. This emerged in America in the 1960s and was endorsed primarily by liberals who were disillusioned by the inability of government action to solve social problems. It entailed a number of ideas which included social authoritarianism. This asserted that contemporary social problems such as crime, disorder, hooliganism, indiscipline among young people, and moral decay were caused by the decline of 'traditional' values, which were being replaced by permissive attitudes and disrespect for authority. Many neo-conservatives apportioned the blame for these problems on the lack of commitment by immigrants to a country's established cultural values. It endorsed a 'law and order' response to social problems and demanded a return to traditional forms of authority such as the family.

Neo-liberalism and neo-conservatism are not necessarily compatible since the former emphasizes self-reliance, which might result in selfish behaviour, whereas the latter views individuals as citizens with a range of civic obligations to fulfill.

FASCISM

Fascism is a political ideology on the right of the political spectrum which, although lacking a coherent body of beliefs, embodies certain common features. These include opposition to communism, Marxism and liberalism (especially individualism, which they advocate should occupy a position subordinate to the national community). Fascism also opposes the operations of liberal democracy, which it seeks to replace with a totalitarian political system in which there is only one party and, ideally, the complete identity of this party with the state. One consequence of this is that civil and political liberties are absent in fascist states.

Fascist parties utilize action and violence as key political tactics, especially when seeking to secure power, and they stress the importance of firm leadership to solve a nation's problems. Prominent leaders of fascist movements, such as Adolf Hitler in Germany, Benito Mussolini in Italy, Francisco Franco in Spain and Antonio de Oliveira Salazar in Portugal, made great use of their personal charisma to secure loyalty from those who followed them. Fascist movements also emphasize the importance of nation and race, the consequences of which can include a desire for territorial expansion and the practice of racism and genocide.

Spotlight

Is charisma important in politics? Winston Churchill once remarked that Clement Attlee was 'a modest man, but then he has so much to be modest about'. However, Attlee was prime minister between 1945 and 1951, presiding over a government whose achievements included the establishment of the National Health Service and the introduction of a range of other social welfare benefits.

Fascist movements appeal to persons of all social classes by using populist rhetoric to secure support. Successful fascist parties attract the lower middle classes when these feel threatened by social and economic changes occurring in a particular country. There was, however, wide variation in the ideas and policies put forward by individual fascist parties whose leaders cultivated support by opportunistically exploiting popular concerns, fears or prejudices. This meant that the success achieved by fascist parties was significantly influenced by events unique to particular countries: in Germany, for example, Hitler's rise to power was aided by factors that included a widespread feeling that the Treaty of Versailles was unfair, the prior existence of nationalist and anti-Semitic beliefs and the economic problems faced by the country after 1919 which resulted in both unemployment and hyper-inflation. In Italy, fascism was aided by the weaknesses displayed by the pre-fascist ruling class.

POPULISM

Populism is not a coherent political ideology, but encompasses a range of right-wing attitudes and opinions.

Populism advocates the pursuance of policies supported by majority public opinion. The concerns and the values which underpin these policies are not derived from any coherent set of political beliefs but are widely varied, although a common strand is that the concerns which are articulated in populist rhetoric are depicted as resting on 'common sense' assumptions. Typically populist politics directs its appeal to the masses over the heads of other established social and political institutions (such as the family, social class, political parties and trade unions) by focusing on a cause which can be depicted as harmful and contrary to the best interests of mass public opinion. This appeal is especially directed at those at the lower end of the social scale, although the leaders of such movements tend to be drawn from higher up the social ladder.

Examples of populist movements include the America People's Party of the 1890s, which voiced the concerns of farmers in the western and southern states, and demanded the increased coinage of silver. Populism is particularly identified with Juan Péron, the President of Argentina 1946–55 and 1973–74. His power rested on his ability to mobilize the poorer elements in society against the institutions of the state. As with fascism, populism is often identified with the strong leadership of a charismatic figure and a distrust of representative institutions.

In Western liberal democracies, populist politics are often identified with extreme right-wing political parties which suggest that the problems of 'ordinary' members of the general public are due to the policies pursued by 'unrepresentative politicians' who have ignored the interests of the masses by pursuing policies such as immigration, and by adopting over-liberal attitudes in areas such as law and order and social policy. Support for such views is often cultivated by selecting a target (usually a weak and vulnerable group in society) that can be scapegoated and depicted as both the root cause and embodiment of the crisis allegedly facing society.

The ability to mobilize public opinion has been enhanced by technological developments, such as the internet, which enable the speedy formation of support for a populist cause. This may exert a significant influence on the conduct of political parties who feel they must follow the expressed views of the general public in order to secure their support.

Dig Deeper

Heywood, A. (2012) *Political Ideologies: An Introduction*. Basingstoke: Macmillan/ Palgrave, 5th ed.

Heywood, A. (2004) *Political Theory: An Introduction*. Basingstoke: Macmillan/Palgrave, 3rd ed.

Leach, R. (2009) *Political Ideology in Britain*. Basingstoke: Macmillan/Palgrave, 2nd ed.

Fact-check

1 Complete the following sentence: 'Proletariat of the world unite. You have nothing to lose but your:
   a Lives
   b Pensions
   c Chains
   d Social welfare benefits

2 The term 'political spectrum' is used to differentiate what:
   a Political ideologies and how they stand in relation to each other
   b The social background of candidates for public office
   c The key policies promoted by the political parties
   d The main characteristics of a political party's electoral support

3 Collectivism is traditionally associated with:
   a Socialism
   b Conservatism
   c Liberalism
   d Progressivism

4 A key contributor to conservative thought in the late eighteenth century was:
   a Thomas Jefferson
   b Edmund Burke
   c John Locke
   d Karl Marx

5 What political ideology links Benito Mussolini, Adolf Hitler and Francisco Franco:
   a Anarchism
   b Dictatorialism
   c Fascism
   d Populism

6 The UK's 1970 Equal Pay Act is an example of a reform inspired by:
   a New Right political ideology
   b Radical feminism
   c Liberal feminism
   d Socialism

4

Elections and electoral systems

Elections are a key aspect of a liberal democratic political system by providing citizens with an opportunity to decide who will govern them and what policies they will pursue. This chapter considers the role of elections and how they empower the public in the conduct of political affairs. It then goes on to discuss the operations of the main electoral systems that are used across the world and evaluate their strengths and weaknesses.

The significance of elections

Key idea (1)

The right to vote is a key political entitlement that allows citizens to choose public office holders and to hold them to account for their actions.

Those of us who live in liberal democracies will periodically be invited to vote. We may be asked to choose representatives for local, state or national office. Elections are the mechanism whereby citizens are provided with the opportunity to select persons to take political decisions on their behalf. They enable public participation in key activities, which include selecting the personnel of government and determining the content of public policy.

Elections further constitute the process whereby public office holders can be made to account for their activities to the general public. It is an essential feature of liberal democracy that sovereignty resides with the people living in each country. Governments must be accountable to the people for their actions. Those that lose the backing of public opinion will be replaced by representatives drawn from another political party at the next round of elections. Elections, therefore, provide an essential link between the government and the governed. They serve as a barometer of public opinion and ensure that the holders of public office, and the policies which they pursue, are broadly in accord with the wishes of the general public.

VOTING AND NON-VOTING

It is sometimes argued that the extent to which citizens exercise their right to vote is one indicator of the 'health' of a system of government. A high level of voter participation (which is sometimes referred to as 'turnout') might suggest enthusiasm by members of the public to involve themselves in the affairs of government in their country and, in more general terms, to express support for the political system which operates in that country. A low level of voter participation might reflect a belief that the outcome will not significantly alter the direction of public policy either because electors believe that all parties 'say the same thing' or because they feel that public policy is controlled by global forces over which individual nations can exert no meaningful control.

In some liberal democracies, voting is compulsory: this is the case in Australia, Belgium and Chile, for example. In others, however, it is optional. Where voting is optional, the level of voter participation varies. In 2010, the turnout for the UK general election was 60.9 per cent. In the 2012 American presidential election, around 129 million persons voted, a turnout of 54.87 per cent of all Americans who were eligible to vote in that contest.

Various reasons might explain non-voting. Factors such as social class, education and income may be influential forces in determining whether a person votes or abstains. Generally, low voting rates are found among persons from low socio-economic backgrounds. Voting laws and registration procedures may also influence turnout. In the UK, for example, local authorities actively seek to ensure that voters are registered. In America, the onus of registration is placed on the individual and low levels of voting are sometimes attributed to the complex registration procedures utilized in some states. In 2012, the American Voting Age Population was around 235 million, but the number of registered voters was only 180 million. However, the turnout of registered voters was high – approximately 71.6 per cent.

Low levels of voting may result in public policy failing to represent the national interest. If public opinion is imperfectly represented, governments may be swayed to act at the bidding of organized minorities. Disinclination by the public to involve themselves in the government of their country may also pave the way for totalitarianism, in which the public become frozen out of participation in government. Alternatively, however, it might be argued that low voting levels are not of great importance. Non-voting may indicate a general level of popular satisfaction with the way in which public affairs are conducted – a popular mentality based on the 'if it ain't broken, why fix it?' approach.

The cost of election campaigns

Key idea (2)

In 2010, it was estimated that total spending by all parties in the UK general election amounted to £31 million and the total cost of the 2012 American presidential and congressional elections was estimated to have been $6 billion.

The perception that financial wealth is the underpinning of success in election contests suggests that only wealthy people can be elected to public office. Accordingly, the spiralling costs of election campaigns have prompted some countries to place limits on the spending of individual candidates and political parties. In the United Kingdom, the 2000 Political Parties Elections and Referendum Act capped the expenditure of political parties in national elections and referendums, and the 2009 Political Parties and Elections Act introduced new limits for spending by individual candidates.

In America, public funding for the campaigns of candidates for the office of president (embracing both the primary elections and general election contest) was introduced in 1974 and first used in the 1976 presidential election. It is administered by the Federal Election Commission.

In practice, however, public funding has failed to prevent excessive expenditure in presidential election campaigns as there are ways to avoid federal limits. Super PACs (a type of political action group – see Chapter 6) first appeared in the 2012 presidential contest and were able to spend whatever money they wished on advertising to promote a party candidate, provided they did not actively engage in that candidate's campaign. Additionally, candidates may opt out of the process and spend whatever money they wish. The 2012 presidential election campaign was the first where both major candidates opted out of public funding arrangements for both primary and the national election contests.

The mandate

Key idea (3)

Those who win elections claim the right to carry out the policies on which they fought their campaign. It is argued that public endorsement of their views gives them a mandate to carry them out.

At national election contests, the political parties put forward a statement of the principles or policies that will guide their future actions should they succeed in taking control of public affairs. In the United Kingdom this statement is termed an election manifesto and in America is referred to as a platform. The party that succeeds in gaining control of a public body through the election of its nominees claims to have a mandate to administer it in line with the statements contained in its election manifesto. Its right to do this has been legitimized by the process of popular election.

Below, we consider some of the **weaknesses** that are associated with the concept of the mandate.

THE ELECTION PRODUCES AN UNCLEAR OUTCOME

Some liberal democracies have parliamentary systems of government. The UK is an example of this, whereby general elections are concerned with returning local representatives for individual parliamentary constituencies. Normally, the party with the largest number of MPs forms the government. However, if no single party possesses an overall majority of seats in the new House of Commons (a situation know as a 'hung parliament') it can be argued that no one party can claim the right to pursue the policies set out in their election manifesto.

THE EMERGENCE OF ISSUES FOLLOWING AN ELECTION

It would be unrealistic for us to expect that a party could include every item of policy that it intended to carry out over a period of several years in a single document prepared for a specific election. Issues emerge, unforeseen when the manifesto was prepared, which have to be responded to even though the public lack the opportunity to express their views on them.

We accept, therefore, that once installed into office, governments need to exercise a certain amount of discretion to respond to pressing problems when they arise. This capacity to act without consulting the general public is referred to as trusteeship.

VOTERS ENDORSE PARTIES RATHER THAN THEIR POLICIES

A party's right to carry out all its promises on the grounds that the public expressed support for them is also a flawed argument. Electors are unable to pick and choose between those policies in a manifesto which they like and those of which they disapprove. It is a question of supporting all or nothing. It is also the case that voters support a party for reasons other than the policies that it advances. Factors such as social class may determine a voter's political allegiance. In extreme circumstances, this may mean that parties secure support in spite of, rather than because of, the policies they put forward.

VOTING MAY BE INFLUENCED BY NEGATIVE FACTORS

It may be argued that the key purpose of elections is to provide a mechanism through which politicians can be held to account by the voters for their previous actions, such as their record in office. We refer to this as *ex post facto* accountability, which suggests that a party or its candidates may secure support for negative rather than positive reasons. For example, it was argued that the outcome of the 2010 UK general election was affected by popular dissatisfaction with the record of the previous Labour government and Gordon Brown's leadership of it. Parties may use smear tactics during a campaign to attack their opponents at the expense of projecting their own policies. Support obtained for negative reasons makes it difficult for parties to claim they have a mandate to carry out their election manifesto promises.

Voting behaviour

Key idea (4)

Psephology is the name given to social scientific examinations that seek to provide an understanding as to why people support a particular political party.

There are a number of factors that may explain a voter's attachment to a political party. These include religion, and local and regional influences. Examples of the latter include the Italian Lega Nord, the Scottish National Party, Plaid Cymru in Wales, the Parti Québécois in Quebec, Canada, and the Catalan Republican Left and Basque National parties in Spain.

Gender and race may also influence party affiliation. The African–Caribbean vote is an important constituent of the support enjoyed by the United Kingdom Labour Party, and the American Democratic Party has also historically enjoyed considerable support from this segment of American society, and also from Hispanic (especially Catholic Hispanic) voters.

The study and scientific analysis of elections is termed psephology, on which models of voting behaviour are based. These models, which were developed after 1945, drew heavily on American political science. Their aim is to provide an explanation for voting behaviour that holds good for a significant proportion of the electorate and, additionally, applies from one generation to the next when a large number of citizens become eligible to vote for the first time, replacing former voters who have died.

The Michigan model was influential and suggested that the basis of voting behaviour was an attachment formed between voters and political parties. It was perceived that an individual's association with a political party was determined by the influences encountered in his or her social relationships. Of these, the major factor was the family. This helped to explain constant attachment to a political party across the generations regardless of factors such as upward or downward social mobility.

CHANGES AFFECTING PARTY AFFILIATION

Social class was often regarded as a key influence of a voter's choice of political party. This dominated explanations of voting behaviour in the United Kingdom from 1945 until 1970 when partisan and class dealignment gave rise to new models of voting behaviour.

'Class is the basis of British party politics; all else is embellishment and detail' (Pulzer, 1967: 98).

'During the 1960s, consistently more than 80% of the electorate had at least a fairly strong attachment to their chosen political party ... the strength of partisanship ... helps to explain the stable two-party system during the 1960s' (Robinson, 2010: 104).

Pulzer, P. (1967) *Political Representation and Elections: Parties and Voting in Great Britain.* New York: Praeger.

Robinson, C. (2010) *Electoral Systems and Voting in the United Kingdom.* Edinburgh: Edinburgh University Press.

▶ Partisan dealignment

'Partisan dealignment' means that a large number of electors either desert the party to which they were traditionally committed, or identify with the party that they historically supported far more weakly. A number of factors may explain this phenomenon. These include increased education and political awareness of many members of the electorate (making them prone to basing their vote on logical as opposed to traditional considerations) and perceptions that the party normally supported by an elector does not reflect his or her own views on key issues. For example, the loss of support experienced by the United Kingdom Labour Party in the early 1980s was attributed to the 'swing to the Left' which occurred after the 1979 general election defeat causing what is termed an 'ideological disjuncture' between the views and values of the party and those of its supporters.

Political crises may also influence partisan dealignment. In America, between 1958 and 1968 key political issues such as the Vietnam War and the Civil Rights Movement resulted in an increased number of voters registering themselves as independents. In France in the same period, however, the perception that the Gaullist Party would defend economic development and political stability in the face of civil unrest resulted in enhanced voter identification with that party.

▶ Class dealignment

'Class dealignment' suggests that the historic identity between a political party and a particular social class becomes of reduced significance. In the United Kingdom, this might be explained after 1970 by the reduced intensity of class consciousness which arose for a number of reasons, including the increased affluence of the working class (which is termed 'embourgeoisement'), the decline in the number of manual workers, and the rise in the service sector of employment. This was perceived to have a particularly damaging effect on the electoral prospects of the Labour Party which failed to win a general election between 1979 and 1997.

The twin effects of partisan and class dealignment had two main consequences for the conduct of politics. It resulted in third parties obtaining increased levels of support, and made the core support given to established major parties less consistent from one general election to the next. These factors make voting behaviour more volatile and gave rise to new models including issue voting, which suggested that specific topical events or policies influenced a person's political behaviour. A further model, the consumer model of voting behaviour built upon the concept of issue-based voting, suggested that a person's choice of political party was similar to a shopper's choice of goods in a supermarket.

▶ Realignment

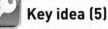

Key idea (5)

Realignment entails a redefinition of the relationship between political parties and key social groups within society that has a fundamental impact on their relative strength.

Partisan and class dealignment, which entail the loosening of traditional bonds attaching individuals and groups to particular parties, may be the prelude to realignment.

The formation of new relationships is usually confirmed in what is termed a 'realigning election', which is seen as the start of new patterns of political behaviour. In the United Kingdom, the 1918 general election evidenced the desertion of the working-class vote from the Liberal Party to the Labour Party. The 1932 American presidential election, which witnessed the birth of the 'New Deal coalition', was a further example of realignment. This coalition was composed of union members, ethnic minorities, liberals and intellectuals, and these newly established patterns of voter loyalties provided the Democratic Party with domination over Congress and the presidency for a number of subsequent decades. In both of these examples, however, the changes in voter loyalty which were evidenced at the realignment elections had been initiated much earlier.

Subsequent examples of realignment have occurred. In America, the victories of Ronald Reagan in 1980 and 1984 were based on the existence of a new coalition. The preference of white male voters in the southern states of America for the Republican Party indicated a major shift in this group's political affiliation that had taken place earlier in the 1970s. In the United Kingdom, the era of Conservative Party dominance (1979–97) rested in part on the defection of relatively affluent members of the working class in south-eastern England (who were dubbed 'Essex Men' and characterized by working in the private sector and owning their own homes) to vote Conservative. However, neither of these changes has been sufficient to bring about a substantial era of political dominance for the parties which benefitted from them. In America, the Democrats succeeded in winning the presidency from the Republicans in 1992 and in the United Kingdom the Conservative Party was voted out of office in the 1997 general election. One aspect of Labour's victory in 1997 was subsequently alleged to have been the defection of white collar professional women (dubbed 'Worcester woman') from the Conservative Party to Labour.

Opinion polls

Key idea (6)

Various forms of opinion polls are put to a wide range of political purposes, which include predicting the outcome of election contests. However, some commentators question the role performed by polls in liberal democratic political affairs.

Election contests are usually accompanied by a wide range of opinion polls that aim to predict the winner. Opinion polls seek to determine the views of the public by putting questions to a small group of people. There are several ways in which this group might be selected. The two main ways are through the use of a random or a quota sample. The first (**random sample**) addresses questions to a segment of the public who are chosen by a method which lacks scientific construction. In Britain, for example, a random sample might consist of every thousandth name on the register of electors in a particular parliamentary constituency. A **quota sample**, however, seeks to address questions to a group of people whose composition is determined in advance. By this method, questions are directed at a group who are perceived to be a cross-section of the public whose views are being sought. It will attempt, for example, to reflect the overall balance between old and young people, men and women and working- and middle-class people.

Opinion polls may be utilized to ascertain public feelings on particular issues. The findings of polls can then be incorporated into the policy proposals put forward by political parties. They are especially prominent in election campaigns. They are used to assess the views of voters on particular issues which may encourage parties to adjust the emphasis of their campaigns (or the content of their policy) to match the popular mood. They are also employed to investigate the outcome of elections by asking voters who they intend to support. The belief that this activity does not merely indicate public feelings but may actually influence voting behaviour (for example, by creating a bandwagon effect for the party judged by the polls to be in the lead) has prompted countries such as France and Italy to ban the publication of poll results close to the actual contest.

The accuracy of opinion polls has also been called into question since they are not consistently accurate especially when seeking to predict the outcome of an election contest. In 1995 the polls wrongly predicted a major victory for Silvio Berlusconi in the Italian regional elections (which his party lost) and a clear victory for Jacques Chirac in the first round of the French presidential election (in which he was defeated by the socialist, Lionel Jospin). In the 2010 UK general election, opinion polls tended to over-represent support for the Liberal Democrats and slightly underestimate support for the Labour Party.

There are several reasons that might explain the shortcomings of opinion polls. Some people may refuse to answer the pollsters' questions. This may distort the result if the refusal to answer is disproportionately associated with one segment of electoral opinion. Polls rely on those who are questioned telling the truth and subsequently adhering to the opinions which they express to the pollsters. The 'last-minute swing' phenomenon suggests that members of the general public may change their minds and depart from a previously expressed opinion. Polls may also find accuracy difficult when the public is evenly divided on the matter under investigation.

EXIT POLLS

Exit polls are a form of opinion poll. They are conducted after an election has taken place and ask citizens as they leave the polling station who they have voted for.

Exit polls are a particular aid to the media who frequently sponsor them in order to be in a position to predict the winner of a contest soon after voting has ended but before the official results are declared. Exit polls are usually accurate, although in the 2000 American presidential election the closeness of the contest between George W. Bush and Al Gore resulted in difficulties. In some states the media predicted one or other of these two candidates as the victor on the evidence of exit polls only to be forced to retract this assertion as the ballots were counted. Problems of this nature also occurred in the 2004 election when the National Exit Poll predicted a 3-percentage point lead for Kerry. In the event, Bush secured a 2.5-percentage point lead and retained the presidency.

The first-past-the-post electoral system and its variants

The remainder of this chapter will consider electoral systems that are used to elect officials to public office: we will start with the first-past-the-post system.

The first-past-the-post (FPTP) electoral system determines the winner of an election contest in similar ways to how the victors in horse races or athletic events are decided.

Under this system, to be elected to a public office it is necessary for a candidate to secure more votes than the person who comes second. But there is no requirement that the winning candidate should secure an overall majority of the votes cast in an election. It is thus possible for a candidate to be victorious under this system despite having secured a minority of the votes cast in an election.

Spotlight

The weakness of the first-past-the-post electoral system is illustrated by the following example.

In the UK parliamentary constituency of Norwich South at the 2010 general election the following result was obtained:

Lib Dem	13,960	29.4%
Labour	13,650	28.7%
Conservative	10,902	22.9%
Green	7,095	14.9%
Others	1,944	4.1%

The Liberal Democrat candidate was elected to the House of Commons for this constituency although he obtained only 29.3 per cent of the votes that were cast by the local electors.

In some countries, electoral systems have been devised that seek to adjust the workings of the first-past-the-post system. These are the second ballot and the alternative vote. Neither of these constitutes a system of proportional representation (a term which we define below) although they do attempt to put right some of the injustices which may arise under the first-past-the-post system.

THE SECOND BALLOT

The second ballot is used in France, both for legislative and presidential elections. The process is a two-stage affair. It is necessary for a candidate to obtain an overall majority of votes cast in the first-round election in order to secure election to public office. In other words, if 50,000 people voted in a constituency it would be necessary for a candidate to secure 25,001 votes to be elected. If no candidate obtained this required figure, a second-round election is held and the candidate who wins most votes is elected. This system seeks to ensure that the winning candidate gets the endorsement of a majority of the electors who cast their votes in the second election.

For presidential contests, the second ballot is between the top two candidates from the first round. For elections to the National Assembly, any candidate who obtains 12.5 per cent of the vote in the first round may enter the second ballot. In practice, however, parties of the Left and Right have often agreed in advance to rally behind one candidate for the second ballot.

A variant of the second ballot is the supplementary vote system, which is used in the UK to elect the Mayor of London, and Police and Crime Commissioners. Under this system, voters select candidates in order of preference (numbering them 1, 2, etc.). If no candidate obtains an overall majority (50 per cent + 1 of the votes cast) there is no second ballot. Instead, the top two candidates remain in the contest and the votes of all of those who are eliminated are redistributed to determine the outcome of the contest.

THE ALTERNATIVE VOTE

The alternative vote is used in Ireland for presidential elections and for by-elections to the lower House, the *Dáil*. It is also used to select members for the Australian House of Representatives. As with the second ballot described above, a candidate cannot be elected without obtaining majority support from the electorate (namely 50 per cent + 1 of the votes cast). Unlike the second ballot, however, there is no second election.

Voters number candidates in order of preference. If, when these votes are counted, no candidate possesses an overall majority, the candidate with least first-preference votes is eliminated and these are redistributed to the candidate placed second on that candidate's ballot paper. This process is repeated until a candidate has an overall majority composed of his or her first-preference votes coupled with the redistributed votes of candidates who have been eliminated.

Proportional representation

Key idea (8)

Proportional representation seeks to ensure that candidates elected to a legislative body, such as the UK House of Commons, at a general election correspond to the proportion of votes each party obtained in that election.

Proportional representation indicates an objective rather than a specific method of election. It seeks to guarantee that the wishes of the electorate are arithmetically reflected in the composition of public bodies such as legislatures and local authorities. This is achieved by ensuring that parties are represented according to the level of popular support they enjoy at an election contest. Various forms of proportional representation are used widely in countries within the EU. This section will consider two of these – the single transferable vote and the party list system.

THE SINGLE TRANSFERABLE VOTE

When used for elections to legislatures, the single transferable vote requires a country to be divided into a number of multi-member constituencies (that is, constituencies which return more than one member to the legislative body). When electors cast their votes, they are required to number candidates in order of preference. They may indicate a preference for as many, or as few, candidates as they wish. To be elected a candidate has to secure a quota of votes. This quota (which is termed the 'Droop quota', after its nineteenth-century 'inventor', Henry Droop) is calculated by the following formula:

$$\left(\frac{\text{total number of valid votes cast in the constituency}}{\text{total number of seats to be filled} + 1}\right) + 1$$

Thus in a constituency in which 100,000 electors voted and there were four seats to be filled, the quota would be 20,001. Any candidate who obtains the necessary number of first-preference votes is declared elected. Further first-preference votes cast for that candidate are then redistributed to the candidates listed second on the ballot paper of the candidate who has been elected.

If, when the count is complete, no candidate obtains the necessary number of first-preference votes, the candidate with fewest is eliminated and these are redistributed to the candidates listed as second choice on the eliminated candidate's ballot paper. This process of eliminating candidates with fewest first-preference votes is continued until the requisite number of seats is filled.

The single transferable vote system ensures that each successful candidate is elected by a similar number of votes. It is used in Ireland for elections to the *Dáil* and for the majority of seats in the Upper Chamber (the *Seanad*). Of the 60 members of the *Seanad*, 49 are elected in this fashion. This system is employed in Northern Ireland for the election of members to the European Parliament and the Northern Irish Assembly. It is also used for elections to the Australian Senate.

THE PARTY LIST SYSTEM

The other main system of proportional representation is the party list system. Its main objective is to ensure that parties are represented in legislative bodies in proportion to the votes that were cast for them. Political parties are responsible for drawing up lists of candidates that may be compiled on a national or on a regional basis.

There are several versions of the party list system. In a very simplistic form (in what is termed a 'closed party list') candidates are ranked in order of preference by political parties and voters place an 'X' against the political party which they wish to support. Countries which include South Africa use the closed party list system.

An alternative version of the party list system is the 'open party list', which is used in countries which include Finland and Brazil. Voters may determine the ranking of candidates put forward by the individual parties by numbering them in order of preference (1, 2, 3, etc.), although their choice is limited to voting for candidates in the list presented by one single party. A third variant of the party list system is the 'free party list system'. This is used for elections in countries which include Luxembourg and Switzerland where voters are able to cast as many votes as there are seats to be filled. The main feature of this system is the 'mix-in' (or panachage) whereby voters are not confined to selecting candidates from one party's list but may support any candidate whose name appears on the ballot paper regardless of which party nominated them.

A number of formulas exist to determine the quotas used in the party list system that successful candidates are required to obtain in order to secure election. A popular one in Europe is the *D'Hondt* system, which is used for national elections in Belgium, the Netherlands, Portugal and Spain, for electing members of the European Parliament representing England, Scotland and Wales, and for selecting the 11 'top-up' members to the Greater London Assembly (the other 14 being chosen by the first-past-the-post system). The D'Hondt formula (named after its nineteenth-century Belgium inventor, Victor D'Hondt) uses the 'highest averages' formula which seeks to ensure a party's representation in the legislative body arithmetically reflects the proportion of votes which it obtained. Thus a party that obtained 20 per cent of the total national poll would be entitled to 20 per cent of the seats in the legislative chamber. If this chamber contained 300 members, that party would be entitled to fill 60 places. When applied to a closed party list, the elected nominees would be those numbered 1–60 on that party's list. When applied to an open party list system, voter preference would determine which candidates filled the party's overall seat allocation.

An alternative formula, Hagenbach-Bischoff (named after its nineteenth-century Swiss inventor, Eduard Hagenbach-Bischoff), determines the quota of votes required to secure an election by dividing the total vote by the number of seats to be filled plus one. This system (which is very similar to the Droop Quota) is used for elections to the Greek Parliament and for Luxembourg's Chamber of Deputies.

▶ The additional member system

The additional- (or mixed-) member system of election blends the first-past-the-post system with proportional representation. This mixed system is used in Germany, for example, and ensures that minority parties that fare badly under the former system can be compensated under the latter. Under this country's additional member system, electors have two votes in parliamentary elections. The first (*Erststimme*) is for a constituency candidate, who is elected under the first-past-the-post system for each of the country's 299 single-member constituencies. The second (*Zweitstimme*) is for a party list drawn up in each state (or Land). The additional members are drawn from this second vote and the *Hare-Niemeyer* system (which replaced the *D'Hondt* system in 1985) is used to allocate the additional members according to the following formula:

$$\frac{\text{total votes obtained by a party} \times \text{number of seats available in the } \textit{Bundestag}}{\text{total number of votes of all parties securing representation in the } \textit{Bundestag}}$$

This formula provides for the proportional allocation of seats in the *Bundestag*: the seats won through the first-past-the-post system are subtracted from the figure obtained by this method and the shortfall is made up from candidates nominated by the states' party lists. This system also gives electors the opportunity of 'split-ticket' voting: that is, they can support a constituency candidate of one party and the party list of another. This is a growing feature in German elections.

In 1992 and 1993, referendums in New Zealand supported changing the electoral system from first-past-the-post to a mixed-member system, whose main features are similar to the electoral system used in Germany. This was first used in the 1996 general election, and a third referendum held in 2011 endorsed the retention of the mixed-member electoral system. Elections to the Scottish Parliament, the Welsh Assembly and Greater London Assembly also use this system. In Scotland and Wales, the additional members are selected from regional party lists drawn up by the political parties and in London from one London-wide party list.

The first-past-the-post electoral system analysed

Key idea (9)

The operation of the first-past-the-post system is easy to understand but it is accused of producing unfair outcomes.

In this section we will consider the strengths and weaknesses of the first-past-the-post electoral system First, the main **strengths** of this system are considered.

ADVANTAGES

▶ **Easy to understand**

The system is relatively easy to understand. Voting is a simple process and it is easy to see how the result is arrived at. The winner takes all.

▶ **Executive strength**

The failure of this system to ensure that the composition of the legislature arithmetically reflects the way in which a nation has voted often benefits the party winning most votes nationally. This is of particular importance in parliamentary systems of government such as the UK where the executive is drawn from the legislature, since it may provide the executive with a larger parliamentary majority than its popular vote justified, thereby enhancing its ability to govern.

One example of how this works occurred in the UK in 2005. In the general election held in that year, a Labour government was returned. Although this party obtained only 35.2 per cent of the votes cast by the electorate, the workings of the first-past-the-post system gave it 355 seats in the House of Commons (54.8 per cent of the total number). This majority guaranteed the government the ability to govern for its full five-year term.

▶ An aid to party unity

The manner in which this system treats minority parties may serve as an inducement for parties either to remain united or to enter into electoral alliances in order to secure political power. This is a particular advantage in countries with parliamentary forms of government since its support within the legislature is likely to be durable.

▶ Enhancement of the link between the citizens and legislators

One criticism of the first-past-the-post electoral system is that it 'is simply unfair. The share of seats that parties receive do not reflect their share of votes; in particular the Liberal Democrats have been severely underrepresented' (Denver, et al., 2012: 208). However, 'supporters of FPTP see its unfairness or disproportionality as a virtue. In particular, it is claimed that in translating votes to seats, the system exaggerates the lead of the winning party in a predictable way and thus ensures that the winner has a clear majority' (Denver, Carman and Johns 2012: 209).

Denver, D., Carman, C. and Johns, R. (2012) *Elections and Voters in Britain*. Basingstoke: Palgrave / Macmillan, 3rd ed.

The first-past-the-post system may strengthen the relationship between members of the legislative branch of government and those who voted for them (their constituents). In the UK, the House of Commons is composed of members elected from 650 single-member constituencies. This aids the development of a close relationship between individual legislators and their constituents. It may also enhance the extent to which legislators can be held accountable for their actions. Local relationships are also of great significance to the conduct of American politics.

WEAKNESSES

In this section the main **weaknesses** of this system are considered.

Key idea (10)

There are a number of problems associated with the first-past-the-post electoral system that relate to the way the electorate's votes are not faithfully translated into representation in a country's legislature.

▶ Distortion of public opinion

It has been suggested that the purpose of elections is to ensure that public office holders and the policies they pursue are reflective of public opinion. A key problem with the first-past-the-post system is that it distorts public opinion by failing to ensure that the wishes of the electorate are arithmetically reflected in the composition of the legislative or executive branches of government. This may therefore result in public policy being out of line with the views or wishes of the majority of the general public.

There are further difficulties arising from the tendency of the first-past-the-post system to distort public opinion. It may produce extreme changes in the composition of the legislatures that do not reflect the political views of the electorate. Major political parties can be virtually wiped out by such a system. An extreme example of this occurred in the 1993 Canadian general election when the ruling Conservative Party was reduced from

157 seats to 2 in the House of Commons. Violent changes in the composition of the legislature or executive branches of government result in the loss of experienced personnel and may create a system of adversarial politics. Parties have less incentive to co-operate when the electoral system may translate them overnight from a minority to a majority.

▶ Unfair treatment of minority parties

A second problem arising from the operations of the first-past-the-post system is the manner in which it treats minority parties. In the UK, the Liberal Party/Liberal Democrats have, for much of the twentieth century, been under-represented in parliament as the electoral system failed to translate that party's national vote into seats within the legislature. Although this party has fared better in general elections held since 1997 than in previous contests (as its support became concentrated in certain areas rather than being evenly spread across the country), its share of the national poll in 2010 (23 per cent) entitled it to 149 seats rather than the 57 it actually won.

Expressing this figure another way, in 2010:

- ▶ It took 33,350 votes to elect a Labour MP
- ▶ It took 34,989 votes to elect a Conservative MP
- ▶ It took 119,788 votes to elect a Liberal Democrat MP

This clearly contravenes the liberal democratic principle of 'one vote, one value'.

▶ Disincentive to voter participation

A further problem with the first-past-the-post system is that it may discourage voter participation. Areas may be considered 'safe' political territory for one party or another and this may discourage opponents of that party from voting on the grounds that if they do so their vote is effectively 'wasted'.

▶ The downplaying of ideology

The first-past-the-post system may discourage parties from fragmenting and thus promote the conduct of politics within the confines of a two-party system. However, this may result in ideology becoming diluted, obscured or played down in order for the parties to serve as vehicles capable of attracting a wide range of political opinions. The absence of a distinct identity may result in voters becoming disinterested in the conduct of politics. The consequence of this is low turnouts in elections and the utilization of alternative ways (such as pressure group activity and various forms of direct action) in order to bring about political change.

Are the benefits of the first-past-the-post system in the UK always realized in practice?

In the UK, the executive branch of government comes from the majority party in the legislative body. However, strong governments (in the sense of the executive having a large parliamentary majority and thus being in a position to ensure the enactment of its election manifesto) have not been a consistent feature of post-1945 politics. Eighteen general elections have been held between 1945 and 2010: in six of these (1950, 1951, 1964, February 1974, October 1974 and 1992) governments were returned with a relatively small majority and in two cases (February 1974 and 2010) a 'hung Parliament' (in which no single party possessed an overall majority of votes in the new House of Commons) was produced.

Result of the 2010 UK general election:

Party	Votes	Seats
Conservative	10,703,700 (36.1%)	306
Labour	8,606,500 (29.0%)	258
Liberal Democrats	6,836,300 (23.0%)	57
Others	3,541,200 (11.9%)	29

In total 29,687,700 electors (65.1 per cent) of the total voted, an increase of 3.7 per cent on the previous general election held in 2005.

Proportional representation analysed

Key idea (11)

Proportional representation is widely used in countries in the EU, but is criticized for consequences that include the production of multi-party systems and coalition government.

In this section we will consider the strengths and weaknesses of proportional representation.

The main advantage of proportional representation is that the system addresses many of the defects of the first-past-the-post system. It ensures that the votes obtained nationally by parties are reflected in the composition of a country's legislature, which is to the particular benefit of minority parties. Legislative bodies throughout Europe contain members drawn from parties such as the Green Party, and thus provide an inducement for such groups to operate within the conventional political system rather than engage in various forms of protest conducted outside the arena of conventional political activity. Proportional representation may also induce parties to co-operate in order to jointly secure political power. This is especially likely to occur in cases where the executive is drawn from the legislative body and may, in turn, be a disincentive for mainstream political parties to endorse extremist views with which no other party would wish to become associated.

However, proportional representation is associated with a number of disadvantages which we will consider below.

REPRESENTATION GIVEN TO POLITICAL EXTREMISTS
Proportional representation may facilitate the representation of the political extremes which, once established within a legislative body, gain respectability and may enjoy a growth in their support. Some countries that use this system seek to guard against this problem by imposing a requirement that a party needs to attain a minimum threshold of national support

in order to secure the return of its candidates to the country's legislative body. In Denmark, this figure is 2 per cent of the national vote; in Sweden 4 per cent and in Turkey 10 per cent.

In Germany, a party must secure 5 per cent of the national vote (or, alternatively, three directly elected members' seats secured from the constituency contests) to qualify for additional members. In the 1998 German national election, this threshold figure enabled the Greens and Communists to secure representation in the *Bundestag*, but denied it to parties on the extreme right of the political spectrum. In 2013, however, the Free Democratic Party (which had been a junior partner in a number of coalition governments since the late 1940s), obtained only 4.8 per cent of the national vote and, as it had no directly elected members either, found itself excluded from representation in the *Bundestag* for the first time in its history.

CREATION OF MULTI-PARTY SYSTEMS

The tendency for proportional representation to aid minority parties to obtain representation in legislative bodies may promote the development of a multi-party system. This is of particular significance for those countries with parliamentary forms of government whose executives are drawn from the legislative body. In these cases, multi-party systems may make it difficult for the electorate to determine the composition of the executive or the policies which it pursues. Additionally, executives may consist of a coalition of parties that are often depicted as being weak and unstable. The high threshold figure used in Turkey (which requires a party to secure 10 per cent of the national vote in order to qualify for parliamentary representation) is designed to avoid the political instability associated with multi-party coalitions.

COMPLEXITY

Critics of proportional representation argue that the system is difficult in the sense that it may not be obvious how the eventual result has been arrived at. This is especially the case with the single transferable vote which requires a process of redistribution (either of the surplus votes of an elected candidate or of the redundant votes of the ones who have been eliminated). Such votes are not randomly redistributed and electors may not fully understand how this process is carried out. A danger with this is that if the process by which the result is arrived at is not fully understood, the result itself may be deprived of popular legitimacy.

ENHANCEMENT OF POSITION OF PARTY LEADERSHIP

Proportional representation has been accused of enhancing the power of the party leadership. This is especially the case with the party list system, which may give regional or national party leaders the ability to place candidates in order of preference and thereby improve the chances of loyal party members being elected by placing them higher in the rankings ahead of those who are regarded as dissentients. This objection is, however, mitigated by the ability of electors to vote for individual candidates in some of the countries that utilize the party list method of election.

MINOR PARTIES MAY OBTAIN UNWARRANTED POLITICAL INFLUENCE

Opponents of proportional representation assert that minor parties may secure a role in a country's political affairs that is out of all proportion to their levels of support. The relatively small Free Democratic Party in Germany enjoyed participation in government between 1969 and 1998 as it held a pivotal position between Christian Democrats and Social Democrats. It could keep either party out of office by siding with the other. The outcome of New Zealand's first national election using proportional representation in 1996 gave the New Zealand First Party (which had obtained 13 per cent of the vote and 17 seats in parliament) a place in a coalition government headed by the National Party, and following the 1997 general election in Ireland the small Progressive Democrat Party was able to enter into a coalition government with *Fianna Fáil*.

IMPACT ON LEGISLATOR AND CONSTITUENT RELATIONSHIPS

It might be argued that proportional representation weakens the link between legislator and constituent, which in countries such as the UK and America is regarded as a crucial political feature. This problem arises as multi-member constituencies are often large. However, this is not a universal feature of proportional representation. The multi-member constituencies used for elections to the *Dáil* in Ireland are small: in the 2011 general election, 43 constituencies returned 165 members. There are at least three MPs to each constituency and the total number of electors in 2011 was around 3.3 million. Additionally, the ability of electors to express support for individual candidates under some versions of the party list system may also serve to enhance the relationship between constituent and representative.

Dig Deeper

Denver, D., Carman, C. and Johns, R. (2012) *Elections and Voters in Britain.* Basingstoke: Palgrave/Macmillan, 3rd ed.

Dummett, M. (1997) *Principles of Electoral Reform.* Oxford: Oxford University Press.

Farrell, D. (2011) *Electoral Systems: A Comparative Introduction.* Basingstoke: Palgrave/Macmillan, 2nd ed.

Robinson, C. (2010) *Electoral Systems and Voting Behaviour in the United Kingdom.* Edinburgh: Edinburgh University Press.

Fact- check

1 The scientific study that seeks to explain why electors vote the way they do is termed:
  a An exit poll
  b Toxicology
  c Philately
  d Psephology

2 An exit poll is carried out:
  a When a government leaves office
  b To determine whether a member state of the EU is allowed to leave
  c After electors have voted in an election contest
  d At the end of a UK Parliamentary Session

3 The erosion of the identity between a political party and a specific social class is known as:
  a Embourgeoisement
  b Class dealignment
  c Partisan realignment
  d Defection

4 The electoral system used in UK general elections is known as:
  a The one man, one vote system
  b The single transferable vote system
  c The first-past-the-post system
  d The party list system

5 The quota of votes that a candidate is required to secure in order to be elected under the single transferable vote system was invented by:
  a Albert Einstein
  b Margaret Thatcher
  c Henry Ford
  d Henry Droop

6 Which of the following countries used the additional member system for elections to their national parliament (legislature):

   a The Irish Republic

   b Germany

   c France

   d The USA

5

Political parties and party systems

Political parties are especially prominent at election times. Their key purpose is to determine the composition of government and the policies that it carries out. To achieve this objective a party may operate independently or it can co-operate with other political parties by participating in coalition governments. In this chapter we will consider the functions served by political parties, the factors influencing their development, and the contemporary problems facing political parties.

Parties and party systems

GENERAL CHARACTERISTICS

Key idea (1)

A political party is a formally organized organization that seeks to secure power and exercise control over government. This may be at national, state, regional or local level.

It has been argued that *'Most democratic parties seek to control the executive function of government … and in democracies they organise themselves to win elections and form administrations (or at least participate in their formation) in order to control the machinery of government'* (Ingle, 2008: 2).

Ingle, S. (2008) *The British Party System: An Introduction.* London: Routledge, 4th ed. revised.

Parties seek political power. A party possesses a formal structure that involves national leadership and local organization. The main role of the latter is to contest elections and recruit party members. This organization is permanent, although it may be most active at election times. The relationship between a party's leaders and its membership varies quite considerably, especially the extent to which a party's leaders can be held accountable for their actions by its rank-and-file supporters. Policy making is frequently the preserve of the party's national leadership, which may also possess some degree of control over the selection of candidates for public office.

Although we tend to regard political parties openly competing for power as the hallmark of a liberal democracy, political parties often exist in countries that do not possess a liberal democratic political system. The ability to inaugurate meaningful change within society is thus an important qualification required by political parties in a liberal democracy. They should be able to carry out their policies without hindrance from other state institutions.

▶ Dominant party systems and one-party states

We might believe that it is essential in a liberal democracy that office should alternate between political parties. However in some countries, one party frequently wins national elections. This was the case for *Fianna Faíl* (which held office in Ireland for 37 of the 43 years between 1932 and 1973), for the UK Conservative Party (which won four successive general elections and formed the government between 1979 and 1997) and the UK Labour Party (which won three successive general elections held after 1997). In Germany, Helmut Kohl's Christian-Socialist-dominated government and was in power from 1982 until 1998.

However, in all these countries, the replacement of the party holding office is theoretically possible and it is the potential of change that separates a one-party state (in which opposition parties are not allowed openly to exist) from one in which a single political party is dominant but that could be replaced through the process of free elections.

One-party dominance has been characterized as *'a competitive (multi) party system wherein one party dominates government, the policy agenda, political competition and discourse, and determines political opinion for a considerable amount of time and without any use of governmental repression, but, wherein opposition parties and societal forces do have a vital function as concerns the shaping of patterns of interaction within the party system'* (Spiess, 2009: 12).

Spiess, C. (2009) *Democracy and Party Systems in Developing Countries: A Comparative Study of India and South Africa.* Abingdon, Oxfordshire: Routledge.

FACTIONS AND TENDENCIES

Key idea (2)

The term faction denotes the existence of a minority group within a larger body that takes issue with the majority over the leadership of that body or the policies that it advocates.

A faction is frequently defined as a group that exists within a political party. It consists of a group with formal organization and a relatively stable membership and is effectively a 'party within a party'. The Italian Christian Democrats and Japan's Liberal Democrats are essentially coalitions of several factions.

Tea Party Movement

The Tea Party Movement (TPM) is a faction within the American Republican Party. It is engaged in conventional political activities in addition to the use of protest to further its aims.

The use of the term 'tea party' refers to the 1773 Boston Tea Party, an episode of direct action by Americans who were opposed to paying a tax on tea to the British government. TEA also is an acronym for Taxed Enough Already. The opposition of the TPM to taxation is underpinned by its opposition to large-scale government spending and it seeks to substitute 'big' government (and the loss of personal freedoms that are claimed to arise from this) for a return to individualist values.

The origins of the TPM date from Tax Day protests in the 1990s. The event that is widely regarded as triggering the establishment of the TPM was a rant by the CNBC on-air editor, Rick Santelli, from the floor of the Chicago Mercantile Exchange on 19 February 2009 where he attacked government bailouts and launched an impassioned attack on the Obama administration's Homeowners Affordability and Stability Plan which sought to enable homeowners facing foreclosure to refinance their mortgages.

The growth of the TPM owes much to social media sites. However, its organizational structure is highly decentralized, reflecting a grassroots movement that has been built from the bottom up: 'Tea Party' is an umbrella term that encompasses a wide variety of localized groups. Insofar as there are national Tea Party policies, they are contained in the 2009 Contract from America. This included a reduction of taxes, a simplified taxation system, a balanced federal budget and the identification of the constitutionality of each law (based on a fundamentalist interpretation of this document). Its dislike of 'big government' underpins opposition to a number of policies pursued by the Obama administration which include the stimulus package, bank bailouts and healthcare reform.

In addition to organizing tax-day Tea Party rallies and related events, the TPM also involves itself in conventional political activity. This aspect of activities is especially associated with the Tea Party Express, a political action committee within the TPM. The TPM Express played a prominent role in the 2010 elections, including asking candidates for political office to endorse the Contract from America. A number of Republican candidates did so and, following the elections, House and Senate Tea Party Caucuses were formed.

Factions need to be distinguished from tendencies. These also exist within a political party and consist of persons who share common opinions. Unlike factions, however, they lack formal organization. During Margaret Thatcher's period of office as prime minister in the United Kingdom (1979–90) the 'Wets' were a tendency within the Conservative Party opposed to many of her policies. Towards the end of the 1990s a further tendency emerged within that party, the Eurosceptics. These were opposed to any further moves towards the pooling of sovereignty and political integration within the EU, and in particular opposed the goal of the Maastricht Treaty of economic and monetary union that came into force in 1993. In 1995, Eurosceptics supported the leadership challenge mounted by John Redwood to the then Conservative Party leader and Prime Minister, John Major.

THE FUNDING OF POLITICAL PARTIES
Political parties commonly secure their income from a variety of sources. These may include sponsors (who make regular donations to party funds) and donors (who make 'one-off' gifts).

Commercial activities undertaken by political parties may contribute towards party funds and parties such as the United Kingdom's Labour Party have traditionally derived much of their income from the trade unions, particularly at a general election. Subscriptions paid by party members also constitute a source of funding for some political parties.

A major problem with donations from private or business sources is a perception that those who give money to parties will expect something in return for their outlay. This may include influence over the content of party policy or its leadership.

In some countries political parties are funded by the state. This was vital in Spain and Portugal where the late transition to liberal democratic politics in the 1970s meant that political parties were unable to raise adequate finance themselves. State funding also occurs in Germany (where parties represented in the *Bundestag* receive finance based on the level of their popular support) and in the USA (where since 1976 public funding has been offered to candidates contesting the office of president provided that they accept an overall capping on their total spending).

There are several reasons for state funding of political parties. This avoids perceptions that wealthy people or organizations are able to buy influence over the operations of a political party in return for their financial support. State funding may also place a ceiling over political expenditure, especially at election times. This last objective was one reason for the introduction of federal funding for presidential candidates in America. However, a danger with state funding is that the parties then become perceived as organs of the state, which have little incentive to recruit a mass membership.

Determinants of party systems

Key idea (3)

The origins of political parties often reflect divisions within society founded on factors that include class, religion and regional identity.

Considerable differences exist within liberal democracies concerning the nature of party systems. Some countries such as the UK, America and New Zealand have relatively few political parties. Scandinavia, however, is characterized by multi-party systems. In order to explain these differences we need to consider what factors influence the development of political parties and party systems.

THE BASIS OF PARTY

The degree of homogeneity (that is, uniformity) in a country is an important determinant concerning the formation and development of political parties. Basic divisions within a society might provide the basis of party, reflecting its key divisions. These can include social class, nationalism, religion or race. Any of these factors are capable of providing the basis around which parties are established and subsequently operate. Some form of partisanship in which groups of electors have a strong affinity to a particular political party is crucial to sustain a stable party system.

Let us consider some examples of this.

SOCIAL CLASS

In the UK, social class was a key factor that shaped the development of political parties in the nineteenth and early years of the twentieth century. The landed aristocracy was identified with the Conservative Party, the industrial bourgeoisie with the Liberal Party and the working class with the Labour Party.

RELIGION

In France, Italy and Germany, religion played an important part in providing the underpinning for political parties. In nineteenth-century France, the basic division was between clericals and anti-clericals. Today the vote for left-wing parties is weakest in countries where the influence of the Catholic Church is strongest, although by the 1960s, social class began to play an increasingly important role in determining party affiliation. In Italy, the Christian Democrats initially relied heavily on the Catholic vote, while in Germany the coalition between the Christian Democrats and the Christian Social Union represented a religious alliance between Catholics and Protestants in opposition to the Social Democrats, who were viewed as representative of the secular interests within society.

Spotlight

Historically, religion played an important role in determining party allegiance in Britain. The Liberal Party was associated with non-conformity, whereas the Church of England's relationship with the Conservative (Tory) Party led to the Church being described as 'the Tory party at prayer'.

REGIONALISM AND NATIONALISM

Regional and national sentiments may provide the basis of a party. These may arise from a perception that the national government pays insufficient regard to the interests of people living in peripheral areas and is often underpinned by cultural factors. Regional or national autonomy is frequently demanded by such parties. Examples include the Italian *Lega Nord*, the Scottish National Party, *Plaid Cymru* in Wales, the *Parti Québécois* in Quebec, Canada and the Catalan Republican Left and Basque National parties in Spain.

THE IRISH PARTY SYSTEM

Political parties may emerge when key social divisions are absent. This is the case in Ireland. Here, a party system developed in the early twentieth century in a country that was relatively unified in terms of race, religion, language and social class. The key issue that divided the country was a matter of policy – support or opposition for the 1921 Anglo–Irish Treaty, which accepted the partitioning of Ireland whereby six Irish counties remained part of the United Kingdom.

In response to this situation, two parties emerged – *Fine Gael* (which supported the treaty) and *Fianna Faíl* (which opposed it). However, as the treaty issue became irrelevant to the conduct of Irish politics, the parties remained as permanent interests. In this sense, it might be argued that the parties became the cause of divisions in Ireland rather than reflections of them.

The role of political parties

Key idea (4)

Political parties perform a range of functions that are vital to the operations of liberal democratic government. These include organizing support for governments and helping to promote national harmony. They also act as the vehicle to select our political leaders.

Political parties are now an accepted way for political affairs within liberal democracies to be conducted. But political parties have not always been accepted as helpful political mechanisms.

The American Constitution contained no provisions for party government and in his farewell address to the nation in 1796, President Washington bemoaned the 'baneful effects of the spirit of party'. In France, the development of political parties was checked by the belief that they tended to undermine the national interest.

However, parties became an accepted feature of political life in both of these countries. The 1958 Constitution of the Fifth French Republic specifically acknowledged their existence.

In the early days of the American republic, political parties were viewed in a negative light: *'parties were denounced as harbingers of treasonable divisiveness and as the sources of fanaticism and violence; "party spirit" was viewed as the antithesis of "public spirit"'* (Belloni and Beller, 1976: 531).

Belloni, F. and Beller, D. (1976) The Study of Party Factions as Competitive Political Organisations. *The Western Political Quarterly*, 29(4) pp 531–549.

In this section we consider the major functions carried out by political importance and explain their significance to the operations of liberal democratic government.

SELECTION OF POLITICAL LEADERS

Parties are responsible for selecting candidates for public office at all levels in the machinery of government. Having selected a candidate, the role of the party is then to secure electoral support for its standard bearer. In particular, a country's national leaders emerge through the structure of political parties. Parties provide the main method for selecting a nation's political elite.

This function is an important one. In the nineteenth century, monarchs frequently exercised their powers of patronage to select members of their country's government. But with the gradual extension of the right to vote, the composition of governments became the subject of popular choice, aided by the operations of political parties.

Below, we briefly consider the various methods that the main political parties use to select their leader in the UK and to choose their nominee for the office of the president in America.

Key idea (5)

All three of the UK's main political parties involve their rank-and-file members in the election of their leaders.

The position of party leader is an important one in the UK since, following a general election, the leader of the party with the largest number of seats in the House of Commons will be appointed prime minister and will head the new government. Leadership elections are generally caused by the death or resignation of the incumbent (that is, the person already holding the post), although there are also formal and informal methods to remove a party's leader and thus trigger an election contest to find a replacement. There is, however, no common procedure whereby the main parties choose their leader.

▶ Labour Party

If there is a vacancy, a nomination for the leader or deputy of the Labour Party has to have the endorsement of 12.5 per cent membership of the Parliamentary Labour Party (PLP). If there is no vacancy, nomination by 20 per cent of the membership of PLP is required. The selection of the leader or deputy leader is then determined by an Electoral College, which is composed of three sections – members of the PLP and Labour Members of the European Parliament, individual party members on basis of One Member One Vote (OMOV), and members of affiliated organizations (such as trade unions) who have expressed support for the Labour Party on a one person one vote basis. Since 1993, each section has possessed one-third of the overall vote. The alternative vote system is used to eliminate candidates until one person has 50 per cent of votes.

The last vacancy for the leadership occurred in 2010 when Ed Milliband was elected leader of the Party, narrowly beating his brother David in the fourth round of voting (when David had been narrowly ahead in the previous three rounds). The final vote was 175,519 : 147,220.

In March 2014, a special Labour Party conference held in London backed further organizational reforms initiated by leader Ed Milliband, the main thrust of which was to further reduce trade union influence in Labour Party politics.

The conference endorsed the main proposals of a review, chaired by Lord Collins, agreeing to abolish the Electoral College and to phase out the system whereby workers in affiliated unions can pay a political levy and vote in Labour Party leadership elections. Instead new categories of 'Affiliated Supporters' (whereby trade unionists would be enrolled by their union in the Party locally but at a reduced rate) and 'Registered Supporters' (which was similar but without members having their fees paid through their union) would be introduced. Alternatively trade unionists could become full members of the Party by paying a higher subscription rate. The conference also agreed to raise the threshold required for nomination to stand for the leadership from 12.5 per cent of Labour MPs in the Parliamentary Labour Party (PLP) to 15 per cent.

▶ **Conservative Party**

In the Conservative Party, a leadership election can be triggered by a vote of no confidence by Conservative MPs in their current leader – 15 per cent of Conservative MPs can request this (which is made to the chair of the '1922 Committee'). If the leader then fails to win this vote he or she must resign.

Formal elections for the post of leader were first introduced in 1965, and between then and 1998 only Conservative Members of Parliament were involved in the process. In 1998, new rules were introduced to broaden the leadership election procedure. Candidates for the leadership must be a Member of Parliament and be nominated by two Members of Parliament. If there are more than two candidates, a series of ballots involving MPs are held in which the candidate with least votes is eliminated. This procedure is continued until only two candidates remain. The Party members are then balloted by postal vote to determine which of these two candidates should become leader of the Party. The last contest for the Party leadership occurred in 2005 when David Cameron defeated David Davis by the margin of 134,446 votes to 64,398.

▶ The Liberal Democrats

A candidate for the leadership of the Liberal Democrats must be a Member of Parliament. He or she requires the support of 10 per cent of his or her parliamentary colleagues together with the signatures of 200 party members in at least 20 different constituencies. Candidates with this level of support are balloted by the party members using the alternative vote (unless only two candidates are put forward, in which case the contest is determined by a plurality vote). The last leadership contest occurred in 2007 in which Nick Clegg defeated Chris Huhne by the margin of 20,988 votes to 20,477.

▶ America

The methods that are employed by the Democrats and Republicans to choose their presidential candidates possess many similarities. In both cases, presidential and vice presidential candidates are chosen at the party's national convention. This is held every four years and its role extends to choosing a platform on which the party will contest the forthcoming national election, and choosing a National Committee to be responsible for organizing the next convention and governing the party until this event takes place.

National conventions formerly played a major role in selecting presidential candidates, and were often characterized by wheeling and dealing conducted in smoke-filled rooms going on into the early hours of the morning, and sometimes lasted several days. In 1924, for example, the Democratic National Convention held in New York lasted for 17 days and conducted 103 ballots before selecting John Davis as the Party's presidential candidate. However, since the 1970s the national conventions have played a more restricted role in selecting presidential candidates. The last occasion when a convention exercised a major role in candidate selection for the Democrats was in 1968 when (in the unusual circumstances following the assassination of Senator Robert Kennedy) Hubert Humphrey (who had not stood in the primary elections) was chosen as the Party's nominee. In 1976, considerable support was given at the Republican National Convention to Governor Ronald Reagan, who mounted a strong challenge to the incumbent Republican President, Gerald Ford. Ford defeated Reagan by the narrow margin of 1,187 to 1,070 votes.

Key idea (6)

In the USA, election contests termed 'primaries' are used in many states to help select a party's candidate for the office of president.

However, in more recent years, the national conventions of both parties have tended to rubber stamp decisions that have been taken elsewhere, in the individual states. This situation is mainly due to the enhanced role played by state primaries (whose role is further considered later in this chapter in connection with the reform of political parties). These contests expose potential candidates to the cut and thrust of electioneering and are now widely used to enable party supporters to express their choice as to who should be the party's nominee for the presidency. Although there are differences in the rules affecting primaries (the Republicans tend to allocate delegates on a winner-takes-all basis in each state, whereas the Democrats favour allocating delegates according to the proportion of the vote obtained by each candidate in the state), this procedure means that the delegates who attend the national conventions are pledged (at least in the first ballot) to support a particular candidate (unless he or she has dropped out of the race before the convention meets) and it is common that a front runner has emerged long before the convention actually takes place.

Some states use caucuses instead of primaries to elect delegates who are pledged to support a particular candidate at the national convention. Caucuses are controlled by the parties whereas primary elections are subject to state and local government control.

ORGANIZATION OF SUPPORT FOR GOVERNMENTS

In addition to selecting political leaders, political parties ensure that governments are provided with organized support. This is especially important in parliamentary systems of government where the executive is drawn from the legislative branch of government. In the UK, the party whip system in the House of Commons ensures that governments have the necessary backing to implement their policies. The whip consists of written instructions indicating how the party leadership wishes its members to vote. Members who disobey such instructions may have the whip withdrawn. This entails expulsion from their parliamentary party and their replacement with an alternative party candidate at the next election.

Without the support of party and its accompanying system of party discipline, governments would be subject to the constant fear of defeat. This organization is also adopted by opposition parties, which are thus able to step in and form a government should the incumbent party be defeated. In this sense, parties may also be said to promote political stability by ensuring that a smooth transfer of power from one government to another can be accomplished.

However, while parties aid the operations of liberal democratic political systems, they are not indispensable to it. In America, for example, candidates for public office often promote themselves through personal organizations, even if they latterly attach themselves to a political party. Neither is membership of a major political party essential for those seeking national office. In the 1992 presidential election an independent candidate, Ross Perot, secured 19.7 million votes. Although Perot failed to repeat this feat in subsequent contests, his showing in 1992 demonstrated that, on that occasion, many Americans were willing to endorse as that country's leader a person who had no association with either of the major political parties.

Further, although governments usually rely on the organized support afforded by a political party (or a combination of parties), there are exceptions to this. In 1995, the Italian President, Oscar Luigi Scalfaro, appointed a banker, Lamberto Dini, to be prime minister and head a non-party government. Although this government was seen as a temporary, stop-gap expedient, it does illustrate that governments can be formed without the initial backing of established political parties. It possessed sufficient vitality to survive a vote of 'no confidence' in October 1995 designed to force an early general election. Dini resigned at the end of that year and subsequently headed a caretaker administration.

STIMULATION OF POPULAR INTEREST AND INVOLVEMENT IN POLITICAL AFFAIRS

Political parties also stimulate popular interest and facilitate public participation in political affairs. They perform this function in a number of ways. Parties need to mobilize the electorate in order to win votes and secure the election of their representatives to public office. This requires the party 'selling' itself to the general public. In theory, therefore, a party puts forward its policies and seeks to convince the electorate that these are preferable to those of its opponents. The electorate thus becomes better informed concerning political affairs.

Second, parties enable persons other than a small elite group of public office holders to be involved in political activity. Members of the general public can join political parties and engage in matters such as candidate selection and policy formulation.

Crucially, parties are a mechanism whereby those who hold public office can be made accountable for their actions. Although elections provide the ultimate means to secure the accountability of public office holders, parties may subject these officials to a more regular, day-by-day scrutiny, possessing the sanction of deselecting them as candidates for future elections if they fail to promote party policy.

PROMOTING NATIONAL HARMONY

Political parties simplify the conduct of political affairs and make them more manageable. They transform the demands made by individuals and groups into programmes that can be put before the electorate. This is known as the 'aggregation of interests', which involves a process of arbitration where diverse demands are given a degree of coherence by being incorporated into a party platform or manifesto. One consequence of this is to transform parties into 'broad churches' which seek to maximize their level of support by incorporating the claims of a wide cross-section of society. This function may be at variance with the view that parties exist to promote a political ideology by suggesting that ideology may have to be diluted in order to win elections.

Such activity enables parties to promote national harmony. Numerous divisions exist within societies, based among other things on class, religion or race. However, in order to win elections, parties have to appeal to as many voters as possible. In doing this, they may endorse policies and address appeals which transcend social divisions. Thus parties might serve as a source of national unity by conciliating the conflicts between diverse groups in society. For example, the UK Labour Party needs to secure support from a sizeable section of the middle class in order to form a government. To do this, it may put forward policies to appeal to such voters. In doing so, it bridges the gulf between the working class (whose interests it was formed to advance) and the middle class. One political party thus becomes the vehicle to further the claims of two distinct groups in society.

PROVIDERS OF PATRONAGE

Political parties provide the personnel of government, and in this sense serve as important sources of patronage. They are able to dispense perks to their members. The party in charge of the national government is in the best position to do this. The chief executive can make ministerial appointments, and so the party becomes the vehicle through which political ambitions can be realized. Party supporters can also be rewarded. In the UK this includes paid appointments to public bodies (quangos) and the bestowal of a range of awards through the honours system.

The decline of party?

Key idea (7)

The reduced level of support obtained by established (or 'major') political parties in recent election contests in a number of countries has been attributed to failures associated with performing their traditional roles, and also to more deep-rooted explanations caused by social and economic change.

In the UK, 97 per cent of the vote cast in the 1955 general election went to the Labour and Conservative parties. In 1964, this figure had declined to 88 per cent. It was further reduced to 76 per cent in 1992, and 68 per cent in 2005. More recently, in the UK, the United Kingdom Independence Party (UKIP) secured 27.49 per cent of the vote in the 2014 elections to the European Parliament and 24 of its candidates were elected. This made it the largest UK party in terms of vote and MEPs elected.

In both France and Italy, similar patterns have emerged affecting the support enjoyed by the major parties and their decline has often benefitted extreme right-wing parties, which include the Progress Party in Norway, the Danish People's Party, the Swiss People's Party, the Freedom Party in Austria, the Italian Northern League and the *Vlaams Blok* in Belgium. However, the most significant achievement of extreme right-wing parties occurred in France in 2002 when the *Front National* candidate defeated the Socialist Prime Minister in the first round of the presidential election.

There are two main explanations for the decline in support experienced by established political parties. One of these is social and economic changes that have helped to erode the support traditionally enjoyed by the major parties. For example, the decline in jobs in the French steel, coal and shipbuilding industries has been cited as one explanation for the reduced support for the Communist Party. Immigration may influence the growth of racist political parties. We considered this issue more thoroughly in Chapter 4 in connection with the discussion on dealignment and realignment. In this section, we will discuss a number of problems affecting the manner in which political parties perform their traditional functions which may have eroded public confidence in their operations.

POLITICAL EDUCATION

Parties may not seek to educate the public in any meaningful manner. Election campaigns may be conducted around trivial rather than key issues. Parties may be more concerned to denigrate an opponent than with an attempt to convince electors of the virtues of their own policies. Or they may decide that the wisest course of political action is to follow public opinion rather than seek to lead it. Thus ideology or policy that is viewed as unpopular might be abandoned by a party in an attempt to win elections.

POPULAR INVOLVEMENT

We may also question the extent to which parties enable widespread involvement in political affairs. Parties do not always have a mass membership. In America, voters do not 'join' a party as they might, for example, in the UK. However, even in countries where individuals can join a political party, they do not always do so in large numbers. French and Irish political parties, for example, lack a tradition of mass membership and tend to be controlled by small elitist groups. Neither are those who do join a party guaranteed a meaningful role in its affairs. The Italian Christian Democrats, for example, has a mass membership, but this has little say on matters such as party policy. The formal accountability of party leaders to rank-and-file activists through mechanisms such as annual party conferences is often imperfectly achieved in practice due to the domination which leaders often exert over their parties.

Centralized control over political parties extends to election contests. In the UK, the recent emergence of stage-managed general elections marginalizes the role of the general public in these contests.

DIVISIVENESS

Political parties do not always seek to promote harmony. Some may seek to make political capital by emphasizing existing divisions within society. France's *Front National* has sought to cultivate support by blaming the country's economic and social problems on immigration, especially from North Africa. The scapegoating of racial or religious groups, depicting them as the main cause of a country's problems, is a common tactic of the extreme right and often serves to create social tension rather than harmony. Racial tension in Germany in the late twentieth and early twenty-first centuries led some politicians to suggest banning the far-right National Democratic Party.

SELF-INTEREST

The role of parties as dispensers of patronage may result in accusations that they are mainly concerned to award 'jobs for the boys'. This may result in popular disenchantment with the conduct of political affairs, with politics being associated with the furtherance of self-interest rather than with service to the nation.

THE CONTINUED VITALITY OF POLITICAL PARTIES

Key idea (8)

Established political parties have undertaken a number of reforms in attempts to counter their loss of electoral support.

Although the position of established political parties in many liberal democracies is weaker than was previously the case, it seems likely that they will continue to carry out important roles within liberal democratic political systems.

Despite problems encountered by political parties, they remain a vital component of the political process: it has been argued that *'political parties in the UK ... remain vital for the functions of interest aggregation, political recruitment and decision-making. We might add that they continue to serve as conduit (though admittedly a shrunken one) of political participation and have long been important to the political integration of social groups, thereby helping to legitimize and stabilize the entire political system'* (Webb, 1995: 322).

Webb, P. (1995) Are British Political Parties in Decline? *Party Politics*, 1, pp 292–322.

One reason to explain the continued vitality of political parties is that they are adaptable and have understood the importance of reform.

Reforms to restore the vitality of parties may take a number of forms. They include attempts to increase the number of citizens joining such organizations. In countries such as America, where local parties have often been controlled by 'bosses', initiatives to increase party membership have sometimes been accompanied by reforms designed to 'democratize' the workings of political parties and ensure that members are able to exercise a greater degree of control over key party affairs, including the selection of candidates and the formulation of policy.

There have been problems associated with such developments. Increasing the membership of local parties has sometimes (although not consistently) resulted in accusations of extremists 'taking over' control of organization, which in turn makes it difficult for parties to appeal to a wide electoral base in order to win elections. What is termed 'coalition building' in America becomes difficult if a party is associated with extremist issues. Similar problems beset the UK Labour Party in the early 1980s that resulted in that party's disastrous showing in the 1983 general election in which it placed a manifesto before the electorate based on left-wing principles. These policies emerged as a result of reforms designed to democratize that organization by giving rank-and-file members a greater role in party affairs, principally the selection of party candidates and the party leader.

REFORM OF PARTIES IN THE UK

Both major parties in the UK implemented reforms towards the end of the twentieth century that sought to streamline party organization in the belief that a modern structure was necessary to attract new party supporters.

▶ The Labour Party

A number of key reforms were embarked upon during the 1990s. These included:

▶ 1990: reforms were initiated affecting the power wielded by trade unions in Labour Party affairs. Traditionally, unions were able to dominate Labour Party affairs (especially the decisions taken at the Annual Party Conference) as each union member was regarded as a member of the Labour Party and thus had a vote at the conference. In practice, the entire union vote was cast as a block by its leadership. In 1990, the National Executive Committee (NEC) voted to reduce the weighting of the union vote to 70 per cent of the entire conference vote and it was proposed to subsequently scale this down further

▶ 1993: trade unionists were required to pay a levy in order to become full members of the Labour Party

▶ 1997: the structure of the NEC was remodelled, the new body consisting of 32 members

▶ 1997: the Joint Policy Committee was established. This includes members from the NEC and – when in office – the government whose role is to develop policy and plan campaigns and elections

▶ 1997: the National Policy Forum was set up: this new body's role was to review Party policy through the mechanism of policy commissions

▶ The Conservative Party

Suggestions for the reform of the structure and organization of the Conservative Party were contained in the document, *Fresh Future*, published in 1997 and implemented in 1998. This was responsible for creating:

▶ A Board of Management (termed the 'Party Board'). This is the ultimate decision-making body in the Party with responsibility for all operational matters, including fundraising, membership and candidates. It is composed of representatives drawn from each section of the Party. It replaced the old National Union of Conservative and Unionist Associations

▶ The National Conservative Convention. This is composed of key local and regional officers of the Party and its main purpose is to facilitate contact between the Party members and the leadership

▶ The Conservative Policy Forum. This is designed to encourage political discussion at all levels of the Party's organization. It supplements the role performed by the Annual Party Conference and the spring assembly

ASSESSMENT OF REFORMS

Many of the reforms pursued by UK parties during the 1990s were contentious and, within Labour circles especially, it was believed that a key aim was to enhance the control wielded over the party by its leadership. An important measure of these reforms is party membership. Although accurate figures are difficult to secure, it is believed that:

▶ the Labour Party's membership in 2013 was around 180,000 (which is about half of the figure it was 15 years previously)

▶ the Conservative's membership in 2012 was around 133,000 (compared with 258,239 when David Cameron became Conservative Party leader in 2005)

▶ the Liberal Democrats had a membership of 45,000–48,000 in 2013 (compared to 65,000 in 2010)

Dig Deeper

Ingle, S. (2008) *The British Party System: An Introduction.* London: Routledge, 4th ed. revised.

Maor, M. (2005) *Political Parties and Party Systems: Comparative Approaches and the British Experience.* Abingdon: Taylor and Frances, e-library edition.

Ware, A. (1996) *Political Parties and Party Systems.* Oxford: Oxford University Press.

Fact-check

1 With reference to a political party, the term 'aggregation of interests' refers to:
   a The ability of bodies such as trade unions to formally affiliate to a political party
   b The manifesto put forward by a party at an election contest
   c The number of pressure groups who formally endorse a political party's election manifesto
   d The need for a political party to win votes from a wide section of the electorate by putting forward policies designed to appeal to a broad cross-section of society

2 A dominant party system is one in which:
   a Only one political party is allowed to field candidates in election contests
   b One political party usually ends up as the victor in an election contest
   c An oligarchic political system in which all political parties are banned
   d Only candidates chosen by formally established political parties are allowed to field candidates for public office

3 In the UK, the government was drawn from which political party between 1979 and 1997:
   a The Labour Party
   b A Conservative–Liberal Democrat Coalition
   c The Conservative Party
   d A Labour–Liberal Democrat Coalition

4 A faction within a political party differs from a tendency in that:
   a A tendency has no formal organization
   b A faction has more members
   c A party's constitution permits a faction to be formed
   d A faction is permanent within a political party whereas a tendency is not

5 In the Irish Republic, the key issue that initially separated the main political parties, Fine Gael and Fianna Faíl was:

a Whether the television programme, *Father Ted*, should be aired on Irish television

b Acceptance or rejection of the 1921 Anglo-Irish Treaty that partitioned Ireland

c The role that the Catholic Church should play in Irish politics

d The rate of income tax to be levied across the country

6 In America, the candidate who is put forward to stand for the presidency of the USA is formally chosen by:

a The parties' leaders

b Primary elections

c The parties' National Convention

d A national ballot of the parties' registered members

6

Pressure groups

Although public policy often stems from political preferences as put forward by political parties at election times, there are other ways of placing ideas onto the political agenda. In this chapter we will consider the role performed by pressure groups in influencing the content of public policy. The activities performed by pressure groups may also, on occasions, be directed at the operations of commercial enterprises.

Definition

Key idea (1)

A pressure group seeks to influence policy making by directly or indirectly influencing the actions undertaken by the formal machinery of government (or on occasions by commercial organizations).

A pressure group (which may also be termed an 'interest group' or an 'advocacy group') is an organization with a formal structure which is composed of a number of individuals seeking to further or defend a common cause or interest. These groups operate at all levels of society. Some seek to influence the activities of local or central government. Others exist within the workplace in the form of trade unions. The factions or tendencies found within some political parties are further examples of such organizations. Many groups perform functions which are not political, for example by providing benefits or advisory services either to their members or to the general public. For the purposes of our discussion, however, we shall concentrate on those seeking to exert influence over national government policy by either seeking to promote reform or by attempting to prevent it.

NGOS AND SOCIAL MOVEMENTS

In addition to the role performed by pressure groups, many reforms are promoted by organizations termed Non-Governmental Organizations (NGOs) and 'social movements'. It is not always easy to differentiate between them.

Examples of NGOs

Médecins Sans Frontières was founded in Paris, France in 1971 and 'is an international, independent, medical humanitarian organization that delivers emergency aid to people affected by armed conflict, epidemics, healthcare exclusion and natural or man-made disasters.' The group is at the forefront of the 'without borders' movement and has been in operation for 40 years.

Oxfam 'is an international confederation of seventeen organizations networked together in 92 countries, as part of a global movement for change, to build a future free from the injustice of poverty'. The well-known organization works to help eliminate global poverty with long-term and sustainable solutions.

Greenpeace is an example of an environmental NGO whose goal is to 'ensure the ability of the Earth to nurture life in all of its diversity'. It operates on a global scale (with almost 3 million members worldwide) and was set up in 1972, emerging from an earlier organization, the Don't Make A Wave Committee. It campaigns (often entailing the use of non-violent direct action) on a range of environmental issues that include commercial whaling, genetic engineering of crops, anti-nuclear issues, overfishing, deforestation and climate change.

NGOs were recognized in the 1945 United Nations Charter in which they were differentiated from governments as organizations that had the right to a voice in the newly created organization the United Nations. NGOs are private bodies, free from government control, that seek to influence the content of national and international policy but are not set up to challenge governments in the sense of seeking their removal from office. They are typically non-profit-making, non-violent and do not have criminal associations. They may be based in a single country, but increasingly operate in the international arena. Their effectiveness has been enhanced by contemporary technological developments (especially electronic forms of communication) and by their tendency to construct coalitions to bring about reforms in areas such as environmental policy, human rights and social reform.

Around 10,000 NGO representatives attended the environmental conference held at Rio in 1992, and NGOs have been active in subsequent events of this type and also in promoting reforms to ban landmines and establish an International Criminal Court. The United Nations has also contracted NGOs to perform services that include the provision of emergency relief.

NGOs may be a component of social movements. Examples of social movements include the peace movement, the women's movement, the environmental movement, animal rights movement and the anti-capitalist movement.

Social movements tend to be loosely organized in comparison to pressure groups and NGOs, and their focus of concern is often broader. Rather than concentrate on one specific policy area, their prime concern is to instill new moral values within society to underpin the reforms they wish to promote. This may bring them into conflict with public authorities or with other organizations that oppose their views. They may, however, embrace the activities of pressure groups, and NGOs whose specific aims are compatible with this overall objective. We would, for example, place the British Campaign for Nuclear Disarmament under the umbrella of the peace movement.

Social movements typically operate outside mainstream political institutions and their tactics are thus dominated by non-conventional forms of political activity. This is frequently carried out on an international stage rather than being confined to any particular country.

The environmental movement is an important example of a contemporary social movement. It has succeeded in bringing together a range of groups engaged in counter-cultural protest (such as new age travellers) and those opposed to hunting, live animal exports, motorway construction and pollution. These seemingly disparate, single-issue bodies are united by a social vision that rejects the culture of advanced capitalist society. All stand opposed to what they view as an alliance of developers, business, the construction industry and government. They have utilized tactics of protest and direct action to project an alternative vision to a modern industrial society that emphasizes environmental considerations over the pursuit of wealth and profit. All groups are concerned with man's damage to the planet and are opposed to materialism and consumerism.

The role of pressure groups

Key idea (2)

Pressure groups seek to influence policy makers. Their actions are thus directed at politicians, civil servants and, in some cases, the general public. The complex and lengthy nature of the policy-making process provides wide scope for group activity.

A major concern of pressure groups is to persuade policy makers to consider their views and then to act upon them. This involves inducing policy makers either to adopt a course of action which they did not initially intend to embark upon or to abandon a measure which they had originally decided to introduce. If a group succeeds in getting its views acted upon it may also become involved in further stages of the policy-making process. These include participating in the formulation of policy to achieve the objective(s) which the group successfully placed on the political agenda. Pressure groups may also be concerned with the implementation of that policy and with monitoring it to ensure that the desired aims are achieved.

PRESSURE GROUPS AND THE PRIVATE SECTOR

Our discussion of pressure groups in this chapter is primarily concerned with their influence on central government policy making. However, pressure groups frequently direct their activities towards alternative targets, such as the practices adopted by commercial organizations. Indeed, a number of Greenpeace activists see business rather than politics as the best arena within which to further environmental aims.

Spotlight

One example of pressure group activity directed at commercial practices was the activity mounted in 1995 by Greenpeace against the decision by the Shell Oil Company to sink a disused oil rig, Brent Spar, in the North Atlantic. Adverse publicity coupled with boycotts of Shell's products organized by other environmental groups resulted in the company's agreeing to examine alternative ways of disposing of its unwanted property.

Political parties and pressure groups

Key idea (3)

Unlike political parties, pressure groups do not seek to control all aspects of government policy but only those areas that are of interest to them.

The key words for us to consider here are 'control' and 'influence'.

Political parties normally seek control over the policy-making process. They may achieve this through their own efforts or in combination with other political parties. They contest elections in the hope of securing power so that they can carry out the policies contained in their election manifestos. Such policies cover all aspects of public affairs and the party seeks to exercise control over a wide range of issues.

Pressure groups, however, wish to influence those who control the policy-making process. They do not normally have an interest in the overall work of government, but only in those aspects of its operations that are of concern to the group and its membership. In order to pursue their aims, groups usually possess a degree of autonomy from both government and political parties. Thus, while a pressure group seeks to exert influence over a relatively narrow aspect of policy making, a political party wishes to control the overall direction of public affairs.

One further distinction between political parties and pressure groups concerns the manner in which they seek to cultivate support. Political parties concentrate their activities on the general public, hoping to convince voters to support them in election contests. Although campaigns directed at the public may form one aspect of pressure group campaigning, the tactics at their disposal are more diverse. Influence may be sought at all levels of the decision-making process.

Classification of pressure groups

Key idea (4)

There are two main types of pressure groups – sectional groups that promote the self-interest of their members, and promotional groups that advocate changes they regard as beneficial to society regardless of whether their members will directly gain from them.

Various ways may be adopted to classify the pressure groups found within liberal democratic political systems. One method is to differentiate according to the relationship that exists between the objective put forward by the group and its membership. This provides us with the two broad categories into which groups might be placed.

SECTIONAL GROUPS

These are groups in which the members have a vested interest in the success of their organization. Sectional pressure groups consist of two broad strands.

Economic (or 'interest') pressure groups advance the causes of their members who stand to benefit materially if the aims of the group are adopted by policy makers. The membership of this type of sectional groups tends to be narrow and restrictive, drawn from people with similar backgrounds. In the UK, examples include employers' associations (such as the Confederation of British Industry), professional bodies (such as the British Medical Association) or labour organizations (such as the Transport and General Workers' Union or the National Farmers' Union). American examples include the American Bar Association and the American Medical Association.

A second type of sectional pressure group consists of **public pressure groups** that seek to represent the views of a section of the general public on a particular issue in which group members have a direct personal interest. This type of sectional group may be defensive (aiming to defend its members' pursuits) or propagandist, seeking to win new supporters to the group's objectives. In America, the National Rifle Association (set up in 1871 to protect the rights of gun owners) is an example of a defensive sectional group, and the Liberty Federation, and the Christian Coalition are propagandist sectional groups.

PROMOTIONAL (OR CAUSE) GROUPS

These are organizations in which the members are united in support of a cause which does not benefit them materially or in terms of advancing interests that would directly benefit them. They tend to view the work of the group as a moral concern and their aim is to change social attitudes and values rather than advance sectional interests. The aims of promotional groups may be designed to benefit specific groups (especially minorities whose needs are often ignored by policy makers) or to be directed at an issue affecting society as a whole. Membership of promotional groups is open to all who share its objectives: members are typically drawn from a wide range of social or occupational backgrounds and are united solely by their common support for the cause advocated by the organization. Examples of promotional groups include animal welfare groups such as the League Against Cruel Sports (which seeks to expose and end cruelty inflicted on animals in the name of sport) and Liberty (which aims to protect civil liberties and promote human rights). Both of these groups are based in the UK.

EPISODIC GROUPS

We should also be aware when classifying pressure groups that activities with which they are associated are not confined to organizations that are specifically established to advance an interest or a cause. Such activities may also be performed by bodies whose existence is concerned with other functions but which may, on occasion, act in the capacity of a pressure group and seek to exert influence within the policy making process. We use the term 'episodic groups' to refer to groups which function in this way.

The Catholic Church in Ireland is an example of a body which sometimes acts as a pressure group. The Roman Catholic bishops played a prominent role in the 1995 referendum campaign opposing a change in the Irish Constitution to permit divorce. In Britain, chief constables and senior members of the judiciary have sometimes made public pronouncements designed to influence the approach adopted by policy makers to the operations of the criminal justice system, and in America, the Pentagon sometimes performs a role akin to that of a pressure group on behalf of the military establishment.

The activities of pressure groups

Key idea (5)

Pressure groups may seek to directly influence the executive, legislative or judicial branches of government, or they may pitch their appeal to the general public hoping that the force of public opinion will be brought to bear on policy makers and induce them to adopt the demands put forward by the group.

In this section, we shall consider how pressure groups seek to exert influence on policy makers.

THE EXECUTIVE BRANCH OF GOVERNMENT

Some pressure groups have the constant ability to liaise with, and be consulted by, key policy makers in the executive branch of government, which consists of both ministers and civil servants.

The relationship between groups and the executive branch of government may be constructed in a number of ways. Some have a permanent relationship with government departments. Members representing a group may be appointed to joint advisory committees, which are mechanisms through which the concerns of a pressure group can be made known to the relevant government department. In France, the access of some groups to government departments is institutionalized through advisory councils. These are composed of representatives of interest groups, technicians and prominent personalities appointed by the government and are attached to individual ministries. Alternatively, some pressure groups enjoy regular access to civil servants and they may also be involved in discussions on appointments to bodies which are responsible to a department. In some countries, contact is secured through the 'old boy' network, in which former ministers or civil servants secure jobs in organizations that may benefit from the contacts in government possessed by such former public officials.

Groups in this position are termed 'insider' groups. This denotes the close relationship and regular consultation that some groups enjoy with key members of the policy-making process. It is a desirable position to occupy in a country such as the UK where political power is centralized in the executive branch of government, although it is of equal importance in some federal countries such as Australia. The relationship between the UK National Farmers' Union and the former Ministry of Agriculture, Fisheries and Food is an historic example of an 'insider' relationship.

The distinction between insider pressure groups – those *'enmeshed in a consultative relationship with officials'* – and outsider groups that were not party to such arrangements was developed by Wyn Grant. Although he argued that *'most groups tend to veer towards an insider strategy because of the potential gains it offers'*, some groups deliberately rejected this approach. These he classified as *'ideological' outsider groups – those which were 'committed to campaigning for radical political change, which cannot be accommodated within existing policy paradigms'* (Grant, 2000: 19 & 20).

Grant, W. (2000) *Pressure Groups and British Politics.* Basingstoke: Palgrave.

Other groups may secure influence through their relationship with the political party that forms the government. The relationship that exists between pressure groups and political parties may be organizational or financial. The American AFL–CIO is associated with the Democratic Party, the French *Confédération Générale du Travail*, (CGT) has close ties with the Communist Party (the PCF) and in the UK, trade unions traditionally had a close relationship with the Labour Party (although this link is now not as strong as it was previously). Between 1964 and 1970 leading trade unionists were frequently invited to Downing Street to discuss industrial affairs over 'beer and sandwiches'. This politically-fashioned link with the ministerial component of the executive is not, however, permanent and may alter when the government changes. This was the case in the UK after 1979 when Conservative administrations adopted a more hostile attitude to the trade unions than had been the case when Labour governments were in power.

These examples illustrate the fact that the insider/outsider distinction is not a rigid one and some groups may adopt either of these strategies at different historical periods. This fluctuation may depend on factors such as group leadership (which may wish to alter group tactics) or (as the examples above suggest) the political environment in which groups operate: historically in Great Britain, trade unions would enjoy a closer relationship with Labour governments than they would with Conservative or Liberal ones.

THE LEGISLATURE

There are a number of ways whereby pressure groups may seek to exert influence over the legislature. Pressure groups may involve themselves in election contests, perhaps by raising money and endorsing candidates which support their policies. In America, Political Action Committees (which we consider later in this chapter) are an important mechanism that seeks to influence the composition of the legislature.

A major mechanism that aims to influence the law-making process is that of lobbying. This describes communication between citizens and policy-makers operating at national or local levels with the intention of influencing the latter's decisions. This communication may be performed directly by organized groups or conducted through intermediaries whom we refer to as lobbyists whom a group employs to further its aims.

Lobbying is the practice of trying to persuade legislators or officials to propose, pass, or defeat legislation or to change existing laws. Lobbying may be done by constituents, organized groups, or other legislators. Lobbying takes place on international, national, state, local, and municipal levels, wherever a government or organization of any kind makes decisions on public policy. A lobbyist may be a professional paid to work on behalf of a special interest group such as a trade association, labor union, or nonprofit organization, or a private individual who acts out personal commitment to a particular cause' Dragojlović, 2010).

Dragojlović, P. (2010) *Lobbying as a Method of Business Communication*. [Online] *http://www.vps.ns.ac.rs/SB/2010/3.13.pdf* [Accessed 21 August 2014].

Lobbying was originally directed exclusively at legislators, but has subsequently extended to the executive branch where politicians and bureaucrats are made the subject of this activity. Its aim is to ensure that law makers are fully briefed and are thus in a position to advance the interests of the pressure group when issues that are relevant to it come before the legislature for discussion or resolution. The importance attached to this activity is much influenced by the independence of action which legislatures possess. Pressure groups may devote relatively little attention to such bodies if they believe them to be dominated by the executive branch of government.

Much lobbying is carried out by pressure groups. Some employ full-time lobbyists to promote their interests while others hire lobbyists on a temporary basis when they wish to advance, or secure the defeat of, legislation that is relevant to their interests. The influence that they are able to exert over policy makers is derived from their being regarded as an important source of information. In the United Kingdom, parliamentary lobbyists (or parliamentary consultants) provide political advice and analysis that may be sought by commercial companies or by other governmental organizations. The most influential lobbyists are those who have established regular contacts in the legislative or executive branches of government, and in this sense they act as a conduit to power.

Lobbying is conducted by a variety of activities, ranging from personal approaches to policy makers to bribery. Concern regarding lobbying has resulted in a number of governments passing law to regulate their activities.

In America, lobbying activities directed at the federal government are regulated by the 1995 Lobby Disclosure Act (which replaced the 1946 Federal Regulation of Lobbying Act and was substantially amended by the 2007 Honest Leadership and Open Government Act). This legislation required lobbyists to register with the clerk of the House of Representatives and the secretary of the Senate within 45 days of having been hired. Lobbyists are required to file quarterly reports and list the issues on which they have lobbied and the institutions they have contacted.

In Germany, lobbying is regulated by the 1977 Members of Parliament Law, and in Canada by the 1988 Lobbyists Registration Act. This was amended by the 2008 Federal Accountability Act, which retitled the 1988 legislation as the Lobbying Act.

Lobbying in America

In America, lobbying is big business. In 2005 over 32,000 lobbyists were registered in Washington DC, three times the number employed in 1995. The expenditure on lobbying (especially by business and commercial interests) has grown from around $800 million in 1996 to $2.2 billion in 2005. Although the number of lobbyists in Washington has subsequently declined, the amount of money spent on lobbying rose to around $3.2 billion in 2013, suggesting that lobbying activities are 'going underground' in order to avoid the legislative controls imposed by the 1995 Lobby Disclosure Act and subsequent amendments to that legislation.

In 2005, a report by the organization Public Citizen estimated that since 1998, 43 per cent of the 198 members of Congress who had left government for private life were registered to lobby. The movement of legislators or members of the executive branch of government into lobbying work is sometimes referred to as 'the revolving door syndrome', and an early reform of President Obama's administration was to bar government officials from taking jobs in lobbying firms while the administration that had appointed them remained in office.

In the United Kingdom, however, the lobbying industry is self-regulating by the Association of Professional Political Consultants. The relationship between lobbyists and members of parliament is controlled by rules drawn up by the House of Commons. The 2014 Transparency of Lobbying, Non-Party Campaigning and Trade Union Administration Act placed restrictions on how much money a voluntary group or trade union could spend while campaigning on political issues before a general election.

Lobbying is one way in which pressure groups impart information to legislators, but they also do this through other ways of communication and in so doing, educate politicians. It has been observed in the UK that *'MPs have benefited, both collectively and individually, from the input of information from interest groups. By giving evidence to select committees, interest groups have ensured that the committees have information independent of ministers and civil servants … Better informed committees and, through them, a better informed House of Commons are able to question government more effectively than would be the case if they had little or no independent information at their disposal'.* (Norton, 1999: 32).

Norton, P. (1999) The United Kingdom: Parliament Under Pressure in P. Norton (ed.) *Parliaments and Pressure Groups in Western Europe.* London: Frank Cass, Volume 2 pp 19–42.

IRON TRIANGLES

In America, some pressure groups enjoy considerable power from the relationship that they have constructed with both the executive and legislative branch of government.

The term 'iron triangle' has been used to describe the close links (governed by ties of interdependent self-interest) that exist between an interest group, the government department or agency concerned with the concerns promoted by that organization and the Congressional committee charged with responsibility for that area of activity. Each element of the 'triangle' provides services, information or policy for the others.

This arrangement provides some groups with a powerful position from which its interests can be advanced. In 1997 a representative of an American consumer group alleged that the Food and Drugs Administration (which regulated the American food industry) was so closely associated with the biotech/pharmaceutical/agri-business complex that it could be described as their Washington branch office. Although a close working relationship between an agency and groups representing industries does not necessarily constitute improper influence, iron triangles have also been argued to be responsible for decentralizing and fragmenting the policy-making process to the detriment of the exercise of central control by the executive and legislative branches of government. In more recent years, the autonomy of such 'sub-governments' has been challenged by alternative centres of power (such as issue networks).

THE JUDICIARY

Pressure groups may turn to the courts to secure the adoption of their aims, usually by challenging the legality of legislation. This approach was crucial to the American Civil Rights Movement. Organizations such as the National Association for the Advancement of Colored People (NAACP) used this mechanism in their fight against segregation practiced by a number of the southern states. A landmark in education was reached in 1954 when the Supreme Court ruled (in the case of Brown v. Board of Education of Topeka) that segregation in schools was unconstitutional and thus illegal throughout the entire country. In more recent years, American consumer and environmental groups have turned to the courts to advance their concerns.

Rules governing the operations of a country's judicial system have a major bearing on the ability or willingness of pressure groups to use the courts to further their objectives. In Australia, for example, legal procedure (termed the rules of *locus standi*) has made it difficult for pressure groups to initiate legal actions since it is necessary for plaintiffs to demonstrate a personal stake or material interest in a case. In America, however, interests groups are permitted to present arguments to courts directly.

The role of the courts is less prominent in countries such as Britain and New Zealand, where judicial challenge to national legislation is precluded by the concept of parliamentary sovereignty, but pressure groups may utilize the courts and launch test cases or challenge the legality of the way in which the law has been implemented.

INDIRECT PRESSURE

Pressure groups may also seek to influence the key institutions of government through indirect means. Pressure groups may focus their activities on the general public, seeking to mobilize public opinion, which then exerts pressure on the formal machinery of government to adopt the issue advocated by a pressure group. This activity may be conducted through a range of protest tactics which we consider more fully in Chapter 7.

The international arena

Key idea (6)

Globalization has affected the operations of pressure groups, many of which operate on an international arena rather than confining their activities to one country.

Pressure groups do not confine their activities to one country, but increasingly operate on a world stage. Groups may be formed in one country seeking influence over policy making in another. Alternatively, they may be international organizations seeking the universal adoption of standards of behaviour throughout the world. Groups such as Amnesty International (which is concerned with human rights) is an example of such a body.

Pressure groups have also adapted to the development of supranational governmental organizations. The policy makers of the European Union are subject to pressure group activity. By 2014 it was estimated that around 30,000 lobbyists were working in Brussels, and that lobbying had become a billion-euro industry. Activities were especially directed at MEPs to influence content of EU legislation. In 2012 it was estimated that the tobacco industry spent more than 5 million Euros a year on lobbying.

Organizations within individual countries may co-ordinate their activities with similar groups in other countries in order to secure overall influence on EU policy. For example, an umbrella body (COPA/COGECA) was established to co-ordinate farming policy at the European level. It represents all European farming unions and has 60 full members from the EU states and a number of partner organizations from non-EU countries. It aims to ensure that farmers and their families obtained income and living conditions that were compatible with those in other sectors of the economy.

Similarly, the Union of Industrial and Employers' Confederations of Europe (UNICE) was set up to provide a European business perspective by lobbying on behalf of all the national business organizations and sectoral federations. Pressure groups may also establish permanent machinery to further their interests within supranational bodies such as the EU. An example of this is the Brussels Office of the Confederation of British Industry, which monitors developments in the EU and seeks to influence the direction of European legislation to the benefit of its membership. The British National Farmers' Union also has an office in Brussels (the British Agricultural Bureau) that gathers intelligence and assists the NFU in lobbying EU institutions.

International institutions, such as the United Nations Human Rights Committee and the European Court of Justice, have also been used by pressure groups that seek to question the actions undertaken by individual governments. In Britain, for example, groups opposed to motorway construction have exercised their right to complain to the European Commission that the government failed adequately to implement the procedures of the 1988 Directive concerned with environmental impact assessments. If the Commission decides that there is a case to answer, then the government can be taken to the European Court of Justice for contravening European law.

Pressure group influence

Key idea (7)

The extent to which pressure groups are able to influence public policy is dependent on a number of factors, which include the resources they are able to muster and the sanctions they can deploy to further their cause through coercive means.

The previous section discussed various tactics a pressure group might utilize to further its aims. The extent to which these tactics succeed in influencing policy makers depends on a range of factors which we now consider.

THE ABILITY OF A GROUP TO MOBILIZE SUPPORT

The level of support enjoyed by a group may be one determinant of its strength. Successful groups need to represent all who adhere to a particular interest or a specific cause. The fragmentation of French labour organizations into a number of competing federations has tended to weaken their influence over policy makers and is in contrast to the organizational unity of business interests (whose trade associations are linked by the umbrella organization, the *Conseil National du Patronat Français*, (National Council of French Employer or CNPF, which was established in 1946, constituting an 'association of associations'). The strength of American labour organizations is reduced by the low affiliation rate of workers to trade unions. The cause of animal welfare in Britain may be impeded by the existence of a wide range of organizations, which include the Royal Society for the Prevention of Cruelty to Animals, People for the Ethical Treatment of Animals (PETA), Compassion in World Farming, the Animal Liberation Front, and the International Fund for Animal Welfare.

EXPERTISE COMMANDED BY A GROUP

A further factor that may affect the influence that groups exercise over policy making is the expertise they are able to command. Governments may be reliant upon such bodies for advice on the technical and complex issues that surround much contemporary public policy, and may further be reliant on a group's goodwill or support to implement policy. Such considerations had a major bearing on the influence possessed by the British Medical Association following the establishment of the National Health Service in 1946.

RESOURCES POSSESSED BY A GROUP

The resources that pressure groups are able to command may also determine the success or failure of a group. Economically powerful groups possess the ability to publicize their objectives and also to resist sanctions that may be deployed against them. Employer organizations are often influential for such reasons. By contrast, consumer groups have traditionally suffered from lack of resources, which may help to explain their difficulties in securing influence over the actions of policy makers. However, some governments (such as the French) and supranational bodies (such as the EU) have contributed towards the funding of pressure groups, which offsets weaknesses that derive from lack of funds.

SANCTIONS AVAILABLE TO A GROUP

The sanctions that an organization is able to deploy are often a factor in its ability to influence policy making. Investment decisions or strikes may be used as weapons by business groups or trade unions to influence the conduct of policy makers. Consumer boycotts may influence the practices of the private sector. Groups involved in the implementation of public policy possess the ability to withhold their co-operation and thus prevent the progress of policies to which they object.

The strengths and weaknesses of pressure group activity

Key idea (8)

Pressure groups enable the public to become involved in policy making. However, their role might be harmful to the conduct of liberal democratic politics for reasons that include the use of inappropriate methods to secure influence and their potential to undermine the capacity of an elected government to govern.

BENEFITS OF PRESSURE GROUPS

Here we consider the main benefits associated with the activities of pressure groups.

▶ Popular involvement in policy making

Pressure groups ensure that the policy-making process is not monopolized by politicians or senior civil servants. The control they are able to exercise is to some extent offset by the operations of pressure groups. Additionally, these organizations aid the participation of members of the general public in policy making whose role in political affairs is thus not merely confined to casting a vote in elections.

▶ Political education

The need for pressure groups to 'sell' their case to secure influence may aid the process of public education in political affairs. Groups may need to explain what they believe in and why they endorse the views that they hold. Groups who oppose government policy may engage in activities such as investigative journalism, which results in enhanced scrutiny and popular awareness of government activity.

▶ Promote reform

Pressure groups may raise matters that the major political parties would prefer to ignore, either because they do not consider them to be mainstream political issues, which generally dominate election campaigns (such as the economy or law and order), or because they are internally divisive to the parties. The emergence of women's issues and environmental concerns onto the political agenda owed much to the activities of pressure groups. This role performed by groups may be enhanced if several align with each other to achieve a common goal. We refer to this as 'agenda building'.

▶ Put forward minority interests

The workings of liberal democratic political systems may also benefit from the ability of pressure groups to advocate minority opinions or concerns. Liberal democracies tend to pay most heed to majority opinion. There is thus a risk that minorities get ignored. Pressure groups provide a vehicle whereby minorities can articulate their needs and encourage policy makers to pay attention to them.

▶ Holding governments accountable

Pressure groups may also assist in the function of holding governments accountable for their actions (or inactions). For example, environmental groups may scrutinize the extent to which environmental regulations are enforced by a government, and put pressure on them to improve their level of performance when deficiencies are unearthed.

DISADVANTAGES OF PRESSURE GROUPS

Let us now consider the main problems associated with the operations of pressure groups.

▶ Pluralism versus hyper-pluralism

Power in a pluralist society is dispersed. Policy emerges as the result of competition, consultation, bargaining and conciliation conducted between groups who are accorded relatively equal access to the policy-making arena. This process is overseen by the government, which is viewed as a neutral arbitrator. Pressure groups thus perform a crucial (and advantageous) role in policy making.

A problem may arise, however, in a society in which a very wide range of groups emerges, some of which hold diametrically opposing views. The processes of consultation, bargaining and conciliation may be long and drawn out. The decision-making process may stagnate and governments find it difficult, or impossible, to take any decisions. This situation (which regards all interests as being on an equal footing) is known as 'hyper-pluralism'. However, the tendency for powerful groups (including the government) to dominate the policy-making process serves to reduce the likelihood of such stagnation occurring in many liberal democracies.

▶ Inequality

One problem associated with pressure groups is that all are not given the same degree of attention by policy makers. The influence they are able to command is considerably influenced by factors including the resources at the group's disposal and the relationships they have constructed with government departments. There are two diametrically opposed problems that arise from the inequality that exists between groups.

First, this situation may result in worthy minority causes making little impact on public policy as they are relatively ignored by the bureaucrats, ministers, political parties, the media and public opinion. Members of groups in such a position may become frustrated and resort to violence, seeking to coerce when they are denied opportunities to persuade.

Second, factors such as resources and sanctions may result in some groups occupying a powerful position within the policy-making process. The ability of some groups to command considerable economic resources and be in possession of powerful sanctions which it can deploy to further its interests may result in them being in a position not merely to influence but to actually dominate the policy-making process. The power of large American corporations has for a long time provided them with a wide degree of autonomy in their dealings with government. In its most extreme form, confrontation may result between the group and the government when the issue is, effectively, one of 'who governs?'

▶ Internal democracy

A further difficulty that we encounter with the workings of pressure groups is the extent to which the opinions or actions of the leadership faithfully reflect the views of the membership. The belief by the UK Conservative governments that trade unions, for example, sometimes endorsed political activity which was not genuinely supported by the rank-and-file resulted in a number of pieces of legislation being enacted during the 1980s designed to ensure that such organizations were responsive to their members' opinions. These measures included requirements for compulsory secret ballots to be held before the commencement of strike action and the periodic election of union leaders. However, most pressure groups are not subject to such internal regulation and are thus susceptible to domination by their leaders. In this situation, pressure groups fail greatly to extend the degree of popular involvement in policy making.

▶ Methods used to secure influence

Concern has been expressed within liberal democracies regarding the expenditure of money by pressure groups in order to achieve influence. The purposes of such spending may go beyond political education and extend into activities that are perceived to approximate bribery or corruption. As we have considered above, lobbying has been a particular cause of concern and has led some countries to introduce measures to regulate these activities.

Political Action Committees (PACs)

In America, pressure group involvement in election contests is performed by Political Action Committees (PACs). These were defined by the 1974 Federal Election Campaign Act as organizations that received or made expenditure of more than $1,000 to influence a federal election. They are registered with the Federal Election Commission (FEC) and act as a mechanism through which corporations and unions can direct funds into the individual campaign funds of candidates for public office who support their aims.

There are two types of PAC – '**connected**', which raise money from people employed by corporations or who are members of unions, and '**non-connected**' (or independent), which raise money by targeting selected groups in society in support of a specific cause or policy. The number of these bodies has risen dramatically – from about 600 in 1974 to over 4,500 in 2010.

The support that can be given to individual candidates has been limited by subsequent amendments to the 1974 Federal Election Campaign Act, but there is no limit on their spending on behalf of a candidate provided that there is no collaboration with the office- seeker. This means that PACs frequently engage in negative political action in which they campaign against candidates whose policies they oppose. One example of this was the opposition mounted by the National Security PAC in the 1988 presidential election against Michael Dukakis. PACs have also been accused of weakening the role of local party organization by reducing the importance of its local fundraising activities and thereby reducing the level of public participation in election campaigns. In an attempt to combat this problem, new legislation enacted in 1979 allowed state and local parties to raise and spend money for 'party-building' activities.

PACs spend considerable sums of money in an attempt to influence the outcome of election contests. According to the FEC, the two-year election cycle of 2007 and 2008 saw record spending of nearly $1.2 billion by PACs, compared with $1.1 billion the previous two years. In the previous presidential campaign of 2003 and 2004, PACs spent $843 million. The number subsequently fell back, but these have been replaced by Super PACS.

Super PACs emerged after the US Supreme Court permitted unlimited corporate and union spending on elections in January 2010 (Citizens United v. Federal Election Commission). Although not directly addressed in that case, subsequent related litigation (SpeechNow v. Federal Election Commission) and FEC activity gave rise to a new form of political committee. These entities, known as Super PACs or Independent-Expenditure-Only Committees (IEOCs), have been permitted to accept unlimited contributions and make unlimited expenditures aimed at electing or defeating federal candidates. Super PACs may not contribute funds directly to Federal candidates or parties.

According to a Congressional Research Service Report in 2013, Super PAC activity increased sharply in 2012; more than 400 active Super PACs spent more than $600 million directly supporting or opposing candidates. This report stated that in 2010 and 2012, between 70 and 80 per cent of Super PAC spending directly supported or opposed federal candidates through independent expenditures (IEs). Super PACs spent $620.9 million on IEs supporting and opposing House, Senate, and presidential candidates in 2012 – almost ten times the approximately $65 million spent in 2010.

▶ Undermine the capacity of a government to govern

Pressure groups may embark on activities that disrupt the conduct of civil affairs and make it impossible for the government to govern. This particular approach uses protest tactics such as direct action. An example of this occurred in the UK in 2000 when protesters who objected to the high cost of fuel blockaded oil refineries and stopped the movement of fuel. This action brought the country to a standstill, with fuel being moved only to those locations approved by the protesters.

THE CORPORATE STATE

A final problem that is associated with pressure groups arises when a relatively small number become incorporated into a state's decision-making machinery. The content of public policy may be heavily influenced by leaders of key pressure groups (especially employer and labour organizations) if they are accorded privileged access to ministers and civil servants through formal institutionalized arrangements. The term 'corporate state' is applied to such political arrangements.

Policy makers frequently consult with pressure groups in liberal democracies. In France, the Constitution requires the government to consult with the Economic and Social Council on socio-economic legislation. This body contains civil servants, trade unions, farmers' organizations, business associations and professional groups. The nature of the political system changes, however, if these consultations preclude the involvement of other parties and lead to consensual decisions being taken that cannot be meaningfully discussed in other forums. Elections cease to enable the public to exert influence over the content of policy, while legislatures may be relegated to bodies that rubber stamp decisions taken elsewhere but over which they possess little or no control. An additional concern is the lack of accountability of policy makers in such corporate structures. Meetings involving pressure groups, ministers and civil servants are conducted in secret, away from the public gaze. It is difficult to ascertain precisely where power resides and who can be held responsible for particular decisions.

Dig Deeper

Coxall, W. (2013) *Pressure Groups in British Politics*. Abingdon, Oxfordshire: Routledge, 2nd ed.

Grant, W. (2000) *Pressure Groups and British Politics*. Basingstoke: Macmillan/Palgrave.

Grant, W. (2008) The Changing Pattern of Group Politics in Britain. *British Politics* 3, pp 204–222.

Thomas, C. (ed.) (2004) *Research Guide to US and International Interest Groups*. Westport, Connecticut: Praeger Publishers.

Watts, D. (2007) *Pressure Groups*. Edinburgh: Edinburgh University Press.

Fact-check

1 Another name for a pressure group is:
   a A sectional group
   b An interest group
   c A trade union
   d A third party

2 The classification of a pressure group as a cause group denotes that:
   a It seeks support for a course of action deemed to be of benefit to society as a whole
   b Its members stand to gain materially if the cause they advocate is adopted as public policy
   c It is concerned only to promote one specific reform
   d It has a diverse range of interests that it seeks to translate into public policy

3 A pressure group that enjoys the status of an 'insider group' secures influence over policy-making by:
   a Engaging in protest
   b Undertaking and / or commissioning research
   c Having access to leading members of the formal policy-making process
   d Being part of a Non-Governmental Organization (NGO)

4 In America, the close relationship between a pressure group, a government department or agency and a Congressional Committee associated with the pressure group's concerns is termed:
   a Corruption
   b Divided government
   c Lobbying
   d An iron triangle

5 In America, the National Rifle Association is opposed to:
   a Private ownership of firearms
   b The use of firearms by terrorists
   c The imposition of restrictions on the private ownership of guns
   d The carrying of firearms in a public place

6 A lobbyist is a person paid by a pressure group to:

a Access key policy makers in order to further a pressure group's interests

b Organize public events to advertise a pressure group's policies

c Stand for election to a public office on behalf of a pressure group

d Act as the leader of a pressure group

7

Protest

The ability to protest is an important feature of liberal democratic political systems. Protest is regarded as a key political freedom and the right to do so is often incorporated into codified constitutions or other legal documents such as the European Convention on Human Rights. However, protest is a broad term that covers a wide range of activities and, although these methods are often peaceful, some activities may entail confrontation either with opponents of the protesters or with the law enforcement agencies. For this reason, governments may pass laws to regulate how protest may be conducted, and agencies such as the police may also adopt measures that are designed to enable them to maintain public order. This chapter examines methods of protest and the state's response to activities of this nature.

What is protest?

Key idea (1)

Protest is a key aspect of 'people power'. It enables citizens to voice their concerns about issues of importance to them, and is conducted outside of the formal political structure that involves political parties, elections and legislatures. It is sometimes referred to as 'extra-parliamentary political activity'.

Protest enables citizens to influence public policy in the period between national elections, and to draw attention to issues that may not feature in such contests. Their aim may be positive (seeking to secure the adoption of a course of action) or negative (aiming to put an end to an existing situation). The focus of protesters' concerns is often public policy, although the commercial practices of business concerns may also inspire protests.

Protest is frequently viewed as a key freedom in a liberal democratic political system. For this reason, the right to peaceful process is embodied in codified constitutions or similar documents. The First Amendment to the American Constitution (ratified in 1791) prohibited Congress from making any law '*abridging the freedom of speech, or of the press; or the right of the people peaceably to assemble, and to petition the Government for a redress of grievances*'. Similarly, Article 11 of the European Convention on Human Rights requires all nations that have signed up to this document to uphold the freedom of assembly and association.

> ### Key idea (2)
>
> Protest is carried out through a wide range of methods that include petitions, demonstrations, direct action, civil disobedience, and industrial disputes. The intention is to secure changes in public or commercial policy.

Petitions

Petitions entail citizens 'signing up' to a proposal that may express opposition to an aspect of public policy protesters wish to change. The aim of this form of protest is that widespread public support for the aims of the petition will convince governments that they need to react in a positive manner in order to reduce the likelihood of the petitioners refusing to support them in the next national election.

The issue(s) raised in the petition may relate to local or national policy, and in many countries is a time-honoured way of conducting protest. In more recent years, issues of global importance have been raised in this manner including Jubilee 2000, which was a coalition of around 100 voluntary groups that organized a four-year campaign seeking to have the debts of 52 of the heavily indebted developing nations cancelled in order to release funds for programmes to eradicate poverty in these countries. Their tactics included a petition that was signed by 24 million people in 166 countries.

Petitions may also be directed at the commercial practices of commercial enterprises. One contemporary example of this is the Sugar Rush petition. This petition seeks to draw attention to the injustices suffered by poor communities in developing countries who are thrown off their land to make way for large sugar plantations that are used in the food and drinks industry dominated by large multinational companies. In cases such as these, the aim of the petition is to convince the commercial concern to alter its practices in order to avoid the possibility that failure to do so may lead the petitioners to adopt further methods of protest, such as direct action in the form of a consumer boycott of the company's products.

Demonstrations

Demonstrations are an important way through which protest is conducted. They entail people who are united behind a particular cause taking to the streets to voice their concerns. They hope that the weight of numbers will convince the government that it needs to change the direction of its policy.

We are all familiar with demonstrations as a means to raise public awareness of an issue. *'A demonstration typically entails a number of people who are united in support of a particular cause and who seek to make others aware of their opinions by undertaking a procession in a public space'* (Joyce and Wain, 2014: 98).

Demonstrations are a collective form of protest which *'implies some physical action – marching, chanting slogans, singing — through which the merger of the individual in the mass, which is the essence of the collective experience, finds expression'* (Hobsbawm, 2003: 73).

Hobsbawm, E. (2003) We are all familiar with demonstrations as a means to raise public awareness of an issue. *Interesting Times: A Twentieth-Century Life*. London: Abacus, new edition.

Joyce, P. and Wain, N. (2014) *Palgrave Dictionary of Public Order Policing, Protest and Political Violence*. Basingstoke: Palgrave / Macmillan.

In recent years, demonstrations have been used to protest against a wide range of issues and the ability to organize protests on a worldwide scale has been aided by technological advances such as the internet. Demonstrations have been used to voice opposition to capitalism and the operations of the global financial system across the world at events that included the Seattle trade talks, the IMF and World Bank Summit in Prague, and the G-20 protests in London.

Austerity measures imposed as a condition of receiving financial aid in the form of bail-out loans from international financial institutions, which some countries needed in order to avoid the nation becoming bankrupt, were the source of demonstrations after 2010 in countries that included Spain, Portugal and Ireland. Large demonstrations protesting against unpopular governments were a feature of protests in a number of Arab Nations after 2010, events that were termed 'Arab Spring', and which led to regime changes in Tunisia, Egypt, Libya and Yemen.

The G-20 Protests (London) 2009

The focus of the G-20 protests was the G-20 summit held in London on 2 April 2009. G-20 is the collective name applied to nations with the world's largest advanced and emerging economies.

Those involved in the protests held on 1 and 2 April came from a wide variety of groups with diverse agendas that included economic policy, the operations of the banking system and bankers' pay and bonuses, climate change, and the war on terror. The banner of 'anti-capitalism' served as an umbrella under which these groups could co-ordinate a protest. The G-20 protest comprised of three separate events. These embraced demonstrations and various forms of direct action, and involved between 9,000 and 11,500 persons.

The G-20 Meltdown Protest embraced four separate demonstrations focusing on war, climate, financial crimes, and land enclosures and borders, which converged outside the Bank of England. This protest was inspired by radical anti-capitalist sentiments. Some damage was caused to property, principally at a branch of the Royal Bank of Scotland, following which confrontations between the police and protesters took place.

A second protest that took place in Bishopsgate was the 'Camp in the City', which sought to draw attention to environmental issues, especially carbon trading. Some scuffles took place between the police and protesters in connection with police actions to clear the camp.

A third event was a demonstration by the Stop the War Coalition. This attracted support from other organizations that included the Campaign for Nuclear Disarmament, and the Palestine Solidarity Committee.

Following these events, a number of complaints were made regarding police actions, which included 185 referrals to the Independent Police Complaints Commission. Many criticisms were voiced concerning the use of police powers. The main issues included the absence of clear standards governing the use of force by individual officers involved in events of this nature, the interpretation of public order law, and the use of public order powers covering actions such as stop and search, photography and obtaining the names and addresses of demonstrators. Containment (or 'kettling' or 'corralling') was used as a police response to these protests whereby the police penned protesters into confined areas from which they were not allowed to leave. It was also observed that some officers had removed their identification numbers, making it extremely difficult for subsequent identification in the event of questions being raised regarding their conduct.

The ability to protest and express dissent is a key aspect of liberal democratic political systems.

One of the most important consequences of the policing of the G-20 protests related to the need to ensure that the future policing of protest reflected the core values of British policing. These values were identified as being *an approachable, impartial, accountable style of policing based on minimal force and anchored in public consent*' whose *key purpose was 'to ensure the safety of the public and the preservation of the peace within a tolerant, plural society'* (HMIC, 2009: 5 and 11). It was argued that when dealing with protest, this model could be eroded by police actions that included *'premature displays of formidable public order protective uniform and equipment'* (HMIC, 2009: 5), which might give the perception of a hardening of the character of British policing. It was further jeopardized by *'poor police communication, uncontrolled instances of force, and the confused and inappropriate use of police powers'* (HMIC, 2009: 12).

Her Majesty's Inspectorate of Constabulary (HMIC) (2009) *Adapting to Protest: Nurturing the British Model of Policing*. London: HMIC. [Online] http://www.hmic.gov.uk/media/adapting-to-protest-nurturing-the-british-model-of-policing-20091125.pdf

Demonstrations may also be directed against businesses engaging in practices that protesters are opposed to. One example of this was the demonstrations waged against the Monsanto multinational company by those objecting to the company's use of genetically modified (GM) crops.

In May 2013, a demonstration against Monsanto's use of GM food took place. This event was termed the 'March Against Monsanto'. It was worldwide in scope (reflecting Monsanto's status as a multinational company) and involved over 2 million people in over fifty countries, spanning six continents.

Direct action

Key idea (3)

Direct action is a form of protest that entails some form of physical action on the part of protesters to achieve their objective.

Whereas demonstrations seek to place pressure on policy makers to change their decisions, either by abandoning a course of action that they were carrying out or to adopt an approach that they had previously rejected, direct action seeks to secure changes by protesters undertaking some form of physical action aimed at advancing their cause. This may be designed to secure a change without any involvement from policy makers being required. An example of this are charities who raise money from the general public that is then put towards a range of humanitarian causes such as housing the homeless or providing aid to alleviate poverty in developing nations.

Spotlight

One important example of an initiative that sought to alleviate a major social problem was Band Aid, which was set up in 1984 by pop artists Bob Geldof and Midge Ure. It sought to raise awareness of the famine in Ethiopia and raise money from the general public to send food and medical supplies to this country. One vehicle through which this was achieved was the release of the song *Do They Know It's Christmas?* which sold 1 million copies in the first week of its release on 29 November. The song inspired similar charity records released in other countries.

Alternatively, direct action may be designed to put pressure on policy makers to adopt a new policy or alter an existing one. Here, direct action will embrace physical action, which may involve the use of tactics such as obstruction or blockades. The target of direct action may be government policy or commercial practices.

In the UK, an important example of direct action occurred in 2000 and was termed the 'fuel crisis'. This entailed action spearheaded by farmers and road hauliers engaged in the agricultural industry who mounted blockades outside oil refineries and fuel distribution depots in an attempt to convince the government to reduce the cost of fuel taxes. Their actions caused petrol filling stations to quickly run out of fuel and the country ground to a halt as workers could not travel to their places of employment, supermarkets were unable to obtain deliveries of food, and hospitals were forced to cancel operations. However, although this protest embarrassed the government, it failed to secure any lasting changes affecting the cost of fuel in the UK.

Subsequent examples in the UK include actions undertaken by the group UK Uncut to oppose the spending cuts that have been initiated by the 2010 Coalition government. They view these cuts as being driven by the rich and powerful at the expense of the poor, disabled and vulnerable within society. UK Uncut utilizes innovative forms of direct action (which include sit-ins, blockades and street parties). One aspect of its protest was the Great British Street Parties held on 26 May 2012, one of which took place outside the house in London owned by the Deputy Prime Minister, Nick Clegg.

Direct action may also be undertaken against commercial practices. One form of this is a consumer boycott that seeks to make commercial organizations change their practices – for example, stopping the testing of cosmetic products on animals. Other examples of direct action include actions undertaken by groups such as the Animal Liberation Front who have mounted raids on places such as farms that breed animals for medical research, or laboratories in which experiments on animals take place. The aim of these raids is to liberate the animals, who are then rehomed.

One difficulty with direct action is that it may entail the use of violence that, in extreme cases, may be viewed as a form of terrorism by those on the receiving end.

Civil disobedience

Key idea (4)

Civil disobedience is a form of direct action in which the physical action that takes place to achieve an objective does not entail the use of violence. It is sometimes referred to as non-violent direct action.

Civil disobedience is a form of direct action that embraces some form of physical activity to advance a cause, but which deliberately rules out the use of violence to secure the desired objective. This form of protest is typically motivated by moral, religious or political perspectives and is directed against actions undertaken by governments (and also those of commercial organizations) that are viewed as unjust or immoral.

The activities associated with civil disobedience include sit-down protests, trespass, and mounting vigils, but it often takes the form of the deliberate flouting of a law that protesters feel to be unjust in the hope that widespread non-compliance will make the law unenforceable and result in the government abandoning it. This aspect of direct action was inspired by actions undertaken by Mohandas Gandhi and his Indian Independence Movement.

> Civil disobedience has been described as an act undertaken by a person in his or her capacity as a citizen under government, entailing disobedience which is *'passive'*, *'non-violent'*, *'courteous'* and *'not uncivil'* (Bedau, 1969: 19). An important aspect of civil disobedience is *'the deliberate and open act of breaking an unjust law'* (Carter, 1983: 13). Civil disobedience entails non-cooperation with the government, and the refusal to pay taxes is viewed as the last stage in this process since *'it is to deny to the government its capacity to govern, to administer and enforce any of its laws'* (Bedau, 1969: 22) since it is dependent on tax revenues to function.
>
> Bedau, H. (ed.) (1969) *Civil Disobedience: Theory and Practice*. New York: Macmillan.
>
> Carter, A. (1983) *Direct Action*. London: Housmans, 3rd ed.

In the UK, an important example of civil disobedience was the 19 year protest mounted outside Greenham Common Air Force Base in Berkshire which commenced in 1981. Women opposed to this base housing American Cruise missiles mounted a constant presence nearby in the form of a number of peace camps to draw attention to the dangers posed by these weapons of mass destruction. The ending of the Cold War led to the removal of the missiles in 1989. The Peace Camp remained as a symbol of opposition to nuclear weapons (in particular the UK's Trident Programme) until its closure in 2000.

A more recent form of civil disobedience is whistleblowing. This refers to an action performed by past or present members of an organization who disclose to the public their employers' practices. They may make such disclosures themselves or provide information to media outlets such as newspapers which publish the material. This issue is discussed in Chapter 11.

Industrial disputes

An industrial dispute commonly takes the form of workers withdrawing their labour – a form of direct action that we usually refer to as a strike. The historic objective of a strike was to secure improved pay and conditions, and it was directed against the employer. A successful strike would alter the power relationship between workers and employers (and in this sense, therefore, could be viewed as a form of political action, empowering the workers).

Strikes may constitute a form of protest against government policy. In the UK, a protest conducted by the National Union of Miners occurred in 1984/85. This constituted a challenge to policies that sought to cut the level of public spending and thus reduce income tax, which were then being pursued by the Conservative government led by Margaret Thatcher. The government wished to close coal mines that they felt were not sufficiently productive and which required subsidies from the taxpayer. The National Union of Miners, led by Arthur Scargill, refused to accept the closure of coal mines, which would have a devastating effect on the livelihoods of workers in the coal industry, and a strike was called that sought to force the government to abandon this aspect of its policy.

Although the nation came close to running out of coal (which was then a key source of the UK's energy requirements), the strike failed and the mining industry was subsequently run down. In 1984 there were 170 pits in Britain employing around 190,000 miners. Twenty years later, the British mining industry consisted of 20 coal mines and 5,000 miners.

Some socialists view industrial action as the key form of political action that will inaugurate a socialist society. They distrust elections as a means of securing a socialist society and instead insist that this will be secured through working-class solidarity arising from industrial militancy. These ideas derive from a doctrine known as syndicalism.

Riots

Key idea (5)

Riots are sometimes depicted as purposeful political action, utilized by communities who feel that conventional political action fails to address the problems that they are experiencing.

Although riots are frequently dismissed by governments as mindless acts of hooliganism underpinned by any purposeful objective, they are also sometimes viewed as a form of protest.

The view that riots are purposeful and constitute a meaningful form of protest is underpinned by the assertion that they are the only means available to poor people to force their concerns onto the political agenda. The needs of those at the bottom end of the social ladder are frequently ignored by governments, who instead are more receptive to dealing with the demands made by other interests such as the middle classes, powerful pressure groups and multinational business companies. Deprived of influence by conventional political action (consisting of political parties, voting and formal law making by legislative bodies), violence is viewed as a mechanism to force the concerns of those at the bottom end of the social ladder onto the formal policy-making agenda and to deal with issues such as social and economic deprivation that policy makers would otherwise choose to ignore.

The view of riots as a method to remedy the ineffectiveness of conventional political activity to address the concerns of those at the bottom end of the social ladder has led to them being depicted as *'the ballot boxes of the poor'* (Bachrach and Baratz, 1970). This suggests that riots are *'a legitimate form of protest directed against injustices that policy makers choose to ignore. The spectacular nature of riots is such that policy makers may be forced to undertake actions that they would otherwise choose not to perform so as to neuter the prevailing dissent and avoid a repetition of the disorder.'* (Joyce and Wain, 2014: 288–289).

Bachrach, P. and Baratz, M. (1970) *Power and Poverty: Theory and Practice*. New York: Oxford University Press.

Joyce, P. and Wain, N. (2014) *Palgrave Dictionary of Public Order Policing, Protest and Political Violence*. Basingstoke: Palgrave / Macmillan.

The state's response to protest

We have argued above that the ability to protest is an important aspect of a liberal democracy that differentiates it from more authoritarian political systems in which protest is not tolerated and those who engage in it run the risk of having severe punishments meted out to them.

The Pussy Riot Protest (Moscow)

The hostile attitude adopted towards protest in an authoritarian political system was illustrated by events that include the coercive response of the Chinese authorities, including the military, to the pro-democracy protests in Tiananmen Square in 1989. More recently this was evidenced in the treatment given to members of a Russian punk rock band, Pussy Riot, who staged a protest at Moscow's Christ the Saviour Cathedral in February 2012. This took the form of performing a political song in the form of a prayer, which commenced with the words *'Virgin Mary, Mother of God, put Putin away'* (in the sense of throwing him out of office). This was performed for less than two minutes before church security stopped them, although the entire event was videotaped by other Pussy Riot members who managed to escape.

The protest was especially designed to highlight the close ties that existed between the hierarchy in the Russian Orthodox Church and the state's political leadership. The 'prayer' attacked *'the Church's*

However, although firm action by a state may end a protest, it may have the opposite effect and, by highlighting the unjust nature of the governing regime, encourage more people to protest, eventually resulting in the downfall of the government. We refer to an event of this nature as 'regime change'. This is one reason why governments often adopt a sceptical attitude towards protest – once large crowds are mobilized on the streets, the established system of law, order and government may be defeated by weight of numbers. This was a feature of the events referred to as 'Arab Spring' which occurred from late 2010 onwards.

Arab Spring

On 17 December 2010, a young Tunisian named Mohamed Bouazizi burned himself to death (we use the term 'self-immolation' to describe a protest of this nature) in the town of Sidi Bouzid. He undertook this action when the authorities confiscated his only means of subsistence, a vegetable barrow, for not having a licence. It led to localized protests that then spread across Tunisia. Facebook played an important part in mobilizing protesters.

The political regime in Tunisia seemed politically stable in the sense that only two presidents had ruled the country since it gained independence from France in 1956 and the incumbent President, Zine El Abidine Ben Ali, had been in power for 23 years. However, there were deep rumblings of discontent below the surface of Tunisian society that could be mobilized to be used against the government. Economic difficulties in the form of high levels of unemployment, inflation, low wages, poverty and poor living conditions affected large numbers of Tunisians. Students who initially spearheaded the protests were especially concerned about their lack of prospects in society. There was also an absence of fundamental political liberties under the rule of the existing political elite. The Islamic movement Ennahda had also been engaged in clashes with the state since the 1990s, wanting it to pursue a more fundamentalist Islamic approach to the country's domestic affairs.

The government responded to the protests with various forms of coercive tactics that included closing schools and universities, and meting out violence against demonstrators. These actions failed to quell the protests which, instead, escalated and the country descended into lawlessness characterized by clashes between gangs loyal to the President and those opposed to his rule.

The inability of the security forces to contain the unrest, and restore law and order forced the President to flee the country on 14 January 2011 – the first Arab ruler to be driven from power by a popular uprising.

Actions in Tunisia then spread to neighbouring Arab Countries and led to the downfall of President Hosni Mubarak in Egypt, Colonel Muammar Gaddafi in Libya (although outside military intervention played an important role in his ousting from power) and to the resignation of President Saleh in Yemen. All of these events occurred in 2011. In Syria, protests against the rule of President Assad escalated into a civil war which was still being waged in early 2015.

However, although protest is tolerated in countries with liberal democratic political systems, it is commonly subject to restrictions. Events such as demonstrations may cause inconvenience to those not protesting and disrupt the conduct of their everyday lives. Protest may undermine the capacity of an elected government to carry out the policies that the electorate endorsed in a general election and hand power over to unelected groups of protesters – a form of 'mob rule'.

Disorder may occur when large numbers of people gather to protest. This may arise from the actions of relatively few protesters participating at a demonstration, or it may be a deliberate tactic that rejects attempts to peacefully convince the general public of the wisdom of protesters' demands and instead seeks to achieve them through coercive means. These tactics may entail the use of violence in order to secure a political objective through intimidation. This is associated with some forms of direct action including picket lines, which are a feature of industrial disputes. It is for reasons such as these that liberal democracies impose limits on the ability to protest by enacting legislation that is enforced by the law enforcement agencies.

Protest is viewed as an essential aspect of a liberal democratic political system – *'The rights of peaceful protest and assembly are amongst our fundamental freedoms: they are numbered among the touchstones which distinguish a free society from a totalitarian one.'* (Home Office, 1985: para 1.7). However, restrictions are imposed upon the exercise of it. It has been argued that *'A balance has to be struck, a compromise found that will accommodate the exercise of the right to protest within a framework of public order which enables ordinary citizens, who are not protesting, to go about their business and pleasure without obstruction or inconvenience'* (Scarman, 1974: para 5).

Home Office (1985) *Review of Public Order Law*. London: HMSO, Cmnd 9510.

Scarman, Lord L. (1974) *Red Lion Square* London: HMSO, Cmnd 5919.

In the UK, the main measures affecting protest are the 1986 Public Order Act and the 1994 Criminal Justice and Public Order Act. Such measures provide the police with a range of powers to deal with protests that include demonstrations, industrial disputes and actions associated with counter culture protest such as trespassory assemblies. These include the ability to ban processions where serious public disorder is anticipated or to re-route events of this nature when problems such as disorder or a serious disruption to the life of the community are expected. Those organizing events such as demonstrations are also expected to give the police advance notice of their intention to protest.

Dig Deeper

Carter, A. (2005) *Direct Action and Democracy Today.* Cambridge: Polity Press.

Joyce, P. (2002) *The Politics of Protest: Extra-parliamentary Politics in Britain since 1970.* Basingstoke: Palgrave Macmillan.

Joyce, P. and Wain, N. (2014) *Palgrave Dictionary of Public Order Policing, Protest and Political Violence.* Basingstoke: Palgrave / Macmillan.

Quill, L. (2009) *Civil Disobedience: (Un)Common Sense in Mass Democracies.* Basingstoke: Palgrave.

Fact –check

1 Another term for protest is:
- **a** Demonstrations
- **b** Public disorder
- **c** Extra-parliamentary political activities
- **d** Direct action

2 The 'pussy riot protest' sought to:
- **a** Draw attention to the plight of lions and tigers kept as exhibits in zoos
- **b** Publicize the close links between Vladimir Putin's government and the Russian Orthodox Church
- **c** Voice opposition to austerity measures which arose from the actions of 'fat cat' bankers
- **d** Express support for environmental causes to avoid what was termed a 'global cat-astrophe'

3 Civil disobedience may entail:
- **a** Using violence to achieve a political objective
- **b** Acting in an uncivil manner towards officers of law enforcement agencies
- **c** Refusing to vote in a general election
- **d** Refusing to obey a law that is felt to be unjust

4 Raids on laboratories that use animals for medical experiments are a form of:
- **a** Direct action
- **b** Animal welfare
- **c** Vandalism
- **d** Theft

5 The 1984/5 UK Miners' dispute sought to:
- **a** Secure higher wages for miners
- **b** Prevent the closure of coal mines
- **c** Obtain higher redundancy payments for miners who lost their jobs when mines were closed
- **d** Prevent the import of coal from abroad

6 The view that riots are purposeful forms of protest means:

   a They occur during the course of a demonstration that gives rise to disorderly conduct

   b They aim to drive the police from an area where they are viewed as 'an army of occupation'

   c They are conscious actions that are designed to draw attention to an issue that politicians are ignoring

   d They enable persons to loot and thus obtain luxury items they could not otherwise afford

8

The media
and politics

The media performs an important role in the government and politics of the state. It acts as an important source of information on current affairs and serves to educate the general public about a wide range of issues related to public policy and commercial practices. When we talk of a 'free press', we are emphasizing the importance of the press acting independently of the state, sometimes providing information on matters that governments would prefer not to make public. The media is diverse in nature, and in this chapter we will examine the main forms of communication embraced by the term 'media' and consider issues related to how the media conducts its operations and the political influence that it wields.

The role of the media in a liberal democracy

WHAT IS THE MEDIA?

Key idea (1)

The term 'media' embraces a wide range of mechanisms that seek to communicate information, ideas and opinions to the general public. It consists of historic means of communication, such as newspapers, and new forms of information transmission, such as the internet and what is termed 'social media'.

The media consists of mechanisms of communication: historically it consisted mainly of newspapers, but today it is more diverse and includes journals, radio, television and newer means of electronic communication using computer technology. The internet is now a major mechanism of international communication, and is widely utilized as a key source of information regarding political affairs. It can also be used as a means to organize extra-parliamentary political activities on a global basis – rallies and demonstrations anywhere in the world can be organized 'by the click of a mouse'.

A more recent development concerns what is termed social media. This entails the sharing of information between groups (or communities) of people through the use of a variety of web-based technologies that include blogs and microblogs, wikis and podcasts, using platforms (or social networking sites) that include Facebook, Twitter, Ning and Flickr. Information placed on such sites is capable of reaching a mass, global, audience in a relatively short space of time and the content is not subject to editing, as is the case with newspapers and the television.

Social media is frequently used for recreational purposes. However, it also serves important political functions through its ability to mobilize communities into some form of political action.

Politicians are increasingly using social media to reach out to voters, especially the younger generations, at election time. It can be used for purposes that include interacting with voters, sending out reminders to turn out and vote, and to raise money with which to finance campaigns. President Obama used it very effectively in his election victories in 2008 and 2012. Protest is now often organized through social media, and was influential in securing regime changes in countries that were affected by Arab Spring. Social media also played an important part in the August riots in England in 2011 when crowds were orchestrated through such means, which was also used to warn them to disperse as the police were observed to be 'coming their way'. For this reason, governments facing disorder may close down social media sites to prevent its escalation (as was the case in Turkey in 2014 when a court order closed down Twitter that had been blamed for causing civil unrest).

The role of the media

Key idea (2)

The media performs a range of functions that are important to the operations of a liberal democratic system of government.

In this section we will consider the functions performed by the media in the operations of a liberal democratic political system. This section, and the remainder of the chapter, primarily focuses on the traditional media (newspapers and television), although some of the issues raised also apply to other forms of media.

A SOURCE OF INFORMATION

The media acts as a source of information concerning internal and international events. By reading, listening to, or viewing the media, we become informed about events about which we have no first-hand knowledge, and thereby the media enables us to become more politically aware. One advantage of this is that public participation in policy making is facilitated. Public opinion is able to exert pressure on governments over a wider range of matters which, but for the role of the media, would be confined to the knowledge of a relatively small, elite group of rulers. The problems facing minorities can be made more widely known in this manner, also.

SCRUTINY OF GOVERNMENT

The media acts as a watchdog and scrutinizes the activities performed by governments. The electorate has information placed at its disposal with which it can judge the record of governments: in particular the shortcomings or errors committed by individual ministers or by the government as a whole may be exposed. Investigative journalism has especially aided this role, and the impact this can have was spectacularly displayed in the downfall of President Nixon in 1974 in connection with the Watergate episode (which was concerned with a break-in at the Democratic National Committee headquarters in 1972 and the subsequent attempt to cover up White House involvement). In this manner, the media performs an important function by ensuring that governments can be held effectively accountable to the electorate.

THE 'FOURTH ESTATE'

In a liberal democracy, the term 'fourth estate' is often used to describe the role of the media as guardians of a country's constitution and the values that underpin it. This implies, however, that the media possess autonomy and is independent of the state, the institutions which comprise it (including the political parties), and the economic interests which underlie it. We sometimes use the term 'free press' to describe this function of the media, emphasizing the importance of media outlets such as newspapers being able to function without interference or hindrance from the state or law enforcement agencies, since one aspect of its work (as we refer to above) is to scrutinize and make public the actions of government. Accordingly, written constitutions in liberal democracies frequently incorporate provisions that guarantee the freedom of the press: the First Amendment to the American Constitution contains such a statement in relation to the freedom of speech, and this principle is also enshrined in the German Basic Law.

Problems posed by the media

Key idea (3)

Information derived from the media may not always be accurate. The information provided may be tainted by political bias or simply be inaccurate.

While it is generally accepted that the media is important to the functioning of liberal democracy, its operations are frequently subject to adverse comment. In this section we consider the major criticisms that have been made concerning the manner in which the media operates.

PARTISANSHIP

The first problem is that of partisanship. Although in countries such as the UK and Ireland, radio and television are subject to legislation that is designed to prevent programmes favouring one politician or political party at the expense of another, other sections of the media, especially the press, are politically biased: they may support one party which they portray in a favourable light while seeking to belittle its political opponents.

Press bias is primarily affected through analysis: that is, newspapers do not simply report events, but seek to guide the public to a particular interpretation of these occurrences and the manner in which problems might be resolved. One way this is done is by blurring fact and opinion. This results in a story that is slanted towards the political perspective the newspaper wishes to advance.

Partisanship is not necessarily a problem: if a country possesses a press that is diverse, a relatively wide range of political opinion will be presented. The biases of one newspaper, for example, can be offset by another presenting a totally different report or analysis of the same issue. Most of us, however, do not read a wide enough range of newspapers to secure such a balanced view. We tend to be selective in our choice of newspaper and thus may be influenced by the interpretation that it puts forward.

Further, newspapers rarely reflect the wide range of political views and opinions found within a particular country. In the United Kingdom, for example, the bulk of national newspapers support the Conservative Party. In Germany, they tend to articulate a moderate conservative political position. This problem of bias has been compounded by recent developments in the concentration of ownership. In many liberal democracies, a number of newspapers are owned by one individual, and this may restrict the diversity of views expressed in that nation's press. Examples of such 'press barons' include Silvio Berlusconi in Italy, the Springer Group in Germany, and Rupert Murdoch, whose worldwide interests cover Europe, Asia and (following the acquisition of Direct TV in 2003) North and Latin America.

SELECTIVE COVERAGE OF EVENTS

A second criticism that is sometimes levelled against the media concerns the process by which events are selected for coverage. Stories that appear in our newspapers or on our television screens are chosen, not according to their importance, but rather their presence is determined by the criterion of 'newsworthiness' applied by media owners or editors. This may mean that stories that are sensational get more media exposure at the expense of worthier events which lack such 'glamour'. Thus war coverage or an inner city riot may get coverage at the expense of events such as famines, simply because editors believe that the spectre of a tenement block being bombed or a police car being burned is more likely to attract readers, or boost listening or viewing figures than is a story of quiet and resigned suffering lacking such drama.

> The extent to which newsworthiness dominates media content is at variance with the media's role as the fourth estate – *as an industry the news media is unequivocally commercial and guided by principles which may be at odds with the independent political purpose of the Fourth Estate rhetoric'* (Schultz, 1998: 16).
>
> Schultz, J. (1998) *Reviving the Fourth Estate*. Cambridge: Cambridge University Press.

This criticism suggests that the media does not always fulfill its role of educating the public, since it is selective in the information provided and how it is presented. This is especially of concern if media owners or editors concentrate on trivia at the expense of key issues of national or international concern.

PRIVACY VERSUS THE 'RIGHT TO KNOW'

Key idea (4)

A key issue affecting the operations of the media is the extent to which it may encroach on individual privacy by confusing the concept of 'public interest' with the broader notion of 'what interests the public'.

The media's watchdog function may lead it to publish information that infringes on the personal life of a public figure. Such information may be obtained in dubious ways, including the use of telephoto lenses or bugging devices. This reveals an important dilemma: where does the public's 'right to know' stop and a public person's 'right to privacy' begin?

This issue entered into public debate following the circumstances surrounding the death of Diana, Princess of Wales, in Paris in 1997. The car in which she was travelling crashed while seeking to avoid the attention of freelance photographers (termed 'paparazzi'). Although these persons were not employed by major media outlets, the willingness of the tabloid press to buy photographs from them encouraged their work. Accordingly, a revised code of practice designed to provide greater protection to members of the public against intrusion by newspapers and magazines was drawn up and came into force in the United Kingdom on 1 January 1998.

The *News of the World* phone-hacking scandal

The need to stay ahead of a rival media outlet may result in the use of practices that are immoral or even illegal. This case study considers events that led to the closure of a major newspaper in Great Britain, the *News of the World*.

The *News of the World* newspaper was published by *News International,* a subsidiary of News Corporation owned by the media tycoon, Rupert Murdoch. Allegations were made that journalists working for this newspaper (and other tabloids published by *News International*) had engaged in a number of malpractices, which included hacking voicemail messages and bribing public officials in order to obtain information that would form the basis of exclusive newsworthy stories.

Initially it was assumed that the victims of such activities were celebrities, politicians and members of the royal family. In January 2007, a *News of the World* editor and a private detective were gaoled in connection with intercepting voicemail messages on the phones of royal aides. However, it subsequently emerged in 2011 that ordinary members of the public had also been targeted in this way. These included relatives of British soldiers killed in action, victims of the July 2005 London bombings, and the phone of the murdered schoolgirl Milly Dowler. Public distaste towards these activities resulted in advertisers withdrawing from the *News of the World* and culminated in a decision by Rupert Murdoch to close the newspaper in July 2011.

One key issue in this scandal was that it appeared that a powerful media outlet with high-powered connections could break the law with impunity. The perception that the newspaper was untouchable was aided by the appointment of a former editor of the *News of the World*, Charles Coulson, as director of communications by incoming Prime Minister, David Cameron in 2010. He resigned from his post in 2011, and it was subsequently alleged that not only was he aware of the extent of phone hacking, but that he also authorized payments to police officers in return for providing information to journalists. He was later arrested in connection with the bribery allegation, and in July 2014 received a prison sentence of eighteen months.

Further calls for the enactment of a privacy law in the UK came in the wake of the *News of the World* phone-hacking scandal, which illustrated the weakness of the revised code of practice and also the power wielded by the media – which was effectively able to operate as a law unto itself.

A PRIVACY LAW

A privacy law is the main alternative to media self-regulation, which is practiced in the UK. This would enable the courts to award damages when such rights were violated. Privacy legislation exists in a number of European countries: a right to privacy is recognized in both French and German law, while in Denmark, unauthorized photography on private property is forbidden. This issue is regulated by state governments in America, and most have some form of privacy law. Privacy legislation to regulate the media in the United Kingdom has been fiercely resisted, though, on the grounds that it would interfere with their ability to act as a public watchdog.

However, the effectiveness of privacy legislation is limited in those countries that have it by broader considerations. In France, for example, the civil damages awarded are usually low and the sanction of the total stoppage of a publication is rarely used. In Germany, privacy is balanced by Article 5 of the 1949 Constitution, which specifically protects the freedom of speech and of the press. The main objections to a specific privacy law in the United Kingdom have been that it would be very complicated to draft and would encounter key problems, including the precise legal definition that could be accorded to 'privacy', thereby possibly preventing the reporting of issues such as corruption in government by investigative journalists.

MEDIA REGULATION IN THE UK

Key idea (5)

The *News of the World* phone-hacking scandal placed the issues of privacy and press regulation firmly onto the political agenda. A public inquiry, chaired by Lord Justice Leveson, led to the introduction of a new system of press self-regulation.

In the wake of the *News of the World* hacking scandal, the Prime Minister set up a public inquiry chaired by Lord Justice Leveson to examine 'the culture, practices and ethics of the press, including contacts between the press and politicians and the press and the police; ... the extent to which the current regulatory regime has failed and whether there has been a failure to act upon any previous warnings about media misconduct'. The report was published in November 2012.

The Leveson Inquiry Report (2012)

The Leveson Inquiry report argued that the existing Press Complaints Commission was insufficient and recommended the creation of a new independent press standards body, created by the industry, with a new code of conduct whose role was to promote high standards in journalism. This new body would have a range of sanctions available including the power to fine, to direct the prominence of apologies, and enforce corrections. Membership would be voluntary, but incentives were put forward to encourage participation, including allowing exemplary damages on libel actions to be awarded against non-participants.

The work of the self-regulatory body would be scrutinized by a recognition body whose role would be underpinned by legislation to assess whether the self-regulation was effective. This legislation would also impose a legal duty on the government to protect the freedom of the press.

Although broadcasters are regulated by Ofcom, which is backed by law, the Prime Minister was not convinced that underpinning self-regulation with a body created by legislation was the right course of action, and ultimately the main political parties agreed that an independent regulator (termed 'Recognition Panel') would be established by royal charter. The charter (Royal Charter on Self-Regulation of the Press) could be amended only if there was a two-thirds majority in both Houses of Parliament.

The new system of regulation entailed self-regulation provided by a new regulator launched by the newspaper and magazine publishers. This was the Independent Press Standards Organisation, which replaced the Press Complaints Commission. This body has powers to demand prominent corrections and apologies from UK news publishers, to determine the nature, extent and placement of these apologies, and impose £1 million fines in cases of 'systematic wrongdoing'.

The Recognition Panel does not regulate the press, but effectively audits the work of the self-regulatory body, in particular to determine whether the self-regulator meets pre-set criteria for regulatory independence and effectiveness.

THE MEDIA AND THE CONDUCT OF POLITICS

Key idea (6)

The media, especially television, exerts a major influence on the conduct of contemporary politics and performs a prominent role in national election campaigns.

In all liberal democracies, the media exerts a profound influence over the conduct of political affairs. In the nineteenth century, the only way members of the general public could see a leading politician was to physically attend meetings which they addressed. It followed, therefore, that oratory was a prized political skill in that period. But this is no longer the case. Initially, the popular press made it possible for politicians to put their case to a wider audience than was able to attend a political meeting. Then the radio, and now television and the social media have enabled leading politicians to address us directly in our own living rooms. This has had a significant influence over the conduct of national election campaigns which may fulfil one of three roles – reinforce a voter's existing loyalty to a political party, attempt to activate its existing supporters to turn out and vote on election day, or seek to convert members of the general public and thus gain new sources of electoral support for the party.

Politicians seize opportunities offered by the media to project themselves to the electorate: the photo opportunity, the walkabout, the press conference, televised debates, and political broadcasts have diminished the importance of the old-style political meeting. The role of the media is especially enhanced in countries such as America, where it is possible for politicians and political parties to buy air time.

Television in particular has had a number of consequences for the conduct of national elections. It provides candidates with an opportunity to address large audiences, and 'head-to-head' televised debates are common in countries with directly elected presidents. This is especially the case in America, where televised debates between the two main contenders for the office of president were introduced in 1960 (between Richard Nixon and John F. Kennedy), and became a feature of all subsequent contests after 1976. They are organized by the Commission on Presidential Debates and often attract large audiences. In the 1980 presidential election, an estimated audience of 81 million people watched the first Jimmy Carter–Ronald Reagan debate. Although social networking sites have become an important source of information for younger people, television remains the main source from which the public obtain information regarding American presidential election contests, and has encouraged other countries to follow suit. In 2012, the French presidential campaign included one televised debate between President Nicolas Sarkozy and his socialist challenger, François Hollande.

Spotlight

In the second 2012 American presidential debate, Obama's Republican challenger, Mitt Romney, referred to his own attempts to appoint women to top jobs when he was governor of Massachusetts. But his choice of words was unfortunate. Romney stated that 'I went to a number of women's groups and said, "can you help us find folks?" and they brought us a whole binder full of women'.

Even in countries with a parliamentary form of government such as the UK, television has tended to focus attention on party leaders and thus transform general elections into contests for the office of prime minister. In such countries, national elections have become 'presidentialized'. This trend was accentuated in the UK 2010 general election when the leaders of the three main parties took part in a series of three televised debates, and a further debate took place between those parties' economic spokesmen. Central control over party affairs has also been enhanced by this development, which has also tended to reduce the importance of activities performed by local party members in connection with the election of candidates to public office.

Additionally, television has placed emphasis on presentation: major political events such as campaign rallies are carefully orchestrated so that viewers are presented with an image of a united and enthusiastic party. Leading politicians are carefully schooled in television techniques since the ability to perform professionally on television has become an essential political skill. Advertising companies play an ever-increasing role in 'selling' political parties and their leaders. The danger with such developments is that content may be of secondary importance to what advertisers refer to as 'packaging'. What are referred to as 'soundbites' are an important consequence of the media's influence on politics and politicians.

Soundbites consist of a short, self-contained phrase or sentence through which a politician seeks to communicate views, opinions, attitudes, or personality traits to the general public. The term was first used in America in the 1960s, but has subsequently been applied on both sides of the Atlantic.

Soundbites may be used to provide the public with a brief statement that encapsulates a politician's or political party's stance on a particular policy issue, or which seeks to provide the public with an image associating a politician or political party with a particular course of action. In this case they are similar to an advertising jingle. The statement in 1993 by the then United Kingdom Home Secretary, Michael Howard, that 'prison works' was a soundbite given with this intention. This was intended to convey the impression of a government that intended to pursue a tough line on crime involving the use of imprisonment rather than non-custodial forms of punishment.

Soundbites may also be used by politicians to summarize their personality traits which they believe might enhance their popular appeal. An example of this was the statement made by the then prime minister of the United Kingdom, Margaret Thatcher, in 1980 that *'the lady's not for turning'* in response to suggestions that her economic policies should be adjusted to combat increasing unemployment and deepening economic recession.

A major problem with soundbites is that complex political issues become abbreviated into catchy words, slogans, or catchphrases designed to cultivate public support without seeking fully to explain to the public the rationale for the course of action proposed.

A soundbite has been described as *'a brief, self-contained, vivid phrase or sentence, which summarises or encapsulates a key point. This is how to communicate effectively with most people, who only take a superficial interest in politics'* (Rosenbaum, 1997: 91).

Rosenbaum, M. (1997) *From Soapbox to Soundbite: Political Campaigning in Britain since 1945*. Basingstoke: Macmillan.

The political influence of the media

Key idea (7)

Although political parties seek to cultivate a good image for themselves in the media, there is debate as to whether the media is able to change political views or merely reinforce existing political habits.

Issues such as ownership and bias are regarded as important in liberal democracies as it is assumed that the media possesses considerable ability to determine the course of political events. In this section we consider various arguments concerning the influence of the media on political affairs.

AGENDA SETTING

It is argued that the media has the ability to 'set the political agenda': that is, the media may publicize a particular issue in the hope of concentrating the attention of their readers, listeners or viewers on this topic. Whether this is a good or a bad development much depends on the motives that lie behind the media's attempts to influence public perceptions. A beneficial aspect of this activity is that the media may lead public opinion in a progressive direction, perhaps securing action on a social problem that would otherwise have been ignored.

Alternatively, however, the media may be guided by partisan motives. Attention may be directed at an issue in order to secure support for a course of action favoured by a media outlet's owner or by the political interests that the owner supports. This may involve whipping up public hysteria to persuade governments to act in a manner advocated by the media or the interests that lay behind it.

Agenda setting theory refers to the ability of the news media *'to influence the salience of topics on the public agenda'* (McCombs and Reynolds 2002: 176) and has been described as the *'creation of public awareness and concern of salient issues by the news media'* (Heath and Bryant, 1992: 279).

Although previous studies had asserted the ability of the press to influence what issues its readers should think about, the actual concept of agenda setting was put forward by McCombs and Shaw who argued that *'In choosing and displaying news, editors, newsroom staff, and broadcasters play an important part in shaping political reality. Readers learn not only about a given issue, but also how much importance to attach to that issue from the amount of information in a news story and its position'* (McCombs and Shaw,1972: 176)

Agenda setting has been described as *'the most important political function the media perform'* (Wasserman, 2003: 234). The influence accorded to the media through the concept of agenda setting is further developed by the concept of media framing, which refers to *'a process through which the media emphasize some aspects of reality and downplay other aspects'* (Miller, 2002: 262).

Heath, R. and Bryant, J. (1992) *Human Communication Theory and Research*. Hillsdale, New Jersey: Erlbaum.

McCombs, M. and Shaw, D. (1972) The agenda setting function of mass media. *Public Opinion Quarterly* 36(2) pp 176–187.

McCombs, M. and Reynolds, A. (2002). News influence on our pictures of the world in J. Bryant and D. Zillmann (eds) *Media effects: Advances in theory and research*. Mahwah, New Jersey: Lawrence Erlbaum Associates.

Miller, D. (2002) *Communication Theories: Perspectives, Processes and Contexts*. Boston, Massachusetts: McGraw-Hill.

Wasserman, G. (2003) *Basics of American Politics*. Harlow: Longman.

THE MEDIA AND ELECTIONS – REINFORCEMENT OR CHANGE?

Agenda setting is, however, only one aspect of media influence. It is sometimes argued that the media has the ability to determine not merely the policies that governments adopt but also, more fundamentally, their political complexion. This accusation implies that the media has a significant influence over voting behaviour at election times. There are two basic schools of thought concerning the ability of the media to influence how we vote. The debate centres on the extent to which the media merely **reinforces existing political behaviour** rather than being able to act as the **agent of political change**.

Those who argue that the media reinforces existing political activity suggest that the power of the media over politics is limited since most members of the general public have preconceived political opinions. People will either read, listen to or view material that is consistent with these existing ideas, or ignore contrary ideas should these be expressed. Further, as the media knows the tastes of their clientele, they will cater for these opinions and not run the risk of losing readers, listeners or viewers. The reinforcement theory thus suggests that issues of media bias are of no significant political importance, even at election times.

A contrary opinion to the reinforcement theory suggests that the media has a profound influence over political activity such as voting behaviour. It is suggested that many people are unaware of the political biases of the media they are subjected to, and may thus be influenced by the manner in which the media portrays events, especially when such exposure takes place over a long period of time.

This potential to be an agent for change may be especially important when the gap between the leading parties for political office is small: in the United Kingdom, the Conservative Party's election victory in 1992 has been attributed to the influence exerted by the pro-Conservative tabloid press on working-class voters. Silvio Berlusconi's victory in the 1994 Italian elections has been explained by the impact of his three television channels on voting behaviour. The perception that the United Kingdom Labour Party needed to convert Conservative supporters in order to win elections considerably affected Labour's stance towards the tabloid press, especially that which was owned by Rupert Murdoch. It was estimated that the support given to the Labour Party by his *Sun* newspaper was an important aspect of Labour's victories in 1997 and 2001. In the latter election, studies suggested that 52 per cent of *Sun* readers voted Labour, while only 29 per cent voted Conservative. Labour was thus keen to retain the support of this newspaper in the 2005 election, which was eventually forthcoming on the eve of the contest.

SPIN DOCTORS

The important role played by the media in determining the outcome of political activities makes it essential that parties undertake measures to ensure that they are favourably projected. Those who undertake this work are termed spin doctors.

A spin doctor is concerned with ensuring that the policies of a political party are effectively presented to the electorate in order to ensure their maximum popular appeal. The term was first used in America in the 1980s. The United Kingdom Labour Party's success at the 1997 general election was heavily influenced by the manner in which spin doctors were able to manage or manipulate the reporting activities of the media, particularly the newspapers, so that their policy and criticisms of the Conservative government received favourable coverage. Following Labour's victory at the 1997 general election, a number of spin doctors were employed in order to secure governmental control of the media's agenda so that journalists would be placed in the position of responding to government initiatives rather than putting forward proposals of their own. The main advantage of this for the government was that it gave it the appearance of being in control of situations that arose.

The position occupied by spin doctors as middlemen between politicians and the electorate provides them with considerable power, since to perform their functions effectively they are required to exercise much control over political affairs and, in particular, a party's media relations. This may have disadvantageous consequences for the operations of liberal democracies. Spin doctors might feel it necessary to dominate elected politicians to the extent of devising policy proposals that they deem to have popular appeal, or imposing censorship on the media. If a spin doctor acts for a party that is in government, this may take the form of seeking to control media activities by bullying journalists into favourably reporting the activities of the government, or denying access to government sources to journalists or publications that adopt a critical stance to the party. Further, the emphasis that they place on presentation and image may become a substitute for policy so that the attention of electors becomes diverted from the contents of government proposals and is instead focused on issues such as delivery, appearance or image. The role of spin doctors may also accelerate a trend whereby official pronouncements on government policy are made in the media rather than in legislative bodies, whose work thus becomes devalued.

ADVERTISING AND MARKETING

The importance attached to presentation in contemporary election campaigns has also ensured that advertising and marketing are important aspects of these contests. In the UK, the advertising firm of Saatchi & Saatchi played a key role in the victories of the Conservative Party in 1979, 1983 and 1987. The poster 'Labour isn't Working' that was produced for the 1979 contest (which mocked the record of the 1974–9 Labour government on unemployment) was widely regarded as having played a key role in securing the victory of Margaret Thatcher, and ensured that aggressive marketing campaigns would become a feature of subsequent UK general elections.

Cross-media ownership

Key idea (8)

Ownership gives media proprietors the potential to influence political outcomes through the biased or selective coverage of events.

Traditionally, media operations were discrete: a 'separation of media powers' existed in many liberal democracies whereby ownership of the print media was divorced from other major forms of communication such as radio and television. While it became increasingly common in the twentieth century for newspaper ownership to be concentrated in relatively few hands by a process of mergers, such processes were solely conducted within the print media. But this has since changed. Increasingly, media owners have financial interests in various forms of communication including newspapers, journals, radio and television. This is what we mean by 'cross-media ownership', which has given rise to extremely powerful media corporations in terms of both economic resources and political clout. In 2013, the three largest American media corporations were Comcast, Walt Disney and Time Warner, with revenues of $64.7 billion, $45.0 billion and $29.7 billion respectively.

PROBLEMS ASSOCIATED WITH CROSS-MEDIA OWNERSHIP

Cross-media ownership has been considerably advanced by the process of deregulation, one consequence of which is that the ownership of all forms of media has become concentrated in fewer and fewer hands. This process occurred in Italy and France during the 1980s, and in the United Kingdom has been facilitated by legislation that included the 1990 Broadcasting Act and the 2003 Communications Act (although the 1996 Broadcasting Act did impose some limitations on cross-media ownership).

Controls do, nonetheless, exist in relation to media ownership. In the UK, control over mergers affecting the media is regulated by the 2002 Enterprise Act and the 2003 Communications Act (which introduced a Public Interest Test). If the Secretary of State for Culture, Media and Sport decides to intervene in a merger bid affecting broadcasting, telecommunications or the postal industries, he or she will take advice from the Office of Communications (Ofcom), which has a statutory duty to represent the interest of citizens and consumers by promoting competition. On the basis of this advice, the Minister will decide whether to refer the bid to the Competition and Markets Authority.

In the USA, the Federal Communications Commission is responsible for ensuring competition in the provision of communication services, both domestically and overseas, within a framework that fosters innovation and offers consumers reliable and meaningful choice in affordable services. In 2013, this body withdrew a proposal to relax the ban on owning multiple media outlets in the same market.

The ability of an individual or a commercial company to have interests in a wide range of media outlets has considerable political significance. These media owners possess a considerable degree of power: as we have already described, they may seek to place ideas on the political agenda, or to influence the manner in which members of the general public think or act. Their ability to do so may be enhanced by a situation in which a wide range of media outlets hammer out a common political line.

Cross-media ownership may further erode the diversity of the media, which is regarded as essential in a liberal democracy. It is important that the media articulate a wide range of opinions in order for members of the public to become politically educated. A similarity of views expressed in various media forms may be more reminiscent of a one-party state than of a society which flourishes on the expression of a variety of opinions.

A further difficulty is that commercial concerns dominate the content of newspapers or programmes. A major fear is that stories or programmes will cater for the lowest common denominator: the practices of the United Kingdom tabloid press, for example, will become the standard form of activity.

While this problem may seem confined to media operating on commercial lines, it has serious implications for public service broadcasting. If they lose viewers to commercial television companies, their case for receiving all, or any, of a licence fee paid by the public is undermined.

Dig Deeper

Franklin, B. (2004) *Packaging Politics: Political Communications in Britain's Media Democracy*. London: Bloomsbury Academic, 2nd ed. revised.

Jones, N. (1995) *Soundbites and Spin Doctors: How Politicians Manipulate the Media – and Vice Versa*. London: Cassell.

Lloyd, J. (2004) *What the Media are doing to our Politics*. London: Constable and Robinson.

Street, J. (2011) *Mass Media, Politics and Democracy*. Basingstoke: Macmillan/ Palgrave, 2nd ed.

Fact-check

1 The term 'fourth estate' refers to:

    a A palace used as an occasional home by the UK monarch

    b A run-down inner city social housing facility

    c The role performed by the media to safeguard liberal democratic political values

    d Media owners whose power enables them to control the political agenda

2 The First Amendment to the American Constitution provides for:

    a The right to bear arms

    b Freedom of speech

    c Presidents to serve only two terms of office

    d Equal treatment of all citizens before the law

3 In 2011, Rupert Murdoch closed down the UK Sunday Newspaper The *News of the World* because:

    a It was linked to a phone-hacking scandal designed to obtain sensational news stories

    b Poor sales

    c Inability to attract advertisers

    d Trade union militancy

4 In the UK, the Leveson Inquiry sought to:

    a Enforce Article 8 of the European Convention on Human Rights

    b Impose a more stringent system of regulation on the press

    c Abolish the television license fee

    d Regulate the internet

5 The role of a spin doctor is to:

    a Write soundbites

    b Manipulate media reporting practices

    c Report to the head of state on the health of astronauts circling the Earth

    d Guarantee the independence of the press

6 Cross-media ownership refers to:

    a A newspaper owner who is angry with the performance of his or her newspaper editor

    b A European Union Law that prohibits one person from owning newspapers in more than one EU country

    c A newspaper that is available in electronic format

    d The ownership of a diverse range of media formats in one set of hands.

9

Constitutions and human rights

Constitutions (or fundamental law as they are sometimes referred to) provide us with information as to how a country's system of government operates. In this chapter we will consider the nature of the information that is contained within constitutions, why states have them, and the distinction between codified and uncodified constitutions.

What is a constitution?

Key idea (1)

A constitution sets a framework within which a country's system of government is conducted. It establishes rules that those who exercise the functions of government have to obey. All future actions performed by the executive and legislature, for example, must be in conformity with the country's constitutional provisions. If this is not the case, the judiciary may set aside these actions through the process of judicial review.

There is usually one document that contains information concerning the manner in which a country's system of government operates. Examples of what we term 'codified constitutions' include the American Constitution, which was drawn up in 1787, the Irish Constitution of 1937, and the French Constitution of 1958. The provisions of codified constitutions have a superior status to ordinary legislation and provide a key point of reference whereby the activities performed by the executive and legislative branches of government, and subordinate authorities such as state or local government can be judged. Actions that contravene it may be set aside by the process of judicial review. Britain, New Zealand and Israel, alternatively, are examples of countries that do not have codified constitutions.

Codified constitutions are traditionally drawn up following some major political event or crisis which necessitates the reconstruction of the apparatus of government. There is a widely felt need to 'start afresh'. In America, new arrangements for government were required when the country secured its independence from the

United Kingdom in the late eighteenth century. A similar situation required an Irish Constitution to be written following the First World War. In Italy and the old state of West Germany, defeat in war and the collapse of fascism necessitated the construction of new governing arrangements. In France, the Algerian war provided the occasion for the drafting of a new constitution in 1958, thus bringing the Fifth Republic into being.

However, it would be impossible to include all the material relevant to the government of a country in one single document. Codified constitutions are supplemented by several additional sources to provide detailed information concerning the operations of a country's system of government. A constitution sometimes establishes broad principles of action whose detailed implementation is left to legislation. Such statutes constitute a further source of information concerning the manner in which government functions. Other sources include declarations made by judges whose work may involve interpreting the constitution. These written sources are supplemented by the adoption of practices concerning the way in which government works. These are usually referred to as conventions which may fundamentally alter arrangements contained or implied in a country's constitution.

For example, the 1958 French Constitution gave the National Assembly the power to dismiss prime ministers. However, their willingness to accept that they could be dismissed by the president, even when enjoying the support of the legislature, facilitated the extension of the president's power. The American Constitution envisaged that Congress would be the main source of legislation. In practice, however, the president subsequently assumed a major role in initiating legislation.

Constitutions as living history

Key idea (2)

Constitutions make provisions for the way in which a country's system of government is organized. Additionally, they provide us with information concerning the ideals of those who were responsible for drawing it up.

A constitution will tell us about the political views, aspirations and values of those who wrote it. The Italian Constitution of 1947 reveals a desire on the part of its authors to organize that country's system of government in order to prevent the return of fascism. This was reflected in the widespread dispersal of political power and the absence of a provision for the direct election of the president. The French Constitution of 1958 displayed a commitment by its authors that strong, effective government was an essential guarantee of national security. They sought to secure this objective by strengthening the executive branch at the expense of the legislature. Parties such as the Socialists, who traditionally viewed a strong legislature as the essence of republicanism, subsequently accepted the enhanced power of the presidency.

An examination of a constitution thus enables us to discover how theory is translated into practice, and how the climate of political opinion at the time when that document was drafted subsequently influences the conduct of a country's governing institutions. It thus embodies a statement of political theory and political history. We shall examine this situation more fully below in relationship to the drafting of the American Constitution.

THE PRINCIPLES OF THE AMERICAN CONSTITUTION

The 55 delegates who assembled at Philadelphia in 1787 to draft the American Constitution were influenced by a variety of political ideas and priorities. These included John Locke's social contract theory and Montesquieu's concept of the separation of powers.

The separation of powers was advocated by Montesquieu in his work *De l'Esprit des Lois*, written in 1748. This held that tyranny was most effectively avoided if the three branches of government (the legislature, executive and judiciary) were separate. This implied that each branch would possess a degree of autonomy and its personnel should be different. This theory appealed to those who drafted the American Constitution. It was widely believed that George III's unreasonable treatment of the American colonists had triggered the War of Independence in 1775. The monarch embodied all three functions of government and was thus prone to tyrannical action. Accordingly, the Constitution placed the legislative, executive and judicial functions of government into the hands of different bodies.

> What we refer to as government is divided into three components, termed 'branches'. The theory of the separation of powers suggests that these three branches should be independent each of the other – *'the legislature is the branch of government that is supposed to make law. The executive branch is charged with implementing or executing the laws and the judicial branch with applying and interpreting them'* (Little and Ogle, 2006: 5).
>
> Little, T. and Ogle, D. (2006) *The Legislative Branch of State Government: People, Process and Politics*. Santa Barbara, California: ABC-CLIO.

However, one difficulty with the separation of powers is that if it were strictly followed, each branch of government would be accountable only to itself. This might result in insufficient restraints being imposed over their actions, enabling each the potential to act in an arbitrary (that is, unreasonable or dictatorial) fashion. The American Constitution thus sought to avoid this situation from occurring by providing for the fragmentation of political power through a system of checks and balances whereby the key functions and operations performed by one branch were subject to scrutiny by the others. Thus the president's power to appoint members of the executive branch of government is restricted by the requirement that senior appointees are subject to the approval ('confirmation') of the Senate. This principle extended to the relationships within the branches of government so that, in the case of Congress, the actions of one of its two Houses could be restrained by the other. The American system of government has thus been described as one of 'separated institutions sharing powers'.

The main problem with a system of checks and balances is that it can result in inertia – the involvement of numerous people in decision making may result in nothing being done as one group effectively cancels out the work of another.

The role of a constitution

As students of politics we need to know how a country's system of government operates. For example, we may wish to ascertain what power is possessed by the head of state. Or we may be interested in the relationship between the executive and the legislature or between the government and its citizens. We get this information from a constitution.

Key idea (3)

A constitution fulfills a number of roles, in particular providing for the division of governmental responsibilities between the executive, legislative and judicial branches of government, establishing the relationships between these three branches of government, and determining the relationship between the government and its citizens.

THE KEY FEATURES OF GOVERNMENT

A constitution describes the essential features of a country's system of government. It contains a formal statement of the composition of the key branches of government – the legislature, executive and the judiciary – and refers to the role that each of these plays in the machinery of government. It also informs us of the relationship between the branches of government. The American president, for example, is required to deliver a State of the Union Address to Congress periodically, and was enabled to put forward legislative proposals for that body's consideration. Below we consider the functions served by a constitution by examining the main features of the American constitution.

THE COMPOSITION OF AMERICAN GOVERNMENT

Key idea (4)

The American constitution provides an important illustration of the way in which a codified constitution is able to regulate the operations of government over a long period of time.

The American Constitution provided for a legislature which is termed 'Congress'. It consists of two chambers – the House of Representatives and the Senate. The Constitution allocated the executive function to the president while the judicial function was given to a Supreme Court and a range of subordinate courts. This Constitution further stipulated the qualifications required for membership of the House of Representatives and the Senate, and laid down conditions governing the presidency, including eligibility to serve in that office and the length of that official's tenure.

The functions of each branch of government were also discussed in this document. A key role given to Congress was that of levying and collecting taxes. One key duty allocated to the president was to be commander-in-chief of the country's armed forces. The federal judiciary was charged with upholding federal law, including the Constitution, and arbitrating disputes between two or more states.

CIVIL RIGHTS

In liberal democracies we usually find statements contained in constitutions concerning the relationship between the government and the citizens of that country. Such documents typically contain safeguards against arbitrary conduct by governments that are designed to protect individual freedom. The German Constitution, for example, contains a prominent statement of basic rights that guarantee its citizens a range of personal freedoms. The omission of such provisions was regarded as a major weakness of the American Constitution. Accordingly, ten amendments (collectively known as the Bill of Rights) were incorporated into this document in 1791. These list a range of personal freedoms which include the freedom of religion, speech and assembly, and the right to petition for the redress of grievances. These amendments also safeguard the right of all citizens to possess arms, include provisions concerning the manner in which citizens or their property can be searched, and provide for the right of an accused person to a speedy and public trial.

Similar provisions are found in many other constitutions. In Ireland, personal rights such as the equality of all citizens before the law, the right of habeas corpus, and the freedom of expression (including the right to criticize government policy) are embodied in the Constitution. In Italy, the right to join a political party or a trade union is enshrined in the Constitution.

Traditionally, personal freedoms focused on the conduct of political affairs and the operations of the criminal justice system. They were designed to prevent governments acting in an overbearing fashion towards their citizens. In the late twentieth century, however, other forms of rights have entered political debates. These include social rights such as the right to a job, the right to be housed, the right to enjoy a minimum standard of living, or the right for a woman to have an abortion. Although legislation may sometimes remove impediments to prevent specific groups of citizens from exercising defined social functions, constitutions rarely contain a fundamental, all-embracing statement of social rights.

GUARANTOR OF A FEDERAL SYSTEM OF GOVERNMENT

In a federal country such as America or Germany, government is jointly exercised by national and sub-national units. The constitution will commonly establish the division of responsibilities that exists within that country between these units of government. The existence of these sub-national bodies is guaranteed by the constitution.

The balance of power between the federal and state governments in America, for example, is discussed in the Constitution, especially in the tenth amendment which stipulated that powers not expressly delegated to the federal government in that document or prohibited from being exercised by the states would be 'reserved to the states respectively, or to the people'. We shall discuss the changing nature of the balance between federal and state governments in America in Chapter 13.

UNCONSTITUTIONAL AND ANTI-CONSTITUTIONAL ACTIONS

An unconstitutional act is one that contravenes either the letter or the spirit of the constitution. The perpetrator usually contravenes one specific constitutional provision or convention. In the United Kingdom, a government refusing to resign following the passage of a 'no confidence' motion in the House of Commons would be accused of acting unconstitutionally.

An anti-constitutional action is one which displays a total disregard for the entire constitutional arrangements that exist within a particular country and may seek to overthrow them. The assassination of the Israeli Prime Minister, Yitzhak Rabin, in 1995 in order to try to alter the direction of government policy towards the Palestinians, was an example of an anti-constitutional action. Military intervention to overthrow a system of liberal democracy and impose a different form of government is a further example. The overthrow of Salvador Allende's government in Chile in 1973 and its replacement by a military regime headed by General Pinochet was an anti-constitutional action.

However, military intervention is sometimes justified by an argument that the government was breaching the letter or spirit of the constitution and the military's actions were designed to uphold the country's fundamental law. This view was put forward by the Egyptian military to justify its ousting from power of President Mohamed Morsi in July 2013.

Keeping codified constitutions up to date

Key idea (5)

An important issue relates to how a document written at an event of historic importance for the conduct of a nation's political affairs can be kept up to date. This is achieved by the processes of amendment and judicial review.

Codified constitutions are designed to be enduring documents. The process of drafting and ratifying (that is, approving) a constitution is a lengthy one. No country can thus afford the luxury of frequently rewriting its constitution.

The question we need to address, therefore, is how a document written at one specific point in time can endure for many years after. In particular we shall consider how a constitution can adjust to subsequent social, economic and political changes that may have a significant impact on the role and operations of government, and how it might respond to eventualities which were not perceived when the document was originally drawn up.

THE PROCESS OF AMENDMENT

Amendments provide one obvious way for a constitution to be kept up to date. Those made to the American Constitution include civil rights issues such as the abolition of slavery, the right of women to vote, and the universal introduction of votes at the age of 18. The power of federal government was enhanced by the amendment which authorized Congress to levy income tax.

Constitutions generally contain provisions whereby additions or deletions can be made to the original document. The process of amendment, however, is subject to great variation. Flexible constitutions are those that can be amended by the normal law-making process. The uncodified British constitution (discussed later) is a good example of a flexible constitution, but the German codified Constitution can also be altered by the normal law-making process.

Usually, however, constitutions can be amended only by a process that is separate from the normal law-making process utilized in a particular country. These are known as rigid constitutions.

The amendment of the Irish Constitution requires a referendum to be held to determine popular support or rejection for any constitutional change put forward by parliament (the *Oireachtas*). Examples of amendments that were made using such a procedure include two in connection with Ireland's membership of the EU (in 1972 and 1987).

The American Constitution can be amended in two ways. The manner usually utilized requires two-thirds of the members of both Houses of Congress to approve a change, following which it is submitted to state legislatures or ratification conventions organized at state level. A proposal needs the support of three-quarters of the states in order to be incorporated into the

Constitution. The alternative method enables the states rather than Congress to initiate the process of reform.

Generally, amendments are most easily secured to flexible constitutions. Changes are more difficult to make when the amending process is lengthy and drawn out. There have only been 26 amendments made to the American constitution since 1789. Well-supported changes (such as the Equal Rights Amendment in the 1970s) failed to secure sufficient support to be incorporated into that document. One potential danger with rigid constitutions is that they fail to keep abreast of social changes.

JUDICIAL REVIEW

A second way, whereby constitutions can be adapted to suit changed circumstances, is through the process of judicial review, which is performed by the judiciary.

Judicial review entails assessing when a contemporary issue or problem is compatible with the letter or spirit of the constitution, enabling judges to strike down actions which, in their view, contravene a country's basic law. In performing this function, judges may draw solely on their legal expertise, or they may, as in the case in Germany, consider submissions from interested parties before reaching a judgment. Judicial review enables the courts to inject contemporary views and values into a country's constitution when they are required to deliver judgment on a specific issue that comes before them. Judicial review may extend the scope of state activity, or it may affect a citizen's civil rights. The American Supreme Court's decision (in Roe v. Wade, 1973) that under certain circumstances a woman had a right to an abortion is an example of judicial interpretation of the constitution.

There are two problems with the process of interpretation. The first is when the core values enshrined in this document lose their appeal because broader social changes make them unfashionable. In such circumstances, the process of judicial review may be unable to adapt the constitution to the new climate of opinion and may have to be replaced by a new document.

The second difficulty is that an acceptance that the constitution is a document whose meaning can be determined by judicial interpretation may result in the loss of its ability to restrain the actions of government. The ability to adjust a constitution in this manner may result in sanction being given to any action that the government wishes to undertake, especially when the latter has the ability to appoint judges. In these circumstances, the constitution does not meaningfully limit the operations of government or force it to subscribe to any basic standard of behaviour. It thus ceases to be an independent source of power, which is essential if it is to act as an impartial arbitrator.

The United Kingdom's uncodified constitution

Key idea (6)

The UK is an example of a country whose constitution is uncodified. Information concerning the operations of government is derived from a range of sources including legislation and judicial decisions.

In contrast to the USA's codified constitution, the UK possesses an uncodified constitution. With the exception of the Commonwealth period, 1649–60, there has been no political revolution or fundamental political crisis to justify the writing of a constitution. The processes of government have been subject to evolutionary adjustments enabling them to accommodate major changes, including the agricultural and industrial revolutions in the eighteenth and nineteenth centuries, and the expanded role of the state after 1945. There is therefore no one document that provides a basic store of knowledge concerning the operations of the branches of government, or the rights and liberties of the subject in the UK. Instead, information of the type normally contained in a constitution is dispersed. There are a wide range of written and unwritten sources to the UK's constitution.

THE SOURCES OF THE UK'S CONSTITUTION

The main sources of the UK's uncodified constitution are as follows.

▶ Statute law

There are numerous examples of acts of parliament that govern the way in which Britain's system of government operates. Examples include the 1911 and 1949 Parliament Acts (which concern the relationship between the House of Commons and the House of Lords, and which specify the powers of the latter chamber) and the 1971 Courts Act (which established the present system of Crown Courts). Devolved government for Scotland, Wales and Northern Ireland was provided in the 1998 Scotland Act, Northern Ireland Act and the Government of Wales Act, and the 1998 Human Rights Act set out the fundamental rights possessed by citizens in the United Kingdom.

▶ European law

There are two sources of European law – primary and secondary legislation. **Primary legislation** embraces EU treaties which, once ratified, take precedence over the national laws of member states. **Secondary legislation** takes the form of regulations, directives and treaties which are issued by the European Parliament acting jointly with the Council of Ministers, by the Council of Ministers, or by the European Commission.

The UK's membership of the European Community in 1973 involved the incorporation of the European Convention, the Treaties of Rome, and 43 volumes of existing European legislation into UK law. These provisions and subsequent European legislation perform an important role in determining the operation of the UK's system of government.

▶ Common law

This is otherwise known as judge-made law or case law. Common law derives from decisions made by judges when trying specific cases. These decisions then became a source of the law through the doctrine of judicial precedent whereby the future decisions of sentencers when trying a similar case should result in the same outcome. Many of the liberties of the subject (such as the freedoms of assembly, speech, movement and privacy) are rooted in common law.

▶ Conventions

As we have observed earlier in this chapter, many matters concerning the operations of government are governed by practices that have become the accepted way of behaving. One example of this concerns ministerial responsibility, which governs the relationship between the executive and legislative branches of government. One advantage of a convention is that it can be disregarded if circumstances justify this course of action. Harold Wilson's suspension of the principle of collective ministerial responsibility during the referendum campaign on Britain's continued membership of the European Economic Community in 1975 was an example of political expediency overriding normal constitutional practice. This enabled the Labour government to avoid having to take a decision which would have had damaging repercussions for the unity of its own party. Below, we will consider the convention of ministerial responsibility in the UK in greater detail.

▶ Ministerial responsibility

There are two types of ministerial responsibility. **Individual ministerial responsibility** concerns the relationship between ministers and the departments they control. As the political head of a department, ministers are expected to be accountable for all actions that their department undertakes. If a serious error is committed by that department, the minister may be subject to the parliamentary sanction of having his or her salary reduced, which would result in resignation. Alternatively, if the error is of the nature that causes the government serious political embarrassment, the minister may be put under pressure by the prime minister to resign.

In extreme circumstances the prime minister may dismiss the minister. In 2006, revelations that the Home Office had permitted over 1,000 foreign prisoners to stay in Britain once they had completed their sentences rather than being considered for deportation to their own countries resulted in the dismissal of the home secretary. The convention of individual responsibility does not apply to ministers who resign (or who are forced to resign) as the result of some form of personal indiscretion. It is solely concerned with the formal role that they occupy within a department.

Spotlight

One example of a ministerial resignation in connection with a personal indiscretion took place in February 2012 when the Energy Secretary, Chris Huhne, resigned from the government (and subsequently also as an MP) in relation to being charged with perverting the course of justice. This charge related to a speeding case in which his then wife accepted penalty points on his behalf. Mr Huhne was gaoled for this offence in 2013.

Collective ministerial responsibility embraces the relationship of the entire executive branch to the legislature. It is assumed that major issues of policy, even if associated with one specific department, have been discussed at cabinet level and thus constitute overall government policy. There are two consequences of this. First, ministers are collectively accountable to the House of Commons for all items of government policy. Theirs is a 'one out, all out' relationship. A vote of 'no confidence' in the government requires the resignation of all of its members. This last happened in 1979 when the House of Commons expressed no confidence in the Labour government headed by James Callaghan. The government resigned and a general election followed.

Collective ministerial responsibility operates differently in other countries. To oust a government in Germany, for example, the *Bundestag* is required to pass what is known as a 'constructive vote of no confidence'. This entails a vote of no confidence in the chancellor coupled with the selection of a replacement (who is required to obtain an absolute majority vote in the *Bundestag*). This process occurred in 1982 when Chancellor Schmidt was replaced by Chancellor Kohl following the decision of the Free Democrats to form a coalition government with the Christian Democrats.

The second consequence of the principle of collective responsibility in the UK is that, while a minister has the right to voice opinions on an issue discussed within the cabinet, once a decision has been reached it is binding on all its participants. A minister who is not in agreement with what has been decided should either resign or 'toe the line' and be prepared publicly to defend the outcome that has been reached.

▶ Human rights

With the exception of European legislation and the Human Rights Act, there is no constitutional enactment superior to ordinary statute law. Other sources of the constitution are ultimately subordinate to this. Accordingly, the constitution is whatever parliament decrees it to be. This has significant implications for the conduct of government. The actions taken by parliament (and the government that exercises control over it) are limited only by adherence to popular conceptions as to what is correct behaviour. The restraints that Britain's constitution imposes on the workings of government are thus spiritual rather than legalistic.

Key idea (7)

The Labour government introduced legislation in 1998 which placed the European Convention for the Protection of Human Rights and Fundamental Freedoms (which was initially drawn up in 1950) into UK law.

Human rights consist of entitlements that should be available to all human beings, no matter where they live. Unlike civil rights of the type referred to above in connection with the first ten amendments to the American Constitution (which are specific to individual countries), human rights are universal in their application and are frequently enforced by international bodies.

'Human rights developed from the tradition of natural rights, which sought to establish boundaries to protect an individual being interfered with by other citizens or by the government and were thus intimately associated with the objective of liberalism that government should be limited in its actions,

> *which was an important aspect of liberal thought. These rights were thus essentially negative, seeking to impose restraints on actions that others might wish to undertake. The English political philosopher, John Locke (1632–1704), suggested that human rights embraced "life, liberty and property" while the American statesman Thomas Jefferson (1743–1826) indicated that they included "life, liberty and the pursuit of happiness". These were rights to which all persons were entitled simply as a consequence of being a human being and which no government could take away since to do so would constitute a denial of their humanity'* (Joyce, 2001: 43).
>
> Joyce, P. (2003) *101 Key Ideas Politics.* London: Hodder and Stoughton.

An important Declaration of Human Rights is to be found in the European Convention for the Protection of Human Rights and Fundamental Freedom, which was drawn up in 1950 by the European Council. It is now referred to as the European Convention on Human Rights and all member states of the Council of Europe are expected to ratify the Convention.

The key human rights that are contained in the Convention are:

▶ The right to life (Article 2)

▶ The prohibition of torture (Article 3)

▶ The prohibition of slavery and forced labour (Article 4)

▶ The right to life and security (Article 5)

▶ The right to a fair trial (Article 6)

▶ The right not to be punished save in accordance with the law (Article 7)

▶ The right to respect for private and family life (Article 8)

▶ Freedom of thought, conscience and religion (Article 9)

▶ Freedom of expression (Article 10)

▶ Freedom of assembly and association (Article 11)

▶ The right to marry (Article 12)

- The prohibition of discrimination (Article 14)
- The protection of property (Article 1 of Protocol 1)
- The right to education (Article 2 of Protocol 1)
- The right to free elections (Article 3 of Protocol 1)

These rights are not, however, of equal standing. Article 3 is absolute and can never be contravened. Articles 2, 4, 5, 6 and 7 and fundamental but may be restricted for specific reasons identified in the Convention. Articles 8, 9, 10 and 11 are qualified rights that may be limited in connection with certain circumstances or conditions laid down in the Convention. The procedure of opting out of the Convention of Human Rights is known as 'derogation'.

THE 1998 HUMAN RIGHTS ACT

The Declaration on Human Rights is an international Treaty whose provisions are enforced by the European Court of Human Rights (ECHR). However, in 1998 the Human Rights Act embodied the Declaration into UK domestic law. Under this legislation, contravention of these rights would constitute an offence: the High Court would be empowered to grant damages to plaintiffs whose complaints were upheld. The new law made it illegal for public authorities (including the government, courts and private bodies discharging public functions) to act in contravention of these designated human rights and required public authorities to act positively to defend the rights included in the legislation. Although these rights would be enforced by the UK courts, it remained possible for an aggrieved citizen to refer the case to the ECHR.

The role played by the judiciary in adjudicating human rights matters considerably added to its powers. In some countries (such as Canada) human rights legislation allows judges to strike down any legislation that conflicts with such basic principles. This is not the case in the United Kingdom (save in the case of legislation passed by the Scottish and Welsh parliaments), thus upholding the concept of the sovereignty of parliament.

The term 'sovereignty of parliament' implies that parliament may pass any legislation it wishes, whose implementation cannot then be challenged by any other body within the state (such as a court or a local authority). This concept is at the heart of the UK's system of government. Initially, this doctrine was designed to provide for the pre-eminence of parliament over the monarchy.

> *The nineteenth-century English constitutional lawyer, A.V. Dicey regarded the sovereignty of parliament as the 'keystone' of the English Constitution. He stated that 'The sovereignty of parliament is from a legal point of view the dominant characteristic of our political institutions ... It means ... that Parliament ... has ... under the English constitution, the right to make or unmake any law whatever; and, further, that no person or body is recognised by the law of England as having a right to override or set aside the legislation of Parliament'* *(Dicey, 1885: 39–40).*
>
> Dicey, A.V. (1885) *Introduction to the Study of the Law of the Constitution.* London: Macmillan.

A further aspect of the sovereignty of parliament is that one parliament cannot bind a successor to a course of action. Any law passed by one parliament can be subsequently amended or repealed by a successor. Thus, while the UK's membership of the EU asserts that European law has precedence over that enacted by the UK Parliament, this apparent undermining of the sovereignty of parliament is addressed by the theoretical ability of a future parliament to withdraw the UK from this supranational arrangement.

The concept of the sovereignty of parliament influences the power wielded by the judiciary in connection with the 1998 Human Rights Act by preventing judges from annulling a law passed by parliament. However, under human rights legislation, judges are empowered to declare a law passed by parliament to be 'incompatible with the Convention'. Although it is unlikely that declarations of this nature by the courts would be ignored by government or parliament – who would be expected to introduce corrective measures speedily to bring such complained-of legislation into line with the Convention of Human Rights – there is nothing to prevent either of these bodies from disregarding such rulings. This might induce an aggrieved person to refer the matter to the ECHR.

The Judiciary and Internment

The manner in which judicial review in connection with human rights issues operates in the UK is illustrated in connection with internment.

Internment is defined as *indefinite detention without trial*. It means that a person suspected of a crime can be indefinitely placed in a prison or similar custodial regime without having first been tried and convicted of an offence. This power was introduced in the United Kingdom by the 2001 Anti-Terrorism, Crime and Security Act as an exceptional measure through which to combat terrorism and which applied only to foreign nationals. This was cited by the government as the 'emergency' that justified it opting out (the technical term is *derogation*) of the European Convention on Human Rights, which would in normal circumstances prevent a government performing an action of this nature. By December 2004, 14 men had been detained in this fashion.

Various legal challenges were mounted to internment, which included assertions that the process was discriminatory in that it treated foreign nationals in a manner different to that of British subjects (who could not be interned).

These culminated in appeals by nine detainees being heard before the Law Lords in December 2004. They ruled (by a majority of 8:1) that the decision by the government to opt out of Article 5 of the European Convention on Human Rights was a disproportionate response to the threat of terrorism, which did not constitute a state of public emergency. One of the Judges, Lord Hoffman, stated that '*the real threat to the life of the nation ... comes not from terrorism but from laws such as these*'. Another, Lord Nicholls, argued that '*indefinite imprisonment without charge or trial is an anathema in any country which observes the rule of law.*'

This judgment that the government's actions were incompatible with the protection that the European Convention on Human Rights afforded to those accused of crime forced the government to rethink its approach to terrorism.

Internment without trial was ended and in its place the 2005 Prevention of Terrorism Act inserted *control orders* which placed stringent conditions affecting issues such as residence and travel on foreign nationals suspected of involvement with terrorism.

Dig Deeper

Bhagwan, V. and Bhushan, V. (2004) *World Constitutions – A Comparative Study.* Sterling Publishers: New Delhi. This is available electronically – *http://books.google.co.uk/books?id=Ya tgyeA5R4sC&pg=PA75&source=gbs_toc_r&cad=3#v=onepage& q&f=false*

Dorey, P. (2008) *The Labour Party and Constitutional Reform.* Basingstoke: Palgrave/Macmillan.

Finer, S., Bogdanor, V. and Rudden, B. (1995) *Comparing Constitutions.* Oxford: Oxford University Press.

Facts on File Incorporated (2006) *Encyclopedia of World Constitutions.* New York: Facts on File Incorporated.

Fact-check

1 Judicial review is a procedure that:
- **a** Vets the appointment of judges
- **b** Ensures that legislation is compatible with the letter and spirit of the constitution
- **c** Scrutinizes the actions of the judicial branch of government
- **d** Determines whether legislation can be introduced.

2 The separation of powers requires:
- **a** Each branch of government to be independent of the others
- **b** Heads of state to be elected presidents rather that hereditary monarchs
- **c** A legislature to be divided into two debating chambers
- **d** A country's armed forces to be controlled by a body that is independent of the government

3 The first ten amendments to the American Constitution are usually collectively referred to as:
- **a** The Ten Commandments
- **b** The Convention on Human Rights
- **c** The Bill of Rights
- **d** The Statement of Personal Freedoms

4 The UK Constitution is:
- **a** Non-existent
- **b** Uncodified
- **c** Rigid
- **d** Otherwise known as Magna Carta

5 In the UK, the doctrine of collective ministerial responsibility requires:
- **a** All ministers to be appointed at the same time
- **b** All ministers to attend meetings of the Cabinet
- **c** All ministers to act in a responsible manner in connection with claiming expenses
- **d** All ministers to resign if parliament passes a vote of 'no confidence' in the government

6 In the UK, Common Law is also referred to as:
  a Case Law
  b The Vagrancy Act
  c Legislation
  d Law relating to the ownership of parks and open spaces

10

The executive branch of government

The executive branch of government exerts political control over a nation's political affairs and is responsible for implementing laws. It is headed by the country's most senior politician who serves as the nation's chief executive. In this chapter we will consider the functions that are performed by the executive branch of government, the specific role that is carried out by chief executives, and the key features of presidential and cabinet government.

The role of the executive branch of government

Key idea (1)

The executive branch of government consists of politicians and permanent officials who are responsible for implementing decisions relating to the conduct of a nation's internal and external political affairs.

The work of the executive branch of government is performed by two distinct sets of people: politicians, and paid, permanent officials. We will consider the workings of the latter, termed 'bureaucracy', in Chapter 11 and the discussion in this chapter will concentrate on the role performed by politicians who give leadership to the executive branch of government and who are usually referred to as 'the government'. For example, in the UK, the government consists of the prime minister, cabinet, and junior ministers. In America it is composed of the president and the cabinet.

Parliamentary and presidential political structures

Key idea (2)

A basic division exists within liberal democracies between parliamentary and presidential forms of government.

Within liberal democracies, governments tend to be either parliamentary or presidential.

In a parliamentary system of government, the executive branch of government is drawn from the legislature and is also collectively accountable to this body for its actions. The office of head of state is separate from the chief executive, the latter being the leader of the largest political party (or coalition of parties) commanding support in the legislature who is called upon by the head of state to form a government. The tenure of chief executives in office is dependent on retaining the legislature's support, and chief executives typically possess the ability to recommend the dissolution of the legislature to the head of state, which triggers a general election. Countries which have this form of government include the UK and Germany.

In the UK, the prime minister, members of the cabinet, and junior ministers are members of parliament (most being drawn from the House of Commons). The government operates with the consent of parliament and especially the House of Commons, which possesses the ultimate sanction: that of passing a motion of 'no confidence' in the government which requires it to resign. In Germany, the chancellor is appointed from the largest party in the *Bundestag* (or the one that is able to construct a coalition possessing a majority in that House). The chancellor commands considerable power, which includes control over economic policy, defence and foreign affairs, and the appointment of ministers who constitute the federal government.

Executive domination of the legislature often gives prime ministers considerable power in such systems of government. There are, however, limitations to this. A government with a small, or no, majority may have to rely on members drawn from other parties to sustain it in office. In this circumstance, the prime minister may have to agree to demands made by other politicians on whom the government is forced to rely, or face the threat of defeat. Coalition governments (an example of which was the one formed between the Conservative Party and Liberal Democrats in 2010) may further restrict a prime minister's power.

A presidential system of government is a political structure in which different personnel compose the executive and legislative branches. This system of government is found in both North and South America. The chief executive is elected for a fixed term and also occupies the position of head of state. The legislature has no formal relationship with the executive branch of government other than its ability to remove the president through the process of impeachment, and the president does not have the power to dissolve the legislature and call a general election.

Presidential powers are limited by the need to secure the legislature's support for certain executive actions. Thus one major problem faced by chief executives is how to mobilize the legislature to secure the attainment of their policy goals.

There are, however, hybrid systems which include elements of parliamentary and presidential systems of government. In Israel, for example, the prime minister has been directly elected since 1996, but is responsible to parliament (the Knesset). The French system of government is also an example of this, where power is shared between the president and prime minister.

Relations within the executive branch

Key idea (3)

Leadership in the executive branch of government may be exercised by one person (the chief executive) or a group of people (the cabinet) headed by the chief executive.

Leadership within the government is exercised by a chief executive. This person appoints other members of the government and usually exercises a pre-eminent position within it, being regarded as the nation's 'leader'.

A chief executive carries out a number of functions that include:

▶ The initiation of proposals for government policy. Often these derive from the party's election manifesto, although chief executives are also required to respond to unforeseen issues which require the government's attention

- Overseeing the administration and execution of policy, and the overall conduct of the government. The exercise of this strategic role may mean that the chief executive intervenes in the specific activities performed by individual government departments. As the result of such activities the work of government is given a degree of coherence

- Mobilizing support for the policies of the government. This may involve liaison with members of the legislature or seeking to rally public opinion in support of government initiatives

- Acting in times of crisis when decisive action is required. Firm leadership is usually best provided by a single person

- Appointing (and dismissing) other members of the executive branch

There are broadly two models that describe the manner in which political power is allocated within the executive branch of government. Power may be held by **the chief executive alone**. This is the case in America where the president is regarded as the main source of power within the executive branch of government. He is separately elected and can thus claim an electoral mandate to initiate recommendations concerning public policy.

An alternative model to power being concentrated in the hands of the chief executive is one where it is **shared by a group of individuals** who include the chief executive and other leading members of the government. We commonly refer to this as a cabinet government and it is more likely to be a feature of parliamentary systems of government.

The cabinet is recognized in Germany's Basic Law and given a number of powers. These include the right to introduce legislation and the power to veto laws that increase expenditure or decrease income. In the United Kingdom, there is a strong tradition of cabinet government. This suggests that political power is shared between the chief executive and other members of the government. Major issues of public policy are discussed by all members of the government as a team, presided over by the prime minister. In recent years, however, the nature of cabinet government in this country has been subject to debates which have questioned the ability of a small group of people to determine major issues of policy. It has been suggested that the United Kingdom's system of government has become 'prime ministerial' or 'presidential' (an issue we will consider in more detail below).

Although the American Constitution made no reference to the concept of cabinet government, George Washington commenced the practice of holding regular meetings with senior members of his administration. Other presidents followed suit and the cabinet has now become an accepted institution of American political life. However, cabinet government (in the sense of a group of equals meeting regularly and making collective decisions concerning policy) has never assumed the importance attached to it in countries such as the United Kingdom.

Spotlight

There is a story that in 1863, President Abraham Lincoln took a vote in a cabinet meeting on whether to sign the Emancipation Proclamation which would release slaves in the Southern, Confederate, states. All his cabinet secretaries were opposed and voted 'nay'. However, Lincoln raised his hand to vote 'aye' and declared 'Seven against and one for. Gentlemen, the ayes have it!' This story may well not be true but it illustrates perceptions regarding the subordinate role of the Cabinet in the American system of government and the responsibility of the President to provide firm leadership.

How chief executives are chosen

Key idea (4)

There is no common mechanism shared by countries to determine how a chief executive is chosen. The way in which chief executives are selected is subject to considerable variation.

In the UK, the chief executive is the leader of the largest party following a general election. This person is formally appointed as prime minister by the head of state, the monarch.

In Germany, the chief executive, or chancellor, is elected by the *Bundestag* from the ranks of the largest party or coalition of parties following a national election. It also elects a cabinet.

In the United States, the chief executive (termed the 'president') is directly elected by popular vote every four years, although this official is technically chosen by a body termed the 'Electoral College'.

The 2012 American Presidential Election

Elections to choose the American president are organized by the states. Each of these is allocated a number of votes in the Electoral College, which comprises the total number of representatives sent by each state to both Houses of Congress. There were 538 Electoral College votes for the 2012 presidential election.

Popular vote determines which candidate wins a particular state and in most of them, that state's entire Electoral College vote is allocated for that victor regardless of the size of his or her winning majority. However, in Maine (since 1972) and Nebraska (since 1992), Electoral College votes can be apportioned. This is called the Congressional District Method where these states allocate two Electoral Votes to the state's popular vote winner and then one each to the popular vote winner in each Congressional district (2 in Maine, 3 in Nebraska) in their state. This creates multiple popular vote contests in these states, which could lead to a split Electoral College vote. This occurred in 2008, when Obama secured one of Nebraska's four Electoral College votes but in 2012 the Republicans won all four of them.

The Electoral College vote is physically cast in Washington by a slate of electors mainly consisting of party officials chosen by the party whose presidential candidate wins the state. These electors are formally approved by each state legislature and are pledged to support the candidate who won their state (although in only 16 states are individual electors required by state law to cast their votes for that candidate). The votes cast in the Electoral College are transmitted to the Senate, which counts them, and formally declares the result of the presidential election.

Result of the 2012 American presidential election

Candidate	Popular vote	Electoral College vote
Barack Obama (Democrat)	65,913,796 (51.06%)	332 (61.7%)
Mitt Romney (Republican)	60,933,500 (47.2%)	206 (38.3%)

In total, according to the Federal Election Commission, 129,085,403 people voted in 2012 and the turnout was around 54.87 per cent. For the first time in American election history, the turnout rate for Black American voters exceeded that for White Americans.

Cabinet government in the United Kingdom

Key idea (5)

The UK has a system of cabinet government, although in recent years the prime minister has occupied a key role in taking key political decisions.

The extent to which the cabinet operates as the decision-making body at the very heart of government, exercising general superintendence over policy and providing cohesion to its affairs, has been questioned. The following arguments have been put forward to explain the *decline* of cabinet government in the UK.

The nineteenth-century political essayist, Walter Bagehot described the Cabinet as a combining committee, *'a hyphen which joins, a buckle which fastens, the legislative part of the state to the executive part of the state. In its origin it belongs to the one, in its functions it belongs to the other'* (Bagehot, 1867: 14).

> The relationship between a prime minister and his or her cabinet has been described as that of *primus inter pares* (first among the equals) *'to mean that, while he or she may be the leader of the team, he or she is of no greater status than ministerial colleagues in the Cabinet'* (Pilkington, 1999: 122).
>
> Manifestations of prime ministerial power in episodes such as reshuffles tend to undermine this perception but *'this myth of equality continues, as does the constitutional theory regarding the collegiate nature of cabinet government, but neither belief is ... completely true in practice'* (Pilkington, 1999: 122).
>
> Bagehot, W. (1867) *The English Constitution*. London: Chapman and Hall.
>
> Pilkington, C. (1999) *The Politics Today Companion to the British Constitution*. Manchester: Manchester University Press.

MINISTERIAL PREOCCUPATION WITH INDIVIDUAL DEPARTMENTS

It is argued that most members of the cabinet are preoccupied with the task of running their departments and thus lack the time or the inclination to involve themselves in affairs other than those with which they are directly concerned. Further, ministers in charge of departments may become parochial and seek to advance their department's interests, which may be to the detriment of concern for overall planning.

CABINET COMMITTEES

It has also been asserted that the extent of the work of contemporary government and its specialized nature means that decisions are made in forums other than at cabinet meetings, which are usually held weekly. These alternative arenas of policy making include cabinet committees, which operate within the framework of the cabinet system. These enable ministers or civil servants to examine issues in depth, perhaps reporting the conclusions of their deliberations to the full cabinet. There are two types of such committees, permanent and ad hoc, and these are serviced by the cabinet secretariat. Key committees are chaired either by the prime minister or the deputy prime minister.

> Cabinet committees assume an important role in the functioning of the modern UK cabinet: in the second half of the twentieth century *'the role of committees has expanded ... to the point where they take most decisions and the cabinet has become a reporting and discursive body'* (James, 1999: 3). However, despite this development, the cabinet remains *'the supreme tier of British government and an aura of importance still surrounds it ... it gives access to confidential information and a seat at the top table ... It is an exclusive meeting where great matters are discussed'* (James, 2009: 3).
>
> James, S. (2009) *British Cabinet Government*. London: Routledge, 2nd ed.

GOVERNMENT BY CLIQUE

Alternatively, decisions may be made using more informal structures which may be divorced from the structure of the cabinet. These include liaisons between ministers, or informal groupings centred on the prime minister that may comprise ministers and other advisers. It is thus asserted that the cabinet becomes sidelined and collective decision making is replaced by cliques organized around the prime minister.

THE CORE EXECUTIVE

In recent years, it has been acknowledged that the prime minister and cabinet do not possess a monopoly of power over decision making. Indeed, a wider range of participants are involved in making policy decisions. We refer to this broader grouping as the 'core executive'. This refers to those bodies, agencies or procedures that are responsible for co-ordinating policy and managing conflict within national government. In the UK, the core executive includes the prime minister, the cabinet and cabinet committees, the treasury, the cabinet office, government departments, and informal meetings which are frequently centred on the prime minister.

> The traditional tendency to focus on the UK prime minister and cabinet (and especially to the debate as to who exercises ultimate power over decision-making) ignores the existence

of other bodies that also play a central role in policy making. The acknowledgement of these additional political players has in more recent years led to an examination of what is termed the core executive – *'the core executive ... acknowledges the existence of a larger and less fixed network of power relationships that embraces Westminster, Whitehall and key players outside of these traditional key areas of power and influence ... Rather than see the cabinet and Prime Minister engaged in a seemingly endless struggle for political supremacy, the idea of a core executive offers us the idea that ... both institutions are embedded in a network of relations with other influential bodies and people. It is the peak, or apex, of this power network that is labelled "core executive".'*

(Buckley, 2006: 185).

Buckley, S. (2006) *The Prime Minister and Cabinet.* Edinburgh: Edinburgh University Press.

PRIME MINISTERIAL GOVERNMENT

Modern prime ministers often dominate the proceedings of their governments. General elections tend to place considerable prominence on the party leader, thus enhancing the status of that person should he or she become prime minister. The prime minister possesses the power to appoint and dismiss other members of the government, and manages the workings of the cabinet through the control of the agenda and summing up its proceedings. The development of a prime ministerial office has further increased the power of this official by providing a bureaucracy that gives advice on major issues of policy. This ensures that the prime minister possesses much information on the key affairs of state. It is thus argued that the UK's government has become prime ministerial or even presidential in nature, whereby the prime minister personally takes major decisions affecting the internal political and external relations of the UK.

THE CONTINUED VITALITY OF CABINET GOVERNMENT

However, the argument that cabinet government has declined in the UK is not universally accepted. The style or character of individual prime ministers has a bearing on the extent to which they wish to exercise initiative or resort to the teamwork of cabinet government to decide major policy issues. Further, prime ministers need to be wary of conduct that can be viewed as overbearing by their cabinet colleagues. Resignations can have a significant impact on the prime minister's hold on office. Sir Geoffrey Howe's resignation from Prime Minister Margaret Thatcher's government in November 1990 had a major impact on the vitality of her administration and her replacement by John Major later that year.

It is also alleged that although the role of the cabinet has changed, it retains an important role in the affairs of modern government. It provides a mechanism for leading members of the government to be made aware of key political issues and provides the semblance of a unified government involved in collective decision making. The cabinet may also act as a final Court of Appeal to arbitrate disputes between ministers.

The power of chief executives

It is often assumed that chief executives occupy a dominant position in the political system from which they are able successfully to advance initiatives designed to achieve their objectives, or those of the government they head. In this section we consider the difficulties that chief executives in the United Kingdom and America may encounter when seeking to advance their political aims, and which thus serve as constraints on their power.

THE UK PRIME MINISTER

Key idea (6)

The power of the UK prime minister is not absolute, and his or her position may be undermined by a number of factors that include possessing a majority of votes in the House of Commons, or being able to maintain control over the parliamentary party.

It is frequently asserted that the prime minister possesses considerable control over the conduct of political affairs in the United Kingdom. However, while there are few formal restraints on this office, the prime minister is subject to a range of informal pressures that may greatly limit that person's power. These are discussed in the sections that follow.

▶ Control of parliament

The parliamentary situation may restrict the ability of a prime minister to achieve political objectives. The prime minister is the leader of the majority party in parliament, which means that the chief executive's ability to exercise control over political affairs is potentially greatest when that party has a sizeable majority in the House of Commons. A government with a small, or no, majority may have to rely on members drawn from other parties to sustain it in the regular votes that occur. In this circumstance, the prime minister may have to agree to demands made by other politicians on whom the government is forced to rely.

▶ Unity of the parliamentary party

A prime minister's power may also be affected by the unity of his or her parliamentary party. Internal divisions may exercise considerable influence on the composition of the government, and a prime minister may be constrained to ensure that party balance is reflected in its make-up. A disunited parliamentary party may make it difficult for the prime minister to secure the passage of policies through the House of Commons. Discontented members may abstain, vote against their own party or even defect to the opposition. This may increase the government's reliance on other parties to secure parliamentary victory. While a prime minister may threaten to quell revolts by the threat of dissolving parliament and holding a general election, this is a double-edged sword and is rarely a credible sanction which can be deployed.

▶ Public opinion

Public opinion may also affect the power of the prime minister. Prime ministers may find it easiest to assert themselves when there is a demonstrable degree of support from the electorate for themselves and the governments that they head. When the level of this support declines (tested in opinion polls, parliamentary by-elections or local government elections) a prime minister is in a weaker position. Accordingly, the ability to manipulate the media is of crucial importance to a contemporary prime minister. Margaret Thatcher's Press Secretary, Bernard Ingham, performed a major role between 1979 and 1990 in bolstering the power of the prime minister and, as Chapter 8 has argued, the Labour government, elected in 1997, subsequently made considerable use of 'spin doctors' in order to maximize the appeal of their policies.

A further response to a government's lack of popularity derives from the prime minister's ability to hire or fire ministers. Cabinet reshuffles involve a prime minister sacking ministers when a government is experiencing unpopularity within the electorate. The implication of this action is that the ministers who have been dismissed are responsible for the government's difficulties. This is a tactic that has been traditionally used by prime ministers in many liberal democracies in an attempt to increase the level of public support for themselves and the governments that they head. In September 1995, the French Prime Minister, Alain Juppé, dismissed 13 ministers in an attempt to reverse the decline in popularity experienced by his government, and in 2006 the British Prime Minister, Tony Blair, dismissed a number of ministers, including the home secretary, in the wake of poor local government election results.

However, the loss of public support may not necessarily affect the conduct of the prime minister. This, to a large extent, depends on that person's nerve as to whether to ignore the loss of support and continue with existing policies or whether to bow to public pressure and make changes in either the personnel or the policy of the government.

THE AMERICAN PRESIDENT

Key idea (7)

The power of the American president is influenced by a number of factors, including relationships with Congress.

The American Constitution placed the executive branch in the hands of a president who is now directly elected. The president serves a term of four years and may be re-elected on one further occasion. The power exercised by a president depends to some extent on personal choice. Presidents may view themselves as an official who should merely enforce the laws passed by Congress, or they may see themselves as a dynamic initiator of public policy. These views are further flavoured by popular opinion.

The belief that American presidents should be strong and assertive in the conduct of public affairs was bolstered by the need for decisive presidential action to cope with the Depression in the 1930s. But this view has subsequently been revised by the perceived failings of strong presidents, as revealed by the outcome of the Vietnam War (which was associated with presidential initiative), and the belief that strong executive action could lead to abuse of power, as was evidenced in Watergate and the subsequent forced resignation of President Nixon in 1974. Such factors have tended to make the public suspicious of presidents who wish to exercise dynamic leadership. Their ability to initiate actions was further weakened by the size of the budget deficit, which grew enormously during the Reagan–Bush years (1981–93) and served as a constraint on policies involving state intervention.

Such considerations have greatly affected the climate within which contemporary presidents operate. But even within such a climate, presidents retain a considerable degree of manoeuvre. They possess a range of formal and informal powers, and may also exploit their position as the only national unifying force to secure the attainment of their objectives. We shall now consider a range of factors that have a bearing on the power of a modern president.

▶ The president's mandate

The mandate that a president obtains in a general election may greatly influence subsequent behaviour. A president may feel it is legitimate to exercise the initiative in public affairs when the outcome of an election provides a clear statement of public support for a stated programme. When the outcome of an election is less clear (for example, the president fails to secure a majority of the popular vote) or it appears that the result was more concerned with the rejection of one candidate than with the popular endorsement of the winner, the president may find it more difficult to promote policy vigorously, especially when this involves initiating radical changes. Recently, it has been argued that the reduced voter turnout in the 2012 presidential election adversely affected President Obama's claim for a mandate to pursue controversial domestic policies embarked upon in his first administration.

▶ **Clearly focused policy goals**

Presidential success in initiating public policy may be most easily realized when policy goals are clearly focused. This suggests a limited set of key objectives that enable both Congress and public opinion in general to appreciate the president's fundamental concerns. It has been argued that President Carter (1977–81) put forward too disparate a range of proposals at the outset of his presidency, which presented a confusing statement of presidential objectives. Accordingly, President Reagan (1981–89) presented a programme that included fewer key issues and emphasized the reform of the economy and moral concerns. Subsequently, relations with Congress were fashioned around achieving these. Presidents do not, however, have complete freedom to set their policy agenda. The initial efforts of President Clinton (1993–2001) to focus on domestic policy issues was impeded by the emergence of defence and foreign policy issues (including the Bosnian crisis) which demanded attention at the expense of the original objectives.

President Obama entered office in 2009 with a very wide-ranging agenda that at home embraced the reform of education and the healthcare system and the need to effectively counter the recession, and abroad included the desire to negotiate with Iran and organize an orderly withdrawal from Iraq. The inevitable lack of progress in attaining all of these policy objectives led to accusations that the new administration was good at launching new policy initiatives but less effective in translating them into effective action.

▶ Relations with Congress

A president's relations with Congress have a fundamental bearing on that official's power. The president (unlike the UK's prime minister) has no direct connection with the legislature and Congress may not be inclined to follow the presidential lead. Congress has become more assertive since the 1970s, which has been to the detriment of presidents seeking to exercise a dominant role in both domestic and foreign affairs.

Theoretically, the party system might secure a degree of support for the president from within Congress, but this does not operate in the same way as it does in the United Kingdom. Changes to the process by which presidential candidates are nominated and the manner in which presidential election campaigns are financed has been to the detriment of the relationship between a president and established party organization. Further, parochialism exerts considerable influence over the conduct of members of Congress. Members of Congress may be more willing to follow the president's lead when they feel this will bring personal political benefits to them, but be inclined to distance themselves from the administration if they feel that association with the president constitutes an electoral liability.

Thus, even when the president's party controls both Houses of Congress, this is no guarantee that all members of that party will support the president on every major policy initiative. President Carter, for example, did not construct good working relationships with his own party, which controlled both Houses of Congress throughout his presidency, and in March 2010, 34 Democrats voted against President Obama's flagship Health Care Reform Bill when it was debated in the House of Representatives.

However, the position of the president is weaker when the opposition party controls either or both Houses of Congress. In France, this situation is referred to as 'cohabitation'. A position of 'gridlock' may arise (in which president and Congress refuse to give way on key policy issues) and the majority party may also utilize its control of key Congressional committees to vigorously scrutinize the policies pursued by the president by the use of their ability to mount investigations.

'Divided government' in America

In a situation of 'divided government' there is no onus on the Congressional majority to aid the passage of the president's programme, and their own leadership might attempt to seize the initiative in policy making. In the period after November 1994 (when the Democrats performed badly in the mid-term Congressional elections) the Republican Speaker of the House of Representatives, Newt Gingrich, and the Republican majority leader in the Senate, Robert Dole, exercised a role in policy initiation which seemed to eclipse the one exerted by President Clinton.

In this situation, presidents may seek to bargain with Congress in order to retain some influence over the legislative process. If Congress puts forward legislative proposals, the president is able to veto them. Although Congress may be able to override this veto, the threat or actuality of using it may trigger off a process of bargaining between the president and Congressional opposition. In 1997, co-operation between President Clinton and the Republican majority in Congress enabled the first nominally balanced budget to be achieved since the late 1960s.

However, divided government may result in neither side being willing to give way to the other. The inability of President Clinton and Congress to resolve disagreements on the budget in 1995 led to a shutdown in government where federal employees were sent home when conditions attached by Congress for the approval of government expenditure were rejected by the president. This shut down in 1995–6 lasted 21 days.

A further shutdown of 16 days occurred in October 2013 when Congress failed to enact legislation appropriating funds for the 2014 financial year and was resolved after an interim appropriations bill was signed into law in the form of the 2014 Continuing Appropriations Act. This situation had arisen because of the inability to resolve a dispute between the Democrat-led Senate and Republican-led House of Representatives. Some Republicans, many of them who identified with the Tea Party, wish to delay, or totally remove, the funding of the Patient Protection and Affordable Care Act (termed 'Obamacare') and the Republicans also insisted on deeper spending cuts, which became the key stumbling blocks to the reconciliation of disagreements.

▶ Conclusion – how presidents may achieve their goals

Contemporary presidents may seek to overcome the difficulties that impede the attainment of their goals in a number of ways. In situations of 'divided' and 'unified' government, a president is required to build coalitions within Congress to secure the passage of key legislation, which may involve securing support from politicians of different political allegiances by lobbying, persuading or even coercing them to support the president.

However, their ability to do this varies. Presidents such as Lyndon Johnson were able to conduct this 'wheeling and dealing' successfully, especially in connection with his 'Great Society' programme. Others whose political experience was different (such as President Carter, who was elected as an 'outsider' to Washington politics) were less successful coalition builders and found problems in persuading Congress to implement their programmes.

Relations with the media may also influence a president's power. A popular president is likely to find it easier to secure support within Congress for the administration's policies, and traditionally presidents went to great lengths to ensure that they received favourable treatment by the media. However, in the post-Watergate period, the media have become prone to subjecting the president to critical analysis, and the ability of the media to subject the president to critical analysis is an important force that may weaken the president in the eyes of the population.

A president may also govern through the use of executive orders which enable the president to act without having to consult Congress. The president's power to issue such orders derives from precedents, custom and constitutional interpretation, and particularly from discretionary powers embodied in legislation passed by Congress. The United Kingdom's equivalent of executive orders is the use of the Royal Prerogative, but its usage is more restricted.

The chief executive's bureaucracy

Key idea (8)

Chief executives possess their own advisers (often organized into formalized machinery of government), who aid them in furthering their political objectives.

The scope of contemporary government requires those exercising control over it to possess detailed knowledge of complex and technical policy areas. Bureaucracies have thus been developed to serve the chief executive, enabling him or her to exert overall control within the executive branch of government. These fulfill a number of functions, which include the provision of advice on policy matters. This gives the chief executive expertise that may provide leverage in dealings with the civil service employed elsewhere within the executive branch. Their role also includes performing functions designed to secure the success of policy initiatives put forward by the chief executive, and may actually implement policy in certain areas.

In America, President Roosevelt established the Executive Office of the President by the 1939 Reorganization Act. This contains three key bodies – the National Security Council, the Council of Economic Advisers, and the Office of Management and Budget. Their work is supplemented by the White House staff, which contains the key aides seen on a regular basis by the president.

The British prime minister has the Prime Minister's Office, which was set up by Harold Wilson in 1974. This contains a policy unit (sometimes referred to as the 'Number 10 Policy Unit') which gives advice, monitors and develops policy. The Prime Minister's Office gives the prime minister detailed knowledge of the affairs of government and enhances his or her ability to initiate policy and exert central control over the affairs of government.

Heads of state

Key idea (9)

The role performed by a head of state is separate from that carried out by a chief executive, and in many countries is carried out by a different person. In the UK, the monarch exercises the role of head of state while the prime minister is the chief executive.

There is considerable variety within liberal democracies concerning the office of head of state. In countries such as the UK, the head of state is a constitutional monarch, whose position is derived from birth. In other countries, the head of state is elected. This may be direct election (as is the case in Ireland) or indirect election (as is the case in Italy where the president is elected by a college of 'grand electors', which includes members of both Houses of Parliament and regional governments). In most liberal democracies, the office of head of state is separate from that of chief executive, although in America the president occupies both roles.

A head of state performs important roles in the functioning of a liberal democracy. This official stands above party politics and constitutes the physical embodiment of the nation. This enables the head of state to provide a rallying point for national unity, which may be especially important in times of crisis or where national unity is undermined by separatist tendencies. Additionally, the head of state ensures that the system of government operates smoothly and efficiently.

Typically, heads of state appoint chief executives or signify the formal approval of legislation. In most cases, these are formal endorsements of decisions that have already been made, but the participation of the head of state to some extent neutralizes the party political dimension of the activity. The involvement of a head of state in selecting a chief executive, for example, seeks to suggest that this official serves the whole nation rather than the political interests which were responsible for securing the office for that person. A head of state usually possesses the ability to intervene in the conduct of political affairs. This intervention may seek to get a particularly contentious issue further examined, or the head of state may possess certain reserve powers (such as the ability to dismiss the government or dissolve the legislature) which serve to make the executive branch accountable to a higher authority for its actions. These powers are particularly important when there is an impasse in government.

An elected head of state may seek to use the authority derived from the position of an apolitical national leader into power, and seek to exercise a major role in a country's political life. Mary Robinson used her tenure as President of Ireland (1990–97) to promote radical politics which improved the position of the needy and remedied the perception of women as second-class citizens.

THE UK MONARCHY

The United Kingdom monarch is head of state and also head of the Commonwealth. Criticisms have been directed at this institution both from within the United Kingdom and also within the Commonwealth, most notably in Australia where a referendum was held in 1999 that narrowly rejected establishing a republic.

Critics argue that the monarchy instills society with values that are inappropriate for a liberal democracy. It transforms 'citizens' into 'subjects' and, in particular, suggests that birth rather than merit is a key determinant of a person's social position. The monarchy has also been condemned on grounds of cost. This has been compared unfavourably with other European constitutional monarchies, for example in Spain or the 'bicycling monarchies' found in Scandinavia.

A key issue concerned the costs of the court and the situation whereby the head of state was above the law in tax matters. In response to such criticisms, it was announced in November 1992 that Queen Elizabeth II would pay tax on her personal income and would assume responsibility for the payments made from the Civil List to most members of the Royal Family. From 1 April 2012 (following the enactment of the 2011 Sovereign Grant Act) the funding provided under the Civil List arrangements was consolidated within the Sovereign Grant. In 2012–13 it was set at £31 million, to rise to £40 million by 2015–16. Public money is provided from other sources, including grants-in-aid from several government departments. In 2008/9 it was estimated that the monarchy cost UK taxpayers £41.5 million.

Further criticisms have been levelled against the monarchy for the role it performs in contemporary government. On the one hand, it is alleged that many actions performed by the monarch are ceremonial (such as the State Opening of Parliament) or are performed at the behest of others (such as granting Royal Pardons, which are determined by the home secretary). On the other, fears are sometimes voiced concerning the monarch's intervention (or potential involvement) in political affairs. The monarch's choice of prime minister in the UK is normally confined to the leader of the largest party following a general election (or to the person elected as party leader should the prime minister die in office, or resign). However, if third parties assume a more dominant role in future years, the monarch may be required to intervene more frequently in the conduct of political affairs, as has been the case in Belgium and the Netherlands. This involvement may extend to decisions relating to the dissolution of parliament or the dismissal of a prime minister.

Chief executives in the UK and USA since 1945

UK PRIME MINISTERS

Name	Date
Clement Attlee (Labour)	1945–51
Winston Churchill (Conservative)	1951–55
Anthony Eden (Conservative)	1955–57
Harold Macmillan (Conservative)	1957–63
Alec Douglas-Home (Conservative)	1963–64
Harold Wilson (Labour)	1964–70
Ted Heath (Conservative)	1970–74
Harold Wilson (Labour)	1974–76
James Callaghan (Labour)	1976–79
Margaret Thatcher (Conservative)	1979–90
John Major (Conservative)	1990–97
Tony Blair (Labour)	1997–2007
Gordon Brown (Labour)	2007–10
David Cameron (Conservative)	2010–

AMERICAN PRESIDENTS

Name	Date
Franklin D. Roosevelt (Democrat)	1933–45
Harry S. Truman (Democrat)	1945–53
Dwight Eisenhower (Republican)	1953–61
John F. Kennedy (Democrat)	1961–63
Lyndon B. Johnson (Democrat)	1963–69
Richard Nixon (Republican)	1969–74
Gerald Ford (Republican)	1974–77
Jimmy Carter (Democrat)	1977–81
Ronald Reagan (Republican)	1981–89
George Bush (Republican)	1989–93
Bill Clinton (Democrat)	1993–2001
George W. Bush (Republican)	2001–09
Barack Obama (Democrat)	2009—

Dig Deeper

Allen, G. (2003) *The Last Prime Minister – Being Honest About the UK Presidency*. Exeter: Imprint Academic, 2nd ed.

Blick, M. and Jones, G. (2010) *Premiership: the Development, Nature and Power of the Office of the British Prime Minister*. Exeter: Imprint Academic.

Buckley, S. (2006) *The Prime Minister and Cabinet*. Edinburgh: Edinburgh University Press.

Greenstein, F. (2009) *The Presidential Difference: Leadership Style from FDR to George W. Bush*. Princeton, New Jersey: Princeton University Press, 2004, 3rd ed.

Jones, C. (2007) *The American Presidency: A Very Short Introduction*. Oxford: Oxford University Press.

Kavanagh, D. and Seldon, A. (2008) *The Powers Behind the Prime Minister: The Hidden Influence of Number 10*. London: HarperCollins, 2nd ed.

Fact-check

1 In a parliamentary system of government, members of the executive branch of government are drawn from:
  a The civil service
  b The cabinet
  c The legislature
  d The Ministerial Select Committee

2 The term 'cohabitation' refers to a political situation in France whereby:
  a Two politicians live together but are not married
  b The legislative and executive branches of government are controlled by personnel drawn from opposing political parties
  c An occasion when the two debating chambers which comprise the national legislature met together in a combined Session
  d Two opposing political parties form a coalition government

3 In America, the Electoral College is used as a mechanism to:
  a Determine who has the right to vote in elections
  b Formally elect the President of the United States
  c Choose and train candidates who intend to stand for national political office
  d Determine when elections to Congress should be held

4 In the UK, the Head of state is:
  a The prime minister
  b The monarch
  c The speaker of the House of Commons
  d The home secretary

5 In the UK, a Prime Minister may seek to quell revolts in his Parliamentary Party by:
  a Threatening to stop their pay
  b Declaring a state of emergency
  c Dissolving Parliament and calling a general election
  d Transferring power to the Head of State

6 In the UK, Margaret Thatcher was unique in the sense that:

a She was not a Member of Parliament when she became prime minister

b She failed to secure a majority of seats in Parliament in the 1979 general election

c She had formerly been a member of the House of Lords

d She was the first woman to occupy the office of Prime minister

11

The bureaucracy

The term 'bureaucracy' refers to the permanent employees of the executive branch who staff the machinery of government. In this chapter we will consider the organization of the machinery of government, the role performed by senior members of the bureaucracy in influencing the content of public policy, and issues related to the reform of the machinery of government. We will also consider the issue of state secrecy and the challenges posed to this by whistleblowing.

The role of the bureaucracy

Key idea (1)

Bureaucrats are the permanent arm of the executive branch of government whose roles are to advise policy makers and implement their decisions.

This aspect of our study concerns the administrative arm of the executive branch of government. Here the work is performed by paid officials whom we term 'bureaucrats'. Many of these are categorized as civil servants. This means that key matters such as recruitment, pay, promotion, grading, dismissal, and conditions of work are subject to common regulations that operate throughout the national government within which they work. Such common regulations are enforced centrally by bodies such as the American Office of Personnel Management, or the United Kingdom's Civil Service Commission.

Civil servants perform a variety of roles in liberal democratic states, but there are two that have traditionally been emphasized: they give advice to those who exercise control of the political arm of the executive branch on the content of policy; they may also be responsible for implementing it. The implementation of policy is carried out at all levels of government and includes the delivery of a service to the public (such as the payment of welfare benefits).

Bureaucracies employ large numbers of people within government agencies and departments. Efficiency in administration requires rational organization. Max Weber suggested that the ideal bureaucracy would be organized according to a number of principles. He suggested that appointments should be determined on the basis of tests and not patronage, that bureaucratic decision making should be characterized by the impersonal application of established rules and procedures (the term 'red tape' being commonly used to describe the consequences of this method of operation), that the structure should be hierarchical with each bureaucrat occupying a defined place in a chain of command, and that bureaucracies should operate on the basis of technical expertise.

The German sociologist Max Weber put forward principles relating to the organization of bureaucracy and the operations of bureaucrats. It has been argued that, for Weber *'the ethical attributes of the "good bureaucrat" – strict adherence to procedure, acceptance of hierarchical sub- and super-ordination, abnegation of personal moral enthusiasm, commitment to the purposes of the office – are the product of definite ethical practices and techniques'* (du Gay, 2000: 28). Additionally, *'The value attached to impersonality by Weber must be understood as itself being an expression of democratic equalization and therefore a more ethically advanced form of authority than that based on personal considerations ("grace and favour", nepotism, cronyism, etc.) which characterized organizational life in public and private spheres before the quickening of modernization in the early twentieth century'* (du Gay, 2005: 173).

du Gay, P. (2000) *In Praise of Bureaucracy: Weber, Organization, Ethics.* London: Sage.

du Gay, P. (2005) *The Values of Bureaucracy.* Oxford: Oxford University Press.

How is the machinery of government organized?

GOVERNMENT DEPARTMENTS

Key idea (2)

The machinery of government comprises a diverse range of agencies. In countries that include Ireland and the UK, government departments constitute a major component of the machinery of government.

The existence of government departments is sometimes determined by legislation. In Ireland, for example, the 1924 Ministers and Secretaries Act (as amended in 2011) provided the legal basis for the establishment of the departments of state and the allocation of work between them. Elsewhere, chief executives may possess the ability to initiate reorganization to the structure of government by abolishing existing departments, creating new ones or reallocating the tasks of government between departments. In the UK, the power to reorganize government departments is derived from the Royal Prerogative rather than through legislation. This theoretically gives the prime minister considerable freedom to reorganize the machinery of government, which may be carried out for a number of reasons that include the desire to direct attention to a particular area of government policy. However, political constraints frequently restrict the scope of such changes. This tends to mean that changes made by a chief executive to the structure of government are often of an incremental nature, marginally adjusting, but not radically overhauling, the organization that existed when the chief executive assumed office.

QUASI-AUTONOMOUS NON-GOVERNMENTAL ORGANIZATIONS

Key idea (3)

The machinery of government in the UK also includes a number of Arm's Length Bodies (ALBs), often termed 'quasi-autonomous non-governmental organisations' (or quangos).

In addition to government departments, in most countries there exists a vast range of alternative mechanisms whereby national public policy is discharged. In America, regulatory agencies, government corporations, and independent executive agencies perform federal government functions. In the UK, a range of agencies exist that operate at 'arm's length' from the government. These comprise non-departmental government bodies, executive agencies, and non-ministerial departments (often collectively referred to as quasi-autonomous non-governmental organisations, or quangos), which deliver services at both national and sub-national levels.

The main advantage arising from the use of such machinery is that it is implemented by organizations that are purpose-built to perform a specific function. It does not have to accord to the organization and structure dictated by normal civil service requirements. Thus people can be recruited with expertise that would not normally be possessed by civil servants (for example, experience in conducting a large-scale business enterprise) and rewarded by a salary which does not have to conform to civil service pay scales. In both the UK and Ireland, these bodies have been used to link the public and private sectors.

Executive Agencies

One example of a quango in the UK is an executive agency that was created to separate policy planning and service delivery. There are two main advantages associated with this reform.

First, it gave key civil servants greater ability to engage in long-term planning by placing the day-to-day administration of services into the hands of bodies other than government departments. It has been argued that, in the United Kingdom, the senior civil service's preoccupation with administration rather than planning resulted in a dislike of change and innovation. This reform would enhance the capacity of senior civil servants to plan. Second, those responsible for implementing services (usually in 'agencies') would exercise a considerable degree of discretion and operational freedom. This would improve the morale and motivation of the staff employed in such work. Within the confines of policy objectives and a budget set by a government department, those who delivered services would be delegated a wide degree of authority as to how they achieved their set goals.

In the UK, this reform took the form of the 'Next Steps' Programme, which was underpinned by a report written by Robin Ibbs in 1988. This report recommended that the national bureaucracy should be divided into a central civil service (which would advise ministers and be responsible for strategic planning within a department) and agencies (which would deliver the services within the framework devised by the department's central civil service).

Agencies exercise an important role within the central machinery of government. In 2000, 60 per cent of civil servants worked in 126 executive agencies, although by 2004 this percentage had fallen to around 53 per cent.

A number of criticisms have been made regarding the operation of agencies. It has been argued that they are insufficiently accountable for their actions. The convention of individual ministerial responsibility is harder to enforce when a wide range of operational decisions are made by civil servants who operate at arm's length from effective ministerial control. Further, such reforms tend to undermine the tradition of a unified civil service. The essence of this principle is that civil servants are able to move across departments and work anywhere within the bureaucracy. Such movement is less likely as the innovations referred promote the view that workers are agency rather than government employees.

There are two major problems affecting quangos.

ACCOUNTABILITY

The extent to which quangos are adequately accountable for their actions has been questioned. They may be deliberately used to avoid the constant 'interference' of politicians, especially in connection with day-to-day policy decisions. It is argued that organizations that pursue commercial activities require a certain amount of freedom so that enterprise can flourish. Others that pursue non-economic tasks may also justify a relative degree of insulation from political control on the grounds that the task with which they are concerned should not be subject to the constant to and fro of political debate: thus such bodies effectively depoliticize the function they are set up to perform. However, accountability remains an important issue as such bodies are concerned with the administration of public policy. Additionally, some rely on state funding to finance some or all of their activities.

Accountability may be secured in three ways – by the chairperson (a political appointee) reporting to the minister, by the chief executive (a paid official) reporting to the department associated with the body (perhaps in the form of an annual report or a corporate plan indicating targets and performance), or through scrutiny exercised by the legislature over the operations which such bodies perform.

The consideration of annual reports might aid legislative scrutiny of such bodies but parliamentary select committees (such as the Irish Joint Committee on State-Sponsored Bodies, established in 1976) possibly possess greater potential for enabling legislatures effectively to examine the activities of these bodies.

PATRONAGE

The second problem associated with the implementation of public policy by bodies other than government departments concerns the manner whereby those who manage these organizations are appointed. The main criterion for the appointment of managers to such organizations often seems to be their political sympathy to the government that appoints them. In the UK this led the Nolan Committee in 1995 to recommend that appointments to quangos should be scrutinized by an independent commissioner for public appointments. The role of this office was extended by the 1997 Labour government to ensure that future appointments were non-partisan and that a much wider group of people (including women and members of ethnic minorities) were encouraged to apply for these jobs.

The civil service as a ruling elite

Key idea (4)

Civil servants perform an important position in government that may be based upon their social background and vocational training.

The description of senior civil servants as an 'elite' particularly refers to their social background. In many countries, such officials derive from a middle- and upper middle-class background. The stereotypical British senior civil servant is middle class, male, educated at public school and at Oxford or Cambridge University. A similar situation exists in France where, despite efforts by socialist administrations to broaden the recruitment base of such officials, a large number derive from socially exclusive backgrounds. There are, however, exceptions: in New Zealand, for example, the main source of recruitment into the civil service is secondary school graduates. Preference is given to internal promotions to fill higher level vacancies.

Concern has been expressed that senior civil servants are able to ensure that policy making is influenced by attitudes and values derived from their untypical social backgrounds. In some countries, however, the influence they possess extends throughout society and is not confined to the machinery of government.

Administrators and politics

Key idea (5)

It is sometimes argued that senior civil servants go beyond their role to advise on and implement policy decisions and instead play an active role in the decision making.

The above question compels us to consider whether the theoretical division between politics and administration is a meaningful one. In theory, senior civil servants give advice to politicians but the latter make decisions. The role of the civil service then becomes that of implementing these decisions. The key issue concerns the extent to which the provision of advice by senior civil servants enables them to dominate the policy-making process. This suggests that the role of civil servants sometimes goes beyond the mere provision of advice and entails the exertion of a considerable degree of influence over the content of public policy, thus undermining the theoretical division between politics and administration.

The accusation that civil servants usurped (that is, took over without lawful authority) the role which ought to be fulfilled by politicians within the executive branch of government has been voiced in the United Kingdom in recent years. An extreme form of this argument has been that senior civil servants might conspire to prevent ministers from pursuing a course of action which they wished to embark upon. We examine this argument in greater detail in the following paragraphs.

Minister–civil servant relationships in the UK

Key idea (6)

In the UK, senior civil servants may go beyond offering advice to policy makers and exercise a major role in policy making.

The aim of this discussion is to consider why and how civil servants might occupy a dominant position in policy making.

Spotlight

The term given to a senior civil servant is 'mandarin'. It is named after a bureaucrat of Imperial China and not the fruit that resembles a small orange.

Civil servants are permanent officials with expertise (either of a policy area or of the workings of the administrative machine). Ministers hold office temporarily. They are 'here today and gone tomorrow'. Additionally, ministers may know little or nothing of the work of a department until they are placed in charge of it by a prime minister. Although they may employ a limited number of policy advisers, these are heavily outnumbered by permanent officials. In theory, therefore, civil servants are in a powerful position to overawe ministers, but in any case many will be voluntarily disposed to defer to the views or wishes of their permanent officials. Some ministers will by choice take little part in policy making and be content to legitimize decisions made on their behalf by their civil servants.

The workload of a minister affects civil service involvement in policy making. A minister is also a member of parliament who needs to devote some time to constituency affairs. He or she is a leading member of a political party who is expected to perform activities to promote that party. A minister may additionally be a member of the cabinet and thus need to devote energy to the overall work of government. It would thus be physically impossible for a minister to supervise all aspects of a department's affairs. Ministers rely heavily on civil servants using their initiative to resolve unimportant or routine issues. These constitute the bulk of a department's work that does not, therefore, come before the minister for consideration. This gives the civil service the ability to make decisions over a very wide range of departmental activities in which the only political guideline might be that of 'knowing the minister's mind' – that is assessing how the minister would act were he or she available to deal with the situation personally.

These arguments suggest that ministers may acquiesce to civil servants playing a significant role in policy making. Problems arise only when ministers perceive civil servants acting improperly by seeking to control the policy-making process by manipulating or obstructing them.

What is termed the 'Whitehall Model of Policy Making' *'contends that civil servants either initiate major policy or so alter it as it passes through their hands as to make it substantially theirs – thus making them the key influence on policy'* (Jones and Norton, 2014: 467).

It has been observed that bureaucrats perform a number of roles – *'an important role of the bureaucracy is its expertise in informing policy formulation as well as its role in the implementation of policy and public service delivery'* (Miller and McTavish, 2014: 55).

Jones, B. and Norton, P. (2014) *Politics UK.* Abingdon, Oxfordshire: Routledge 8th ed.

Miller, K. and McTavish, D. (2014) *Making and Managing Public Policy.* Abingdon, Oxfordshire: Routledge.

Many ministers make decisions by selecting from options presented to them by the civil service. This gives the civil service ample opportunity to guide the minister in the direction in which they wish him or her to go. They may do this, for example, by producing an incomplete list of options designed to direct the minister towards the course of action favoured by the department. Alternatively they may attempt to 'blind a minister with science' – that is, making an issue seem so technical that the minister, as a layperson, feels uncomfortable and thus disposed towards accepting the preferred view put forward by the civil service.

However, some ministers wish to exercise a more prominent role concerning policy making. They enter office with clearly defined policy objectives and an appreciation concerning how these goals should be accomplished. However, this does not guarantee that the civil service will follow the minister's lead. They may utilize an array of devices to stop, or slow down, the implementation of the minister's wishes. Such tactics include deliberately delaying the implementation of ministerial directives or mobilizing opposition to the minister's policy. The latter may involve the use of machinery such as interdepartmental committees (which are staffed by senior civil servants and from which ministers are excluded) to mobilize opposition to a minister's policy from civil servants drawn from a number of departments.

Alternatively, civil servants might manufacture political pressure against a minister designed to secure the abandonment of the politician's preferred course of action. They may do this by appealing over the head of the minister to the prime minister or the cabinet, possibly utilizing the argument that the minister's intended actions are contrary or damaging to overall government policy. The success of such a tactic is considerably influenced by the minister's standing among his or her political colleagues.

Thus the argument that civil servants conspire to dominate the policy-making process is not totally accurate. Apparent attempts by civil servants to thwart the objectives of their ministers may indicate the existence of multiple accountabilities whereby civil servants acknowledge the authority of others within the machinery of government over his or her own minister.

Additionally, although there may be occasions when ministers and their civil servants have clashed, the relationship between them is frequently harmonious. Each needs the other. The minister relies on the civil service for advice and the handling of routine business to ensure a manageable workload, but the civil service relies on the minister to promote the department's interests. This may involve defending the department when its interests or activities are scrutinized by the cabinet or within parliament. It may also involve performing an ambassadorial role to convince the general public that the department fulfills a vital role in civil affairs.

MINISTERIAL ADVISERS

Ministers may seek to offset domination exerted by civil servants by employing their own advisers. In 2013, there were 98 of these costing £7.2 million a year. Advisers are governed by a code of conduct that seeks to define the role and set out their relationships with the permanent civil service. A separate ministerial code sets out rules for their appointment and their status in relation to ministers.

There are, however, a number of difficulties with this situation. Ministerial advisers are employed as temporary senior civil servants and have thus been accused of politicizing the civil service even though they are appointed only for the lifetime of the government. Civil servants may resent the role of these 'outsiders'. Clashes between the Permanent Secretary at the Treasury, Sir Terence Burns, and the Chancellor of the Exchequer's special adviser, Ed Balls, resulted in the former vacating his post in 1998.

DELEGATED LEGISLATION

In addition to arguments that imply civil servants may illicitly perform policy-making functions, they also may perform the task quite legitimately through their ability to draft what is termed 'delegated legislation'. This arises when an act of parliament (termed 'primary legislation') establishes broad principles whose detailed substance is left to civil servants to implement through means such as statutory instruments.

An important example of delegated legislation is the Codes of Practice governing the use of police powers that are issued (and regularly amended) under the provisions of the 1984 Police and Criminal Evidence Act.

There are many advantages of this process. The ability of civil servants to draw up or amend delegated legislation means that the law-making process is speedier than would be the case were parliament required to carry out this process by introducing new legislation. This means that the law can be speedily updated. Additionally, civil servants may be better equipped than politicians to devise detailed and technical regulations. The importance of delegated legislation was enhanced in 2001 when the Regulatory Reform Act provided for the reform of primary legislation through regulatory reform orders. Subsequently, the 2006 Legislative and Regulatory Reform Act simplified the procedure involved in this process.

Nonetheless, parliament retains a scrutinizing role over delegated legislation. All statutory instruments must be referred to parliament (although very few are actively considered by this body) and some require an affirmative resolution to be passed by both Houses of Parliament before they become law. Scrutiny is also carried out by parliamentary committees. The House of Commons has a Regulatory Reform Committee, and the House of Lords a Delegated Powers Scrutiny Committee and a House of Lords Secondary Legislation Scrutiny Committee. A joint committee of both Houses of Parliament, the Joint Committee on Statutory Instruments, was re-established following the 2010 general election to perform work of this nature.

Political control of the bureaucracy

Key idea (7)

In liberal democratic political systems, the bureaucracy is not autonomous, but is subject to a number of political controls wielded by the executive and legislative branches of government.

There are various ways whereby the operations of the bureaucracy can be made susceptible to political control. As we have argued above in connection with the UK, ministers may appoint their own advisers to offset the activities of civil servants. One problem is that if these advisers are outsiders they may effectively be 'frozen out' of the operations of a department by its permanent officials. In France, this difficulty is solved by ministers appointing existing civil servants to act as their advisers. These are located in the *Cabinet Ministériel* (Cabinet of France). They often derive from the *Grand Corps de l'Etat*, operate under the minister's direct control, and may revert to their previous posts when their service to the minister has ended.

Chief executives may also seek to exert influence over civil service actions. They may do this through involvement in the appointment, promotion and removal of civil servants. A major difficulty with these activities is that the civil service might become politicized. This means it becomes so closely identified with the policies of a particular political party that its neutrality (which is essential if it is to serve governments of other political persuasions) is questioned.

The legislature may also exert influence over the conduct of the bureaucracy, a function which is termed 'oversight' in America. In the United Kingdom, special investigations may be launched by bodies such as parliamentary select committees into the operations of particular departments or agencies.

In assessing the effectiveness of political control over the bureaucracy, however, we must be aware of a potential conflict between accountability and managerial freedom. Although those whose activities are financed by public money need to account for what they do, excessive accountability tends to stifle initiative and make civil servants operate in a cautious manner dominated by adherence to stipulated procedures. Ideally, therefore, agencies should be accountable for their results but given a degree of discretion as to how these are achieved.

Reform of the civil service

Key idea (8)

Civil service reform has been pursued vigorously in a number of countries in recent years and has taken a number of different directions.

The growth in the role of the state in a number of countries after 1945 resulted in a large civil service (or bureaucracy) to administer the services associated with it. This was costly. Thus governments wishing to prune public spending cast a critical eye at the workings of the bureaucracy. The reform of the civil service has been advocated in many countries. In Ireland, the Devlin Report put forward reform proposals in 1969. In the United Kingdom, the Fulton Report in 1968 and the Ibbs Report in 1988 influenced significant changes within the civil service. In America, this subject was considered by Vice President Al Gore's National Performance Review published in 1993. This initiated reforms to the federal bureaucracy that sought to improve customer service, cut red tape and decrease the number of federal employees. It was estimated that when the Clinton administration left office in 2001, savings of around $136 million had been made arising from the review, including a reduction of around 377,000 federal employees.

Governments influenced by 'New Right' ideology have been especially interested in civil service reform in recent years. While it would be impossible to chart the directions that civil service reform has taken in various countries, there are certain developments that have occurred widely. One important underpinning of these reforms is New Public Management (NPM).

NEW PUBLIC MANAGEMENT

Key idea (9)

Initiatives such as NPM have underpinned reforms of the working practices and performance culture of the civil service.

NPM is the underpinning for a number of reforms which have sought to remodel the way public policy is implemented and has led to the fragmentation of government, with policies now being implemented by a range of agencies rather than being the preserve of bodies which are arms of the state. This approach is especially identified with the New Right.

NPM embraces a number of key features. It is rooted in the New Right's support for the free market, one consequence of which is to question the desirability of service provision by the public sector: this may require those agencies implementing public policy being required to prove which aspects of their work must remain in the public sector, and which need to be transferred to the private sector. It has sought to reorganize the operations of public sector agencies through the use of management techniques associated with the private sector such as performance indicators, business plans, and a shift of emphasis towards the attainment of objectives at the expense of compliance with bureaucratic rules and procedures. It has emphasized the importance of value for money being maintained by those who provide public services: this may be secured by a number of initiatives, which include procedures to enable the private sector to compete for the right to deliver services that were formerly solely associated with the public sector through the process of contracting out.

The emphasis on efficiency, value for money and quality of service are integral aspects of NPM, which seeks to transform citizens into consumers whose power rests not upon the political sanction of accountability but, rather, upon their ability to shop around and go elsewhere if a public service is being provided inefficiently. NPM was also identified with the twin forces of centralization and decentralization: this entailed organizational goals being set by central government (whose attainment may also be measured by centrally set performance targets) while leaving their fulfullment to agency heads who possess considerable operational freedom, but who must operate within a budget that is also centrally determined. The delegation of power downwards within organizations was a key aspect of NPM in America.

In the UK, post-1997 Labour governments adopted and developed NPM. They retained many features of NPM (such as targets and performance indicators) but innovations included the introduction of best value to assess efficiency and effectiveness in service delivery and to enhance the quality of service.

Freedom of information and official secrecy

Key idea (10)

The flow of information to the general public regarding the operations of government is essential if the government is to be held accountable for its actions. However, the release of official information may be restricted by legislation that is justified by the argument that it is necessary to protect state secrecy.

In a liberal democracy, members of the general public need to be in a position to evaluate the performance of a government in order to give or deny that government political support. To do so requires access to information by which public policy can be judged. In many liberal democracies this is provided by freedom of information legislation.

Freedom of information legislation requires public bodies or officials to make available to citizens a wide range of public documents. Public access was first granted in Sweden in 1766, but in other countries it has been a twentieth-century development. Freedom of information legislation exists in America and Germany where it is a considerable aid to investigative journalism. In America, the 1966 and 1974 Freedom of Information Acts provided citizens and interest groups with the right to inspect most federal records. Although access to some information may be denied, an appeal to the courts may secure the production of the desired information. New Zealand also has an Official Information Act that permits public access to a wide range of information. In the United Kingdom, the 2000 Freedom of Information Act gave the public access to information held on them by public authorities. The operations of the measure are overseen by an information commissioner.

The 'right to know' is viewed as an important civil right in liberal democratic countries, enabling citizens to hold their governments to account for the actions they have taken. There are, however, limits placed on the public's ability to have access to official material. Typically, this is constrained by the desire to prevent unwarranted intrusion into an individual's privacy and also to safeguard national security. Legislation exists in a number of liberal democracies to restrict the release of official information that may be used to prevent the media from publishing material which is deemed to be contrary to state interests. This includes Ireland's 1939 Offences Against the State Act, America's 1976 Government in the Sunshine Act, the 1986 Omnibus Anti-drugs Abuse Act, the 2002 Intelligence Authorization Act, and an Executive Order signed by President Reagan in 1982.

The UK's Official Secrets legislation (initially enacted in 1911) made any disclosure of official information a criminal offence. This posed dilemmas for some civil servants who sometimes believed that politicians confused state interests with their own political considerations and sought to use the former grounds to suppress information that might have damaging political consequences. This gave rise to the phenomenon of whistleblowing, which involved a civil servant deliberately leaking information to bodies such as the media when he or she believed that the public's right to know superseded the concern of a government to keep such material secret.

Whistleblowing refers to an action performed by past or present members of an organization who disclose their employers' *'illegal, immoral or illegitimate practices'* to persons or organizations *'who may be able to affect action'* (Miceli and Near, 1984: 689). The motives of the person making the disclosure (the whistleblower) *'are typically driven by a belief that it is in the public interest to reveal the information that is disclosed and that the public's right to know should be given precedence over individual or corporate claims of the need for confidentiality or secrecy in the conduct of their affairs'* (Joyce and Wain, 2014: 347).

Joyce, P. and Wain, N. (2014) *Palgrave Dictionary of Public Order Policing, Protest and Political Violence*. Basingstoke: Palgrave.

Miceli, M. and Near, J. (1984) The Relationships Among Beliefs, Organizational Position and Whistle-blowing Status: A Discriminant Analysis. *Academy of Management Journal*, 27(4) pp 687–705

A danger posed by whistleblowing is that it erodes the trust between ministers and civil servants. It might result in the politicization of the bureaucracy whereby politicians appoint persons to its upper ranks whose trust and loyalty can be relied upon.

One interesting example of whistleblowing occurred in the 1980s. Clive Ponting, a civil servant, leaked a document concerning the sinking during the Falklands War of the Argentinian cruiser, the General Belgrano, to a Labour member of parliament, Tam Dalyell. He justified his action by arguing that the government was misleading parliament, and hence the country. He perceived that his duty to the nation as a public servant outweighed his loyalty to the government. Civil servants who engage in this activity run the risk of dismissal and imprisonment. Ponting was charged with breaking the Official Secrets Act but was acquitted in 1985 by a jury sympathetic to his arguments.

In the wake of this trial, a new Official Secrets Act was enacted in the UK in 1989. The sanction of a criminal prosecution was limited to certain categories of official information, which were broadly associated with the interests of the state. Within these categories, an absolute ban was imposed on disclosure of some information (for example, by intelligence officers discussing the operations of the security services), while in other areas (such as defence) it would be necessary to demonstrate that the disclosure resulted in 'harm' or 'jeopardy' to state interests. The act contained no public interest defence which might be used by civil servants or investigative journalists who publicized government activities in these restricted areas.

Julian Assange and WikiLeaks

Technological advances have further facilitated whistleblowing whereby information can be published on websites that can be set up (and accessed) anywhere in the world. One important contemporary example of this is WikiLeaks, which had been set up in 2006 with the aim of making public classified documents. Its editor-in-chief was Julian Assange.

On 28 November 2010, WikiLeaks commenced publishing a series of US State Department cables. Eventually over 250,000 cables were released. The majority of them were unclassified, but a significant proportion (around 40 per cent) were classed as confidential and around 6 per cent as secret. Some of these related to the corruption of the governing regime in Tunisia and their release has been seen as a factor in that country's 'Arab Spring' revolution in December 2010. Others related to the war in Afghanistan where the release of personal information relating to informants was argued to have put their lives at risk arising from retaliation by the Taliban.

Although some people might view the actions of WikiLeaks as an acceptable form of civil disobedience seeking to expose secrecy and injustice in the operations of government, many senior American politicians, including the American Vice President, viewed Assange as a 'high tech terrorist'. Later that year, a European Arrest Warrant was issued in connection with a request by the Swedish police to question Assange in connection with an investigation into cases of sexual assault involving two women in August 2010.

Assange sought to challenge the enforcement of this Warrant through the British Courts arguing that its real purpose was to secure his extradition to America to face charges in connection with the WikiLeaks disclosures. He was initially placed in prison in December 2010 but later released on bail. Following the final rejection of this attempt by the Supreme Court of the United Kingdom in June 2012, he entered the Ecuadorian Embassy in London where he was granted diplomatic asylum. It remains the intention of the UK government to enforce the Warrant whenever he leaves the Embassy and a police presence has been placed there to implement this.

One of WikiLeaks' key sources was Bradley (now Chelsea) Manning, a soldier who served as an intelligence analyst in Iraq and who had access to databases used by the American military to transmit classified information. In total, Manning sent WikiLeaks more than 470,000 Iraq and Afghanistan battlefield reports, 250,000 State Department Diplomatic cables and other material that included battlefield video clips.

Manning was arrested in Iraq in May 2010. His defence was that he aimed 'to expose war crimes and deceitful diplomacy, that the information was not harmful to the US, and that the vast majority of the material he released was not classified, and was more embarrassing than damaging for the government'. In July 2013 Manning was found guilty of 17 charges and was sentenced to 35 years' imprisonment.

Dig Deeper

Barberis, P. (1996) *The Elite of the Elite*. Aldershot: Dartmouth.

du Gay, P. (2000) *In Praise of Bureaucracy: Weber, Organization, Ethics*. London: Sage.

du Gay, P. (2005) *The Values of Bureaucracy*. Oxford: Oxford University Press.

Page, E. and Jenkins, B. (2005) *Policy Bureaucracy: Government with a Cast of Thousands*. Oxford: Oxford University Press.

Page. E. (2012) *Policies Without Politicians: Bureaucratic Influence in Comparative Perspective*. Oxford: Oxford University Press.

Fact-check

1 The term 'red tape' refers to:
   a The process used to approve the appointment of senior civil servants in the UK
   b The application of established rules and procedures to bureaucratic decision-making
   c The delay in implementing a decision arising from the process of judicial review
   d A procedure used in the UK to speed up a Bill's progress through Parliament

2 In the UK, the power to reorganize government departments is derived from:
   a The Royal Prerogative
   b Legislation
   c Common Law
   d A Motion approved by both Houses of Parliament

3 In the USA, legislative influence over the conduct of the bureaucracy is termed:
   a Congressional control
   b The hearings system
   c Executive orders
   d Oversight

4 In the UK, the attempt initiated in the late 1980s to divorce policy planning and service delivery gave rise to:
   a Chaos
   b Executive agencies
   c New Public Management
   d The downfall of Margaret Thatcher as prime minister

5 A person who makes public information derived from his or her employment as a public servant is known as:
   a A criminal
   b A discloser
   c A whistleblower
   d An enemy of the state

6 In the UK, a Statutory Instrument is:

   a A medieval instrument of torture

   b A form of delegated legislation

   c An Act of Parliament that can never be repealed

   d A procedure used to dismiss a minister from his or her office

12

The legislative branch of government

The main purpose of legislatures is to make law but they also perform other important activities. In this chapter we will examine the key functions performed by legislatures, consider the problems that contemporary legislatures face in carrying out these duties and the initiatives that have been put forward in an attempt to overcome these problems.

The functions of legislatures

Key idea (1)

The key role of the legislative branch of government is to approve law which citizens are subsequently required to obey.

Elected legislatures are viewed as the symbol of representative government: as it is not possible for all citizens to directly share in policy making, we elect persons who perform these duties on our behalf. These representatives convene in the country's legislature (which is referred to as Congress in America, Parliament in the United Kingdom or the *Oireachtas* in Ireland). This is thus the institution that links the government and the governed. In addition to this symbolic function, legislatures undertake a number of specific tasks which we consider now.

LAW MAKING

Legislatures constitute the law-making body within a country's system of government. Thus making the law (or amending or repealing it) is a key function that they perform. A specific, although important, aspect of this role is approving the budget and granting authority for the collection of taxes.

Below we will consider the process of law making in the UK parliament.

Key idea (2)

Law making is a complex process that typically involves a number of stages through which a legislative proposal (termed 'bill' in the UK and USA) must proceed in order to be transformed into a law that is binding on a nation's citizens.

In the UK a difference exists between public and private legislation. The former constitutes the general law of the land, but the latter is limited in jurisdiction (often being promoted by public bodies such as local authorities to extend their powers). A number of stages are involved in translating a proposal into law. The following outline applies to public legislation. We are assuming that this legislation is first introduced into the House of Commons, which is generally (but not exclusively) the case. Money Bills (which raise or spend public money) are required to originate in the House of Commons.

First reading

This is merely the announcement of an intention to introduce legislation on a particular topic. No debate occurs at this stage.

Second reading

This is a debate on the general principles embodied in the legislative proposal (termed a 'bill'). If these principles are approved, the bill progresses to the next stage in the legislative process.

Committee stage

This involves a detailed examination of the contents of the bill. Amendments can be made provided that they do not destroy the bill's fundamental principles, which have been approved in the second reading. This stage usually takes place in a standing committee, which involves a relatively small number of MPs who are appointed by the Committee of Selection. However, a committee of the whole House or a special standing committee (which takes evidence in public) may be used instead.

Report stage

Here any changes to the bill proposed by the committee are considered by the full House of Commons and either approved or rejected.

Third reading

This is a consideration of the bill as amended in its progress through the House of Commons.

If the bill receives its third reading, it then goes through a similar process in the House of Lords, although the committee stage is usually a committee of the whole House.

In the United Kingdom, the two chambers of parliament are not co-equal in power and, in the case of disagreement between them, the views of the directly elected House of Commons will ultimately prevail. This situation is provided for in the 1949 Parliament Act, which gave the House of Lords the power to delay the progress of non-financial legislation that has been passed by the House of Commons for the maximum period of one year (spread across two parliamentary sessions), after which (provided the measure is reintroduced in the House of Commons) it will become law. This procedure is used relatively infrequently but was put into operation to secure the enactment of the 1991 War Crimes Act, the 1999 European Parliamentary Elections Act, the 2000 Sexual Offences (Amendment) Act, and the 2004 Hunting Act.

When such differences are reconciled, the bill is passed for Royal Assent. This is granted automatically (the last refusal being in 1707), but is the process by which the 'bill' becomes an 'act'.

It was formerly necessary for a bill to complete all of these stages in a single Parliamentary Session. If this failed to happen, the bill could be reintroduced in the following Session, commencing at the first reading stage. However, since 2002 it has been possible for government bills to be 'carried over' from one Session of Parliament to the next if all stages have not been completed in the Session in which the bill was introduced. The 'carry over' procedure allows for the discussion of a bill to be resumed in the second Session of Parliament where it was left off in the first Session, although bills are usually required to complete all Parliamentary stages within one year of the measure having obtained its first reading.

Reform of the House of Lords

The major problem with the House of Lords (which is often referred to as the 'Upper Chamber') was that the majority of its members inherited their right to be there. Although the power wielded by this hereditary element was to some extent diluted after 1958 by the presence of life peers (that is, persons nominated to sit in the House of Lords by the prime minister, and whose title was not passed on to other family members) no members of the House of Lords were elected by the general public. A further problem was that the vast majority of hereditary peers supported the Conservative Party, thus giving the House of Lords an inbuilt Conservative majority.

Post-1997 Labour governments proceeded cautiously with reforming the House of Lords. The 1999 House of Lords Act removed almost all of the hereditary peers (only 92 out of 750 remained) and in the same year, a Royal Commission chaired by Lord Wakeham was set up to consider the future role, functions and composition of this body. Its report in 2000 (*A House for the Future*) proposed that the House of Lords should be a revising and advisory body whose role was to complement, but not undermine, the House of Commons. It also proposed that most appointments should be made by an Appointments Commission.

Following this report, an Independent House of Lords Appointments Commission was established in 2000 to take over the nomination of all members to the House of Lords other than those who were nominated by the political parties, and to scrutinize the suitability of all nominations including those made by the political parties.

In 2002 a Joint Committee (composed of members of the House of Commons and House of Lords) on the House of Lords reform was set up, and their first report in that year considered a number of options related to that body's composition. Subsequently, in 2007 the Government published a White Paper, *The House of Lords: Reform*, which proposed a House of Lords where 50 per cent of members were elected and 50 per cent appointed. In March 2007, the House of Commons voted in support of an elected House of Lords, and a week later the House of Lords voted in favour of a fully appointed House.

In 2012, the Coalition government introduced the House of Lords Reform Bill that would have resulted in most members of the House of Lords being elected. However, opposition from within the Conservative Party promoted the government to abandon this reform.

The various stages that are involved in the law-making process means that numerous people are involved in the production of an Act of Parliament: *'a bill as it enters Parliament may be, and as it emerges frequently is, a compromise between divergent views. It is the work of many minds, and the product of many hands'* (Ilbert, 2000: 195).
Ilbert, C. (2000) *The Mechanics of Law Making*. Clark, New Jersey: The Lawbook Exhange Ltd.

▶ Law making in the American Congress

As with the UK, the legislative process in America involves a proposal being considered at a number of stages. Legislation may be introduced in either the House of Representatives or the Senate (although the Senate does not have the power to initiate bills imposing taxes and – in practice – also lacks the ability to put forward bills authorizing the expenditure of federal funds (termed 'appropriation bills').

The key stages that are involved are:

▶ Introduction

▶ Consideration by Committee

▶ Consideration by all members of the House or Senate

▶ Resolution of differences between the House and the Senate. This may require the formation of a conference committee to resolve them. If a bill is passed in different versions by the two Houses, a committee composed of members of each House is appointed to resolve the differences and draw up a single bill, which is then returned to each House for a vote. It is not necessary to resort to this mechanism frequently, but when it is used it may provide a forum in which 'trade-offs' between the House of Representatives and the Senate are made

▶ Final passage whereby a bill approved by both House and Senate is 'enrolled'

The final stage of the law-making process rests with the president, who may sign the 'enrolled' measure into law, veto it and return it to Congress, or let it become law without signature. At the end of a Session, the president has a further option – that of the 'pocket veto', whereby a bill approved by Congress is not signed into law and is thus killed off.

SCRUTINY OF THE EXECUTIVE

Key idea (3)

Legislatures perform a number of other functions in addition to law making. In particular they scrutinize actions that have either been carried out or which are proposed as future actions by the executive branch of government.

In addition to law making, legislatures scrutinize the actions of the executive branch of government. Governments are required to justify their actions to the legislature, which may thus exert influence over the government's conduct. This scrutiny may be retrospective (that is, it occurs after a decision has been implemented and seeks to examine whether it was justified). In some cases, however, the legislature may be required to give its consent to an action that the executive branch wishes to undertake. In America, for example, Congress has to approve a declaration of war.

In parliamentary systems in which the legislature provides the personnel of government, scrutiny facilitates ministerial responsibility. Governments are collectively responsible to the legislature. Perceived deficiencies in the overall activities of the government may result in its dismissal by the legislature (usually through the mechanism of a vote of 'no confidence'). Individual ministers may also be individually responsible for the performance of specific aspects of the work of the executive branch. However, the ability of legislatures to force individual ministers to resign varies. In Germany, for example, the *Bundestag* lacks such a sanction, although criticism by the legislature of a minister may result in that person's resignation.

▶ Confirmation of governmental appointments

Scrutiny may also extend to approving the nomination of individual members of the government put forward by the chief executive. This form of legislative scrutiny operates in some parliamentary systems of government such as Ireland. The scrutiny of nominations for public office by the legislature is also a feature of some presidential systems of government such as America, where the Senate is required to confirm a wide range of presidential appointments. The rationale for such a process is to ensure that those nominated for high government office have the relevant credentials to occupy such a post. In practice, however, this form of scrutiny might involve delving into a person's private life (to demonstrate personal failings that are allegedly incompatible with office holding) or might be determined on political grounds.

INVESTIGATORY FUNCTIONS

The investigation of issues of public importance is an important function of many legislative bodies, which is usually performed by committees. This role may be separate from the exercise of scrutiny over the actions of the executive. In America, Congress has the right to subpoena – that is to force persons to appear and answer questions on the topic that is the subject of investigation and to secure the production of documents to aid the investigatory process.

SUPERVISORY FUNCTIONS

Legislatures may concern themselves with the manner in which an institution of government or an activity that is reliant on public funds is being performed. This function (which in America is termed oversight) is concerned with monitoring the bureaucracy and its administration of policy. It entails ensuring that an agency is meeting the goals specified, that the public money provided for it is being spent for the purposes for which it was intended, or that an operation is conducted in accordance with any restrictions that were initially placed upon it by the legislature. The American Congress actively performs supervisory functions through committee hearings and the review of agency budgets, but these procedures are less prominent in other legislatures such as Britain. An example of this was the hearings held by the Senate Finance Committee in 1997 into the operations of the Internal Revenue Service.

RAISING ISSUES OF LOCAL AND NATIONAL IMPORTANCE

Legislatures debate policy and other issues of public importance. Such debates are published in official journals and through the media, thus providing a source of information for the general public. This enables the electorate to be politically informed and educated. These bodies further provide a forum in which representatives can advance the interests of their constituencies and intercede on behalf of any of their constituents who have encountered problems in their dealings with the executive branch of government. Much work of this nature takes place in private, but it is usually possible to raise such issues publicly within the legislative chamber.

JUDICIAL FUNCTIONS

Legislatures may also perform judicial functions whereby members of all three branches of government may be tried and sentenced for offences connected with the performance of their official duties.

In America, for example, Congress has a judicial power: that of impeachment. This is a formal charge where a member of the executive or judicial branch of government has committed an offence while in office. The accusation of inappropriate conduct is laid before the House of Representatives and, if they believe that there is a case to answer, a trial takes place in the Senate. If guilt is determined by this body the official would be dismissed from public office.

Legislatures may also exercise judicial-type functions in relation to the conduct of their members. The processes used vary. In America, for example, each House of Congress has an Ethics Committee to which accusations of wrongdoing contravening the rules of either body are referred. Members of Congress cannot be impeached, but wrongdoings by legislators may be punished by an alternative process of censorship. This rarely involves removal from office, but embraces alternative sanctions which adversely affect the status of the condemned legislator.

INITIATING CONSTITUTIONAL CHANGE

Legislatures play a key role in the process of changing a country's constitution. In countries with a flexible constitution (that is, one that can be altered by the normal law-making process) the legislature is solely responsible for initiating and determining constitutional change. This is the situation in the United Kingdom. In countries with rigid constitutions (where amendment involves a separate process from the normal law-making procedure), the role of the legislature in providing for change is reduced.

In America, for example, two-thirds of both Houses of Congress (the House of Representatives and the Senate) must separately agree either to call a constitutional convention to determine change when asked to do so by two-thirds of the states (which last occurred in 1787), or themselves propose a specific amendment to the Constitution, of which two-thirds of the states must then approve. A recent example of this process was the Equal Rights Amendment proposed by Congress in 1972, which failed to secure the required level of support from state legislatures since only 35 approved it.

The operations of legislatures

Legislatures conduct their affairs through a number of mechanisms. We discuss the main ones in the sections that follow.

DEBATE

Legislatures are first and foremost debating institutions. This means that functions such as the consideration of legislation, the articulation of constituency issues, or the discussion of matters of national importance are performed orally. Members of the legislature deliver speeches in which they put forward their views and listen to the judgements of their fellow legislators on the same issue. To facilitate debate, members of legislative bodies may enjoy certain immunities that ordinary members of the general public do not possess. In the UK, for example, members of the House of Commons enjoy freedom of speech. This is one of a number of 'parliamentary privileges'. This means that in parliament members may effectively say what they want (subject to the speaker's rulings) to facilitate the maximum degree of openness in debate. Speeches made by a member of parliament, no matter how defamatory, cannot be subject to an action for slander.

COMMITTEES

Key idea (4)

To avoid being overloaded with work, legislatures devolve many of their functions onto committees.

Much of the work performed by contemporary legislative bodies is delegated to committees. In turn, these bodies may devolve responsibilities to sub-committees, which have become increasingly influential in the US Congress since the 1970s. These are useful devices as they enable a legislature to consider a number of matters at the same time, and thus cope with increased volumes of work that is associated with the expanded role of the state in years following World War II and membership of supranational bodies. They further enable small groups of legislators to investigate the affairs of government in considerable detail, and through their reports the entire assembly becomes more knowledgeable of these matters and thus less dependent on government for the provision of information.

There are various types of committee existing in modern legislatures. In the UK's House of Commons, a key division is between standing committees (which are used to consider legislation) and select committees (which are used for various purposes, including – following reforms introduced in 1979 – examination of the work performed by key government departments). A similar division exists in the American Congress, although here, standing committees are the most widely used form of committee. Both Houses use standing committees to consider bills in different policy areas. In 2010, there were approximately 20 standing committees in the US House of Representatives, each of which had a number of sub-committees. Select committees may also be set up to investigate special problems. In countries whose legislatures consist of more than one chamber, joint committees may be established to enable the two chambers to co-operate for specific purposes.

Committees are an especially useful means for considering legislation. In countries such as America, the examination of legislative proposals is aided by a system of hearings in which the committee or sub-committee considering the proposal invites interested parties to give evidence before it to ensure that their decisions are based on a wide range of informed opinion. The decision whether to report a measure out of committee with a favourable recommendation or to 'kill' it is influenced by this procedure.

In some countries, the work of committees extends beyond the consideration of legislative proposals. Legislation may be initiated by these bodies. The committee system of the German parliament is particularly influential in this respect.

▶ The party system and committee membership

The party system may have an important bearing on the effectiveness with which committees operate in modern legislatures. The appointment of members to committees usually involves the party leadership, and the fact that committee members are affiliated to a political party may influence the manner in which issues before a committee are viewed by its members.

In countries with parliamentary forms of government such as the UK, the party system may help the executive branch dominate committee proceedings, since the governing party usually possesses a majority on committees considering legislation. In countries with presidential systems such as America, committees may exercise a far greater degree of autonomy since the executive branch is not directly involved in appointments. There, appointments are allocated by the party apparatus that exists in both Houses, although a member's desire to serve on a particular committee may be taken into account.

Membership is not confined to a particular Session of Congress: once appointed to a committee, a member will usually sit on it for the remainder of his or her career. The chairmanship of such bodies is largely – although now not exclusively – determined by seniority. This was a procedure whereby the longest serving committee member whose party controlled Congress headed the committee.

QUESTIONS

Questions are a further means through which the work of the legislature is transacted in countries with parliamentary forms of government. These may be oral or written and are addressed to members of the executive branch of government. They can be of use in eliciting information, clarifying an issue, or seeking to secure action by the executive branch of government, although they are rarely of importance to the process of policy making. They provide a mechanism whereby civil servants (who prepare the answers to these questions) respond to an agenda set by legislators as opposed to members of the executive branch of government. In the German *Bundestag*, questions aid the process of ministerial accountability. The oral questioning of a minister may be followed by a vote, which enables members of the legislature to express whether they are satisfied with the answers with which they have been provided.

Bicameral and unicameral legislatures

Key idea (5)

Legislatures may consist of one body or debating chamber (termed 'unicameral') or consist of two bodies (termed 'bicameral'). The UK has a bicameral legislature, composed of the House of Commons and the House of Lords.

In most liberal democratic political systems, the legislature is divided into two separate bodies. These bodies form separate debating chambers. For example, in the United Kingdom, parliament consists of the House of Commons and the House of Lords. In America, the legislative branch is divided into the House of Representatives and the Senate. In Ireland, parliament (the *Oireachtas*) consists of the *Daíl Éireann* and the *Seanad Éireann*, while in France the legislative function of government is shared between the *Assemblée nationale* and the *Sénat*. All these countries have what is termed a bicameral legislature.

The opposite of this is a unicameral system in which the legislature consists of only one body. Examples of this are found in New Zealand, Finland, Denmark, Sweden and Israel.

The following section considers the advantages of having a legislature composed of two bodies or debating chambers.

A REVISING CHAMBER

An important benefit of a bicameral legislature is that one chamber can give the other an opportunity to think again, to reconsider its position. On occasions when the content of legislation is contentious and the period surrounding its passage through the first of the legislative bodies is charged with emotion for and against the measure, it is useful that a second chamber can coolly and calmly re-evaluate what has been done and, if necessary, invite the first chamber to reassess the situation by either rejecting the measure or proposing amendments to it. In this case, the second chamber performs the function of a revising chamber.

DIFFERENCES IN COMPOSITION

In bicameral systems, the two chambers of the legislature are often drawn from different constituencies (that is, composed in different ways). This may be an advantage in that it enables issues to be examined from different perspectives.

In some countries, one chamber of the legislature is designed to represent public opinion while the other is concerned with territorial representation – advancing the more localized views of the areas, states, or regions into which the country is divided.

This was originally the justification for creating the American Senate. When the constitution was being drafted, a conflict of interest emerged between the sparsely populated states and those in which large numbers of persons resided. Thus the constitution adopted a compromise position (which was termed the 'Connecticut Compromise'). This resulted in representation in one chamber (the House of Representatives) being based on population, which gave the populous states a greater voice in that body. However each state, regardless of size, was given equal representation in the second chamber, the Senate.

In Germany, the *Bundestag* consists of representatives elected by the voters for a four-year term of office, whereas the *Bundesrat* provides a forum at national level in which the views of the states (or *Länder*) can be put forward. Members of the *Bundesrat* are not elected but are nominated by the 16 individual state governments. Each state sends delegations to this body, which are mandated to act in accordance with the instructions given to them by the state government. Each state is allotted three votes in the *Bundesrat,* with extra votes being given to the more populated states.

In France, members of the National Assembly are elected for a five-year term and, since 2004, Senators serve a six-year term. They are indirectly elected by an Electoral College composed of around 150,000 officials (termed *grands électeurs*), which includes regional councillors, department councillors, mayors, city councillors in large towns and members of the National Assembly. However, 90 per cent of the electors are delegates appointed by councillors.

FUNCTIONAL REPRESENTATION

Second chambers may also articulate concerns other than territorial ones. They may represent the interests of specific groups within a country. This is referred to as functional representation. The Irish *Seanad* is theoretically constituted in part on this basis. Members of this body are not directly elected, but are supposed to reflect vocational interests. The majority of its members are chosen in *Seanad* panel elections. In the 2002 *Seanad* elections, the electorate consisted of 971 persons, comprising members of the *Daíl*, outgoing members of the *Seanad,* and members of county councils and city councils. These constituted an Electoral College that elected members from five panels using the single transferable vote. These panels are the Cultural and Education Panel (from which five members are elected), the Agricultural Panel (eleven members), the Labour Panel (eleven members) the Industrial and Commercial Panel (nine members), and the Administrative Panel (seven members).

A further three members are chosen from graduates of the National University of Ireland and another three from Dublin University graduates. The prime minister (*taoiseach*) appoints a further eleven members. Although this process is designed to ensure representation in parliament from key vocational groups in Irish society, in reality party affiliation is an important qualification for election to this body.

The Thirty-Second Amendment of the Constitution (Abolition of *Seanad Éireann*) Bill 2013 proposed to amend the constitution of Ireland by abolishing the Senate. However, this proposal was rejected by the electorate in a referendum held in October 2013 by 51.7 per cent to 48.3 per cent.

Changes affecting the power and authority of legislatures

Key idea (6)

The power of legislatures has been affected by factors that include the executive branch of government assuming a dominant role of key legislative functions such as law making.

Changes affecting the power and authority of legislatures have occurred in a number of countries, and in this section we seek to understand the nature of these Developments. First we will analyse changes affecting the power wielded by legislatures.

MEMBERSHIP OF SUPRANATIONAL BODIES
The membership of supranational bodies has implications for both the law making and scrutinizing role performed by

national legislatures. In the United Kingdom, for example, membership of the EU has resulted in the loss of some of parliament's traditional legislative functions, but has also added to the volume of governmental activity that this body is expected to monitor. Membership of international bodies such as the International Monetary Fund and the World Trade Organization also imposes restrictions on the conduct of nation states in key policy areas and may additionally dictate obligations to them.

One example of the power wielded by supranational bodies concerned the conditions imposed on countries seeking bail-out funds in the wake of the international debt crisis that affected a number of countries after 2008. In order to stave off a nation's bankruptcy, financial aid in the form of 'bail-out loans' was provided by bodies such as the International Monetary Fund, the European Central Bank, and the EU. These three bodies were often collectively referred to as the *troika,* and the nations receiving aid of this nature were Greece, Spain, Portugal and Ireland. However, these loans were given with severe conditions attached to them, in particular that countries receiving financial aid should implement a raft of austerity measures that entailed cuts in public spending (including the reduced provision of public services, welfare benefits, and the implementation of pay cuts and redundancy of public sector workers). The objective of these policies was to reduce the nation's budget deficit regardless as to whether these policies secured public approval within the nation on whom they were forced, and is an example of how international bodies can override national sovereignty.

DEVELOPMENTS DEVALUING THE LAW-MAKING ROLE OF LEGISLATURES

The role of legislatures as law-making bodies has been undermined by a number of contemporary developments. These include the referendum (whose usage has increased in countries such as the UK, which traditionally made little use of them) and other aspects of 'people politics' in which citizens seek to secure changes in legislation by engaging in various forms of extra-parliamentary political action.

The role of legislatures as law-making bodies is also affected by what is termed 'neo-corporatism'. This denotes a close working relationship between government, unions, and business interests. One example of this was the National Economic Development Council (usually referred to as NEDDY) that was set up by the United Kingdom Conservative government headed by Harold Macmillan in 1962. It brought together ministers, civil servants, trade union leaders, and representatives of employers, and its key role was to plan for industrial growth. Parliament thus became devalued as key economic and industrial policies were determined in this alternative body. This principle was subsequently applied elsewhere, being associated, for example, with reforms initiated by Robert Reich, who was US Secretary of Labor under President Clinton.

THE ROLE OF THE MEDIA

The ability of legislatures to scrutinize the actions of the executive, to air grievances, or to educate the public concerning political affairs is often more effectively conducted by the media. Television interviews with leading politicians and investigative journalism perform important roles in enabling the public to be informed of political matters. Additionally, politicians may decide that the media offers them better opportunities to present arguments to the electorate than a debate which takes place in a legislative body.

DOMINATION BY THE EXECUTIVE BRANCH OF GOVERNMENT

A major explanation for the decline in the power of legislatures is the tendency for these bodies to be dominated by the executive branch of government. In many countries, the initiation of policy and the control over finance has passed to the executive branch. In the UK, for example, the bulk of public legislation is initiated by the government. Parliament thus responds to the agenda set for it by the government. It may subsequently be able to influence the detailed content of this legislation, but it is not the driving force behind it. Additionally, governments may be able to utilize procedural devices to expedite the progress of their legislation. In the UK, one such device is the guillotine. This is a mechanism that limits the time devoted to a debate, ensuring that the progress of a government measure is not halted by unnecessary or excessive parliamentary debate. Since 1999, however, agreements between the political parties embodied in programme motions have been used to stipulate the time to be devoted to a bill in its committee, report and third reading stages.

The domination of legislatures by the executive branch of government is a feature of the operations of government in a number of countries. It has been observed that:

'Even though the executive is responsible ... to the legislature, the cabinet and its ministers retain wide-ranging power to govern the country as long as they remain in office. This power comprises both effective political control over the administrative departments of state and a firm grip on the day-to-day activities of the legislature ... Executive control of the entire legislative process, from the drafting of bills to the determination of the order of business, combined with the almost universal provision that the executive may recommend the dissolution of the legislature and the holding of fresh elections, gives any incumbent administration considerable power over the legislature' (Laver and Shepsie, 1996: 3–4).

Laver, M. and Shepsie, K. (1996) *Making and Breaking Government: Cabinets and Legislatures in Parliamentary Democracies*. Cambridge: Cambridge University Press.

Executive dominance of legislatures has occurred in both parliamentary and presidential forms of government. There are three reasons that might account for this development.

The first is the ability of the executive branch of government to act independently of legislatures in certain circumstances. This has enhanced the power of the former, eroding the latter's ability to initiate public policy or scrutinize the activities of government. In the UK, the government may make use of the Royal Prerogative and undertake certain actions without having to first obtain parliamentary approval. In other liberal democracies, chief executives are given emergency powers with which to act as they see fit to deal with an emergency, or may govern by some form of decree. The American president, for example, may issue executive orders and thus act in certain matters without the approval of Congress.

The second explanation for executive domination of legislatures concerns the ability to cope with the volume of post-war state activity, much of which is of a complex and technical nature. This has made it difficult for members of legislatures to keep abreast of the affairs of modern government and has tended to result in ministers and civil servants within the executive branch exercising a dominant position in policy making because of the superior information they have at their disposal.

The final explanation for executive dominance of legislatures is the development of the party system. The party system possesses some obvious advantages for legislative bodies. It helps to prevent legislative anarchy (in the sense of members seeking to pursue individual interests to the exclusion of all else) and organizes the work of these bodies, thus ensuring that specific goals and objectives are achieved. But there are also disadvantages for legislatures that arise from the party system.

The party system aligns members of the executive and legislative branches. Members of both branches, when belonging to the same party, have common ideological and policy interests. They have a vested interest in successfully translating these common concerns into law. These mutual interests are influenced by party discipline, which serves to induce members of the legislature to follow the lead given by their party leaders within the executive branch of government. In extreme cases, where party discipline is strong, disobedience to the wishes of the executive might result in expulsion from the party, as happened to the 'Eurorebels' in the UK Conservative Party in 1994.

The emergence of disciplined political parties has the effect of ensuring that legislatures do not act as corporate institutions exercising their functions on behalf of the nation as a whole. Instead, they operate under the direction of the executive branch of government.

Key idea (7)

In addition to legislatures suffering a reduction in their power, many have additionally experienced a loss of authority derived from factors that include accusations of 'sleaze' and corruption.

In this section we consider some of the main factors that have had an adverse effect on the authority of legislatures.

▶ **Adversarial politics**

The operations of the party system have one further consequence that may devalue the workings of the legislature. Party systems often give rise to adversarial politics. Britain and New Zealand are examples of countries whose political affairs are traditionally conducted in this manner. The political parties which compete for office put forward policies that are significantly different from those of their opponents, typically formulated on contrasting ideology.

Adversarial politics denotes a situation in which one party is automatically disposed to oppose the views and suggestions of another as a point of principle. If this style of politics influences the operations of the legislature it means that this body lacks any sense of common purpose. The work of the legislature is less concerned with a genuine search for the best solutions to issues and problems regardless of party affiliation but is mainly activated by the furtherance of partisan acrimony and the pursuit of party advantage. Members of the legislature who are supporters of the same party from which the executive is drawn are likely to back that government and deride proposals made by the opposition party (or parties), regardless of the merits of the cases put forward. Similarly, those who are not supporters of the government are likely to make destructive rather than constructive assessments of initiatives put forward by the executive branch.

Thus, party systems may erode the ability of legislatures to take dispassionate consideration of a range of ideas and then support those whose overall opinion within that body agrees is the best course of action in the national interest. This situation may affect the way in which members of the general public feel towards the legislature.

▶ The economic climate

Public confidence in legislatures may be especially affected by the economic climate. Factors such as recession and (more recently) the international debt crisis are likely to have an adverse impact on the way the public view all institutions of government, especially when it appears that their country's problems are incapable of being resolved by internally promoted initiatives. Recession is further likely to reduce the capacity of institutions of government to act as innovators: rather than act as dynamic proponents of reform (that may enhance the standing of such bodies in the public eye) both executives and legislators are disposed towards negative measures such as pruning public spending. This is a less adventurous exercise than initiating new programmes and may have an adverse effect on the way in which the public view the machinery of government.

▶ Performance of a diverse range of functions

Legislatures perform a wide range of functions. However, not all of these are compatible. In particular, prominent attention to the role of promoting local considerations (termed parochialism) may detract from the legislature's ability to exercise superintendence over national affairs, and provide the appearance of a fragmented body with no overall sense of purpose. This may also result in the decline of the aura and prestige of that body and thus its authority.

Although the service that legislators provide to their constituents is an important one in many countries, it may detract from that body's ability or willingness to view matters from an overall national perspective. This argument has been directed at the parochialism of members of the American Congress.

Parochialism in the American Congress

Although American Congressional elections are fought by candidates who represent the nation's major parties, the main influence on the outcome of these elections is the personal vote a candidate can attract. This personal vote may be secured on the basis of that person's campaigning style and how they 'come across' to local voters. However, the key basis of a personal vote is the candidate's previous record when in office. This record can be based on factors which include accessibility to local constituents (especially the provision of help to those with problems), the voicing of support for local interests or causes, and particularly the ability to attract government resources into the constituency the candidate represents.

It follows, therefore, that incumbent candidates (that is, those who were elected at the previous contest and are seeking re-election) are in a far better position to win seats in the House of Representatives or Senate than a candidate who has no record to advance and is seeking to win a seat for the first time. Only factors such as a dilatory record in advancing constituency interests or being involved in some form of scandal are likely to offset the incumbent's advantage. Although sitting candidates do sometimes lose, a key feature of elections to Congress is that incumbents are in a good position to win and usually do so.

In the 113th Congress (which met in 2013), the average length of service for a member of the House of Representatives was 9.1 years (4.6 terms), and 10.2 years for a member of the Senate (1.7 terms). In the Congressional elections that were held in 2012, only 27 incumbents in the House of Representatives were defeated in the election (and a further 13 in the primaries). A total of 93.8 per cent of incumbent Democrats and 92.1 per cent of incumbent Republicans were re-elected. In the 2012 Senate elections, only one incumbent out of 33 contests was defeated (and a further one in his primary election).

It has been argued that parochialism results in Congress having a dual character: it is at one and the same time a body composed of politicians with a keen interest (or even a preoccupation) with local affairs, but is also a forum for making national policy. Concern with the former consideration may detract from the latter function and reduce Congress's effectiveness in responding to current or future problems.

In connection with incumbency in American politics, it has been observed that: *'Compared to figures in other countries, turnover rates in American legislatures are low. The average turnover in the US House of Representatives over the past 50 years is 16.5% ... In the US House, turnover is largely a product of voluntary retirement since, on average, over 90% of incumbent house members who run for re-election win, although rates are lower somewhat in the US Senate'* (Montcrief, 2002: 56).

Montcrief, G. (2002) Recruitment and Retention in US Legislatures in G. Loewenberg, P. Squire, and R. Kiewiet, (eds) *Legislatures: Comparative Perspectives on Representative Assemblies*. Michigan: University of Michigan Press, pp 46–79.

▶ Sleaze

The authority of legislatures may be adversely affected by perceptions that members of these bodies are motivated by a desire to further their own self-interests rather than to serve the public. Allegations of corrupt behaviour or 'sleaze' have been made in connection with the behaviour of public officials in a number of countries in recent years, and is an important factor eroding the trust that we have in those who exercise power on our behalf.

Sleaze describes the abuse of power by elected public officials who improperly exploit their office for personal gain, party advantage (which may especially benefit party leaders to secure or retain their hold on power), or for sexual motives. The term also embraces attempts to cover up such inappropriate behaviour either by those guilty of misconduct or by their political colleagues.

In the United Kingdom problems included the 'cash for questions' accusation in 1994 that a small number of

Conservative members of parliament had accepted money to table parliamentary questions. This resulted in the appointment of a Committee on Standards in Public Life whose recommendations (contained in the first report of this body in 1995) included establishing an independent Parliamentary Commissioner for Standards.

However, the reforms that were initiated during the 1990s did not eliminate perceptions of sleaze. Towards the end of the 1990s, problems surfaced in respect to the activities of lobbying firms who had been implicated in the 1994 'cash for questions' episode. It was alleged that aides to ministers either joined these firms and were able to use their former contacts to secure access to ministers, or were prepared to use their position inside government to offer access to ministers or to confidential information. This resulted in the government bringing forward a new code to regulate lobbying in 1998 whose provisions included prohibiting a minister's political aides from leaking confidential information to lobbyists. However, this failed to end problems associated with the activities of lobbying firms and in 2010 three former Labour cabinet members were accused of involvement in an 'influence for cash' scandal which alleged that they were willing to use their past contacts in government to secure changes in legislation sought by lobbyists.

Additional problems surfaced in 2009 when a national newspaper published details of MPs' expense accounts. Although in most cases MPs had broken no law relating to their expense claims, public opinion was concerned regarding the wide range of expenses that an MP could legitimately claim for. This issue resulted in the resignation of the Speaker, George Martin, in June 2009 and ensured that the desire to 'clean up politics' received a high profile in the 2010 UK general election.

Spotlight

By the end of 2013, five Labour MPs and two Conservative Peers were gaoled following convictions that related to submitting false expense claims.

The issue of sleaze has dealt considerable harm to the image of legislators. It has been argued that: *'There has in recent years been a damaging erosion of public trust in the government and in the probity of those who occupy positions of influence in public life ... In general the public trusts public servants far more than its elected representatives, and those they appoint'* (Livesey, 2007: 149).

In the UK public trust in politicians was dented by the expenses scandal that initially broke in 2009: *'In addition to mortgages on MPs second homes, claims included the cleaning of a moat, the upkeep of a swimming pool, the maintenance of a "helipad", the tuning of a piano, the purchase of horse manure as a garden fertilizer and a contribution towards the wages paid to a housekeeper'* (Joyce, 2012: 114).

Actions undertaken by governments that the public deem to be immoral have played a major role in the erosion of trust in public officials – *'An NOP poll in October 2000 found that 49 per cent regarded "financial sleaze in government" as a major problem with 39 per cent calling it "a minor problem".'* Other issues that this poll found problematic (whether as major or minor issues) were *'ministers appointing friends to important public posts'* ... *'the government using spin doctors to manipulate the media'* ... *'the granting of peerages and honours to large donors'* ... *'government ministers putting interests of business before people'* ... *'government ministers not being truthful'* (Marwick, 2003).

Joyce, P. (2012) *Criminology – A Complete Introduction*. London: Hodder and Stoughton.

Livesey, T. (2007) Honesty in Public Life in P. Riordan, *Values in Public Life: Aspects of Common Good*. London: Transaction Publications, pp 143–156.

Marwick, A. (2003) *British Society since 1945: The Penguin Social History of Britain*. London: Penguin Books, 4th ed.

However, this problem did not end at the 2010 general election. In May 2010, the Liberal Democrat Cabinet Member, David Laws, resigned from the government following newspaper revelations that he had claimed around £40,000 in expenses as second home costs between 2004 and 2009 during which time he had been renting rooms from his partner. In 2012, another Liberal Democrat Cabinet Member, Chris Huhne, also resigned from the government following a decision by the Crown Prosecution Service to charge him with perverting the course of justice in connection with claims that his wife accepted speeding penalty points on his behalf. In 2013, he and his former wife were both convicted of this charge and sentenced to eight months in prison.

The continued vitality of legislatures

Key idea (8)

Despite the emergence of developments that have undermined both the power and authority of legislatures, they remain important aspects of the machinery of government in countries with liberal democratic political systems.

In the two previous sections, we have referred to difficulties faced by contemporary legislatures. We have argued that they face two related sets of problems – changes affecting the power of these bodies that have hindered their ability to discharge traditional functions effectively, and changes in public perceptions of the aura and prestige of such bodies that have had an adverse effect on their authority. These arguments can be amalgamated into the suggestion that there has been a decline in legislatures.

However, although we have charted major developments that have contributed to arguments alleging the decline of such bodies, it is important to appreciate that they continue to perform valuable and vital roles in political affairs. Some of the problems to which we have drawn attention are neither universal nor insuperable. For example, the dominant hold that governments exercise over the law-making process is greater in some countries than in others. In both Germany and Italy, for example, there remains a considerable degree of scope for legislation to be initiated by ordinary (or 'backbench') members of the legislature.

We have drawn attention to the impact of the party system on the role of legislatures. However, the strength of party varies from one liberal democracy to another, and this has an obvious bearing on the subservience of legislature to the executive. For example, the nature of the American party relationship between Congress and the president is one factor that explains why Congress has retained an extremely significant role in law making.

Additionally, the dominance that governments possess over the conduct of legislatures through the operations of the party system is not always a constant feature in the political affairs of a country. There are occasions on which legislatures may assert themselves to a greater degree. For example:

▶ Labour governments in the UK suffered 16 'backbench rebellions' between 1997 and 2001, and 19 between 2001 and 2005 where a number of Labour MPs failed to vote in accordance with their leader's wishes. The most serious rebellion came in 2003 when 121 Labour MPs defied a three-line whip, voting against the government and in support of a resolution that declared the case for military action against Saddam Hussein was 'as yet unproven'

▶ Between 2010 and July 2014, the UK's Coalition government suffered four defeats in the House of Commons, the most significant of which occurred in August 2013 when the House rejected a motion provisionally authorizing military intervention in the Syrian Civil War

Legislative assertiveness is especially likely to occur when (in a parliamentary system) no one party possesses overall majority support in the legislature or when (in a presidential system) the executive branch of government is controlled by a different party to that which controls the legislature. In France, this latter situation is termed 'cohabitation' and occurred between 1986–8, 1993–5, and again between 1997–2002. On this latter occasion, President Chirac (of the conservative RPR party) was obliged to appoint his defeated opponent in the 1995 presidential election, the socialist Lionel Jospin, to the office of Prime Minister. In such situations, governments become accountable to the legislature rather than to the president, thus enhancing the power of the former at the expense of the latter.

Dig Deeper

Foley, M. and Owen, J. (1996) *Congress and the Presidency: Institutional Politics in a Separated System.* Manchester: Manchester University Press.

Hughes, A. (2013) *A History of Political Scandals: Sex, Sleaze and Spin.* Barnsley, Yorkshire: Pen & Sword History.

Loewenberg, G., Squire, P. and Kiewiet, R. (eds) (2002) *Legislatures: Comparative Perspectives on Representative Assemblies.* Michigan: University of Michigan Press.

Ritchie, D. (2010) *The U.S. Congress: A Very Short Introduction.* Oxford: Oxford University Press.

Fact-check

1 In the UK, the purpose of Royal Assent is to:
  a Authorize the collection of taxes
  b Authorize the grant of money to the monarch
  c Transform a bill into an Act of Parliament
  d Formally declare an end to a Parliamentary Session

2 In the USA, the role of a Conference Committee is to:
  a Reconcile differences between the House of Representatives and the Senate regarding the content of a bill
  b Choose the Speaker of the House of Representatives
  c Scrutinize the conduct of the president of the United States
  d Scrutinize the expense claims made by members of Congress

3 A bicameral legislature is one that:
  a Meets twice a year
  b Consists of two debating chambers
  c Consists of one debating chamber
  d Is subject to election every two years

4 In the UK, the guillotine is a procedure that:
  a Enables the length of a Parliamentary Session to be reduced if this suits the government
  b Provides for the execution of MPs who cheat on their expense claims
  c Places a limit on the volume of legislation that can be introduced into Parliament in any one Parliamentary Session
  d Places limits on the time devoted to debating a measure before Parliament

5 In the UK Parliament, standing committees are:
  a Used to consider the content of legislative proposals
  b Held in rooms where no seating is provided in order to limit the time spent in discussion
  c Responsible for exercising oversight over government departments
  d Committees composed of members of both Houses of Parliament

6 The term given to a system whereby a legislature is composed to represent the interests of specific groups within a country is known as:

  a Cronyism
  b Proportional representation
  c The corporate state
  d Functional representation

13

The judicial branch of government

In this chapter, we will consider the operations of the judicial branch of government. In particular we will examine the functions and operations of the courts and the role performed by judges who administer the law.

What do the courts do?

Key idea (1)

The main role of the courts is to adjudicate a dispute between two parties. These two parties may be private citizens who are in dispute with each other. Alternatively, the state may be party to a case that comes before the courts.

No two liberal democratic countries have an identical judicial system. Differences especially exist concerning the conduct of trials. The UK and America utilize the adversarial system in which two parties seek to prove their case by discrediting that put forward by their opponents. The trial is presided over by a judge whose main function is to ensure fair play. Many European countries utilize an inquisitorial system. Here the gathering of evidence is the responsibility of the judge and the main function of the trial is to resolve issues uncovered in the earlier investigation. The judge will actively intervene in the trial in order to arrive at the truth.

CIVIL AND CRIMINAL LAW

There are two types of dispute that may come before a court – civil and criminal. Civil law is concerned with the resolution of disagreements in which, typically, one party seeks some form of redress (such as damages) from a second party. Criminal law embraces activities that have broader social implications and which thus require the state to initiate a prosecution with a view to punishing the offender. Slander is an example of a civil action, murder is a criminal charge.

In many countries, civil and criminal matters are heard in different courts. This is not invariably the case, however. In France civil and criminal matters are heard in the one court, the *ordre judiciaire,* utilizing the same judicial personnel. In England and Wales a circuit judge may hear both civil and criminal cases and magistrates' courts perform some civil functions.

The organization of the courts in England and Wales

Key idea (2)

The civil and criminal courts in England and Wales are organized in a hierarchical fashion so that the least serious criminal offences are heard in the lowest court in the judicial hierarchy.

Most criminal cases (around 95 per cent) are tried in magistrates' courts, the majority of which are staffed by laypersons termed justices of the peace. There are around 30,000 lay magistrates in England and Wales who are responsible for trying summary offences – minor crimes that carry the maximum penalty of a fine of £5,000 and/or a prison sentence of up to six months.

The more serious crimes, carrying heavier sentences, are heard in Crown Courts presided over by a judge and making use of a jury. Appeals against the verdicts reached in Crown Courts are heard by the Court of Appeal (Criminal Division).

Minor civil matters may be handled by the small claims procedure, which seeks to resolve a dispute without the need to take it to open court. Most civil cases that go to court are heard by county courts, although the High Court of Justice may hear cases in which large sums of money are claimed. Appeals against a verdict reached in a County Court or the High Court will be heard by the Court of Appeal (Civil Division).

The House of Lords formerly acted as the final Court of Appeal for both criminal and civil cases. The 2005 Constitutional Reform Act replaced the jurisdiction of the House of Lords with a new body, the Supreme Court, which became operational in 2009. This Court is composed of 12 justices and hears appeals on points of law for all civil cases in the UK and relating to criminal cases in England, Wales and Northern Ireland. It also adjudicates on devolution issues arising from the 1998 and 2012 Scotland Acts, the 1998 Northern Ireland Act, and the 2006 Government of Wales Act.

Scotland has a legal system which is different from that in England and Wales, and the courts in Northern Ireland also function differently from their English and Welsh counterparts.

INTERNATIONAL COURTS WITH JURISDICTION IN THE UK

The International Criminal Court is responsible for trying cases related to genocide, crimes against humanity, and war crimes committed anywhere in the world. It was created in 1998 and became operational in 2002. Individual nations are required to endorse its operations through a process of ratification which, in the case of the UK, was the 2001 International Criminal Court Act.

There are two European courts with the power to overrule decisions made by British courts of law. These are the European Court of Justice and the European Court of Human Rights.

▶ The European Court of Justice (ECJ) / Court of Justice

This Court is staffed by 25 judges and 8 advocates drawn from member countries of the EU, who serve for 6 years. It was established in 1952 and its main purpose is to ensure that EU law is adhered to within member countries. Disputes between states, between the EU and member states, between individuals and the EU, or between the institutions of the EU are all referred to this Court. It has the power to declare unlawful any national law that contravenes EU law, and also has the power to fine companies in breach of this legislation.

The ECJ embraced two subordinate courts. One of these, initially referred to as the Court of First Instance, determined direct actions brought by 'natural and legal' persons. Appeals against its decisions will be heard by the ECJ. The 2009 Treaty of Lisbon renamed the ECJ the 'Court of Justice' and the Court of First Instance became the 'General Court'.

▶ The European Court of Human Rights (ECHR)

In 1950, the Council of Europe (whose membership is wider than that of the EU, with which it should not be confused) drew up the European Convention of Human Rights. This is enforced by the ECHR, which was reorganized in 1988 (a reform that entailed the new Court incorporating the work previously performed by the European Commission of Human Rights). It is based in Strasbourg.

The ECHR investigates complaints concerning breaches of human rights that may be made by signatory states or their citizens. Decisions of the ECHR are binding on member states, unless the Court's opinion is advisory, related to an interpretation of the Convention or its Protocols. However, the only penalty that can be exacted for non-compliance is expulsion from the Council of Europe.

Critics of the power of the ECHR have argued that judges at Strasbourg have stretched the original text of the European Convention on Human Rights to fit situations that were outside the expectations of those who drafted and ratified it. Criticism has also been voiced at the tendency of ECHR judges to apply a one-size-fits-all interpretation of the Convention that fails to take into account the specific cultural and other differences of participating nations.

TRIAL BY JURY

Juries are designed to provide a trial by one's peers (that is, equals) and they are an important feature of the judicial process in the UK and America. In the UK, jurors serve in Crown (but not magistrates' courts), and are chosen from the electoral register drawn up by local government. Their role is to listen to the evidence that is put forward in a trial by the defence and prosecution and come to a decision as to whether the defendant is guilty or not guilty.

Juries possess a number of advantages. Their ability to pronounce a not guilty verdict in the face of overwhelming evidence to the contrary may bring about reform of the law if public opinion feels that the law and the penalties that it imposes are unjust. Juries may also take the motive of the law breaker into account when deciding on his or her guilt or innocence.

Nonetheless, there are problems associated with juries. They are not necessarily socially representative and this may lead to perceptions that racial or gender bias underpins their decisions. In 1992, a jury's acquittal of white Los Angeles police officers who had been caught on camera severely attacking a black American, Rodney King, resulted in serious riots. It is also possible that jurors may be swayed by the conduct of lawyers, which poses the problem that rich people can hire the most effective performers in court, effectively buying their acquittal from crimes they have committed. In the UK, successive home secretaries have sought to reduce the crimes that are eligible for trial by jury so that they can be heard in magistrates' courts. The cost of jury trials has been one motive for this reform, which has been vigorously resisted by civil libertarians who view trial by jury as a key aspect of civil rights.

ADMINISTRATIVE LAW

Administrative law is concerned with the relationship between a government and its citizens. In the UK, challenges mounted by the general public to the actions or operations of the executive branch of government may be heard in the courts. The legality of delegated legislation or accusations of abuse of power may be challenged in this manner. Minor issues (such as a challenge to a decision taken by a civil servant) may, however, be resolved by tribunals. Complaints of maladministration (an accusation that incorrect procedures were followed to arrive at a decision) may be submitted to the ombudsman.

In other countries, however, a separate court system exists to adjudicate upon such matters. France has a distinct system of courts concerned with administrative law, arising from a belief that the executive branch of government would become subordinate to the judiciary if the ordinary courts were able to review actions undertaken by the executive. This belief resulted in the establishment of a separate system of administrative courts. These have exclusive jurisdiction in a wide range of cases covered by public law, which involve disagreements between individuals and the workings of the state including allegations of illegal actions undertaken by ministers, civil servants and public bodies.

The French system of administrative courts is headed by the *Conseil d'État*, which acts as both an advisory and a judicial body. It advises the government on legal affairs in general and on the preparation of bills, ordinances and some decrees, and acts as the Supreme Court for administrative justice.

Below this are the *cours administrative d'appel*. This court possesses judicial powers alone and hears appeals from the *tribunaux administratifs*. The latter operates on a regional level and handle the largest share of disputes between individuals and government (state, local authority, or a public or private organization that delivers a public service).

CONSTITUTIONAL LAW

Key idea (3)

Courts may be responsible for ensuring that the constitution is obeyed by national and sub-national governments. They do this through the process of judicial review.

In some countries the courts may be also called upon to adjudicate disputes arising from the constitution (or what is often referred to as fundamental law). This is termed 'judicial review'. Typically, it involves assessing whether acts passed by the legislature accord with the statement of fundamental law contained in a country's constitution. But it may also scrutinize actions undertaken by the executive branch (such as the executive orders issued by the American president). If the courts decide that legislation or executive decisions are in breach of the constitution they may be declared 'unconstitutional'. This has the effect of overturning these measures and rendering them 'null and void'.

Additionally, the courts may be required to determine the constitutionality of actions undertaken by sub-national bodies such as state governments. This form of adjudication is frequently required in states with federal systems of government. The courts may also have to ensure that the allocation of responsibilities within and between the institutions of government remains as was provided for in the constitution.

In America, the process of judicial review is performed by the Supreme Court. This consists of nine judges appointed by the president subject to the consent of the Senate. Their intervention occurs when cases are referred to them on appeal either from the highest Courts of Appeal in the states or from the Federal Court of Appeal. Judicial review provides the Supreme Court with considerable political power. In the 1950s and 1960s its decisions were influential in establishing the civil rights of black Americans.

In France, the *Conseil Constitutionnel* is responsible for ensuring that the principle and rules of the constitution are adhered to, in particular to determine whether statutes approved by parliament conform to the constitution before the president signs them into law. This body was instituted in the 1958 Constitution. Its members are not required to be legally trained judges. Three of them are appointed by the president of France, three by the president of the National Assembly and three by the president of the Senate. They serve for nine years and may not be renominated. Former presidents of the republic may also serve on this body. The quorum for the *Conseil Constitutionnel* is seven. Unlike the American Supreme Court, there are some limitations placed on the jurisdiction of this body and it further exercises a range of advisory power (including the requirement that it has to be consulted if the president intends to exercise emergency powers).

A country that lacks a codified constitution (such as the UK) does not have any process whereby the actions of bodies such as parliament can be overturned. This procedure would be contrary to the concept of the sovereignty of parliament. This doctrine insists that parliament is the sole source of law-making power whose actions cannot be overruled by any other body. In countries with uncodified constitutions, judicial review has a more limited scope: that of scrutinizing the actions undertaken by the legislature, executive or other tiers of government to ensure that they accord with the requirements imposed upon them by legislation, in particular that the correct legal procedures related to a decision have been correctly followed.

In addition to dealing with criminal offences, the courts also perform the function of judicial review: '*Judicial review in the UK comprises an assessment of a decision made by a public body (which includes government departments, local authorities, tribunals. Or any other organization that exercises a public function ...)... The basis on which judicial intervention is founded is the doctrine of ultra vires which suggests that a public body has acted beyond its authorized limits ... In countries that possess codified constitutions, the judiciary are responsible for ensuring that the constitution is upheld. Senior courts (such as the American Supreme Court or the French Conseil Constitutionnel) perform this function*' (Joyce and Wain, 2010: 112–113).

Joyce, P. and Wain, N. (2010) *A Dictionary of Criminal Justice*.
London: Routledge.

However, in the UK, the 1998 Human Rights Act provided the judiciary with the ability to warn parliament that a piece of legislation was contrary to the European Declaration of Human Rights. The Courts were not able to annul or strike down legislation that they considered to be contravening the Declaration but, instead, were able to issue a Declaration of Incompatibility which urged the government and parliament to reconsider the issue. We considered this matter in Chapter 9.

Judicial interpretation

Key idea (4)

The role of judges may sometimes extend beyond administering the law and entail them determining its content. This is known as judicial law making (or judicial activism).

In theory, the role of judges is to apply the law to the matter that comes before them. However, it is often argued that judges go beyond this role and effectively determine its contents, which are subsequently binding on courts dealing with similar cases. This situation arises as a result of judicial interpretation of such documents that may effectively give judges the ability to act in a law-making capacity. Judges differ, however, in the principles which they apply when interpreting the law or constitution. These are now discussed.

THE STRICT LETTER OF THE LAW

Some judges rigidly apply the wording of the statute or constitution to the case that is before them. The judge's interpretation, therefore, is little more than the citation of existing sources as the basis for the decision which they reach. A case is determined according to the strict letter of the law. This strict interpretation view of the role of the judiciary tends to promote a conservative approach to judicial interpretation. It suggests that issues that are not contained in a country's law or constitution cannot be inserted into it by judges. Those who endorse such a view regard this as either the work of legislators or as a matter which should be responded to by the process of constitutional amendment.

JUDICIAL ACTIVISM

Other judges, however, exercise a wider degree of discretion when interpreting the law. Some who are faced with a situation that is not strictly covered by existing law may believe it to be their responsibility to bring the existing law or the constitution up to date. Alternatively, the law under consideration may lack precision (containing words such as 'normally' or 'reasonable') or be ambiguous and thus capable of having more than one meaning. The judge will therefore be required to give an opinion as to the correct course of action that should be pursued in the case with which they are dealing. In these situations, judicial interpretation departs from the precise wording of the law or constitution. It may be guided by one or other of the following two principles.

Judges may decide a case according to the spirit of the law or constitution. That is, they reach a verdict based on what they view to be compatible with existing law or constitutional enactments rather than what is actually contained in them. In reaching their decision, judges may seek to determine what was in the minds of those who initially drafted the law or constitution and apply this to the case before them. Other judges may go beyond this. They may consider it their duty to adjudicate a case according to what they believe should be contained in the law or constitution rather than what actually is there.

Both of these principles enable a judge to advance beyond the mere administration of the law and, instead, to act in the capacity of a legislator. That is, they advance existing law or create new law through the ability they give themselves to interpret laws and constitutions. The term 'judicial activism' is applied to the situation in which judges exercise a positive role in policy making.

> Judicial activism embraces the possibility that judges may act in a law-making capacity. The following quotation was written in connection with America, but the general principles extend elsewhere – *'how much freedom do judges possess to create new laws? In theory, the legal duty is to find out what the law states, relate this to the facts of a given case, and provide a ruling. But … the process of interpretation is open to different approaches, which can result in courts effectively initiating new policies in a manner traditionally performed by elected legislatures. In general, the less deference that judges show legislatures, and the more expansively and creatively they read the Constitution, the more likely it is that courts will engage in making new policies under the guise of judicial interpretation – not merely interpreting laws but initiating new public policies'* (Singh, 2003: 181).
>
> Singh, R. (2003) *American Government and Politics: A Precise Introduction.* London: Sage.

Judicial interpretation may help to ensure that the law or constitution is kept up to date, or accords with changing public sentiments as to what constitutes reasonable conduct. However, critics of this role argue that judges ought to distinguish between interpreting the law and actually writing it. They assert that judicial interpretation leads judges to perform a role that ought to be carried out by the legislative branch of government or through the process of constitutional amendment.

The politics of the judiciary

Key idea (5)

It is sometimes alleged that the decisions of judges are influenced by factors other than a dispassionate application of the law.

We know from our own experiences that it is difficult to act in a totally detached and neutral manner. Our actions are likely to be based upon our personal values. Judges are no exception to this. In the following section we will evaluate some of the factors that might influence the way in which judges discharge their responsibilities, and the extent to which they are sufficiently accountable for their actions.

PERSONAL VALUES

The personal values of judges may exert considerable influence on the way in which they perform their duties. These values may be influenced by factors including the judges' social background or legal training. This suggests that it is desirable that judges should be representative of the society in which they operate in terms such as class, gender or race. If judges are socially unrepresentative they may be open to the accusation of discriminatory conduct towards those from a different background.

POLITICAL OPINIONS

The political opinions held by a judge may also influence how that official operates. These may derive from the position which the judiciary operates in the machinery of the state. In a liberal democracy, judges may regard the preservation of this system of government to be of paramount importance. This may influence the attitude which judges display in cases when state interests are involved. Alternatively, these opinions may consist of the judge's own political preferences. In many countries the executive branch of government has the ability to appoint judges.

In America, all federal judges and justices of the Supreme Court are appointed by the president. Inquiries into a candidate's background are initiated on behalf of the chief executive. Following this, however, they are required to be confirmed by the Senate whose Judiciary Committee conducts hearings into a nominee's suitability. Between 1789 and 2006 presidents submitted 158 nominations for judges to the Supreme Court, of which 122 were confirmed (and in 7 other cases the nominee declined to serve). Judges of the Supreme Court serve for life subject to 'good behaviour'. The ability of this body to overrule state and federal legislators and the chief executive influences presidents to appoint judges whose political views closely correspond to their own. For similar reasons, the Senate may pay regard to issues other than the professional competence of a nominee who comes before them for confirmation.

Spotlight

Following his victory in the 1936 presidential election, President Roosevelt decided to confront the Supreme Court that had been blocking some of his New Deal initiatives. His plan was to increase the nine judges of the Supreme Court (perhaps by as many as six new members) to dilute the influence of those conservatives serving on the court who opposed him. However, one of the serving judges, Justice Roberts, changed sides to support the President's initiatives, giving rise to the suggestion that 'a switch in times saves nine'. Subsequently, he used the historic appointments procedure to nominate judges favourable to the New Deal and by the time he died in 1945, he had secured the nomination of eight judges who were sympathetic to his New Deal policies.

Some presidents have the opportunity to appoint a large number of federal judges and others very few. However, when one party has filled the office of president for a number of years, it is likely that the composition of the Federal courts will reflect this control. Thus, when President Clinton entered office in 1992, he was faced with a conservative Supreme Court whose personnel had been mainly chosen by previous Republican presidents. During his eight-year period in office he was able to nominate only two members of this nine-member court. In contrast, his successor, George W. Bush was able to nominate four judges in his eight-year presidency. By the end of August 2014, President Obama had nominated two Justices to the Supreme Court.

Judges and the 2000 American Presidential Election

The ability of the executive branch of government to appoint members to the judicial branch may be of considerable political importance. In 2000, the US Supreme Court was able to determine the outcome of that year's presidential election.

Concern about voting practices in the state of Florida (especially in connection with discounted votes) resulted in manual recounts being commenced. The Supreme Court intervened in this process, first by halting this process and then by ruling that there was no time to stage proper recounts of disputed ballots. This decision meant that Florida's 25 Electoral College votes were given to the Republican candidate, George W. Bush, who obtained a majority of 537 votes out of the almost 6 million votes that were cast in that state. These 25 Electoral College votes gave Bush a narrow majority in the Electoral College and he thus became president.

This decision contravened the traditional reluctance of the Supreme Court to intervene in elections (which were regarded as functions administered by the states) and eroded the defence of state rights that this court had upheld in recent years. Some commentators believed that party politics were a factor in the decision of the court (seven of whose nine members had been nominated by previous Republican presidents).

Judicial office holding

Key idea (6)

The appointment procedures, tenure and accountability of judges bear an important relationship to the manner in which they perform their duties.

APPOINTMENT

Judges in England and Wales are organized in a hierarchy: recorders are the most junior judges in the courts handling criminal offences and the Law Lords (the twelve Lords criminal offences and the Justices of the Supreme Court are the most senior. Vacancies are advertised for all but the most senior appointments (the Lord Justices of Appeal who serve in the Court of Appeal and the Justices of the Supreme Court) and those eligible on grounds of professional experience may apply. The views of serving members of the judiciary have traditionally been sought on applicants (through what is referred to as the 'soundings system') before a shortlist was produced of candidates to be interviewed.

The perception that the 'soundings' procedure resulted in a socially unrepresentative judiciary (since those who were asked for an opinion on an applicant might favour a person whose background was similar to their own, thus potentially discriminating against women and members of minority ethnic groups) has resulted in reforms to the appointment process, in particular the establishment of an independent Judicial Appointments Commission for England and Wales in the 2005 Constitutional Reform Act that took the selection of judges away from the Lord Chancellor and his department (then called the Department for Constitutional Affairs).

THE TENURE OF JUDGES

Liberal democratic political systems usually give judges considerable security of tenure. This is designed to ensure that these public officials cannot be placed under pressure to determine cases according to the wishes of the government of the day. In the UK, for example, senior judges can only be removed by an address of both Houses of Parliament to the Queen. In Ireland, judges can only be dismissed for misbehaviour and incapacity, and to do this requires resolutions from the *Daíl* and the *Seanad*. Additionally, an Irish judge's remuneration may not be reduced during that official's continuance in office.

Security of tenure tends to make judges insufficiently accountable for their actions. They are able to say and do more or less what they like in the sure knowledge that they do not have to answer directly to politicians or to the public at large. This is particularly a problem when judicial interpretation effectively gives judges a key role in the determination of public policy.

An informal control over judges is exerted by the media – *'The media acts as a powerful check upon the judiciary by reporting the courts' activities; media reporting supports the principle of open government which, in turn, feeds public confidence in the courts'* (Shetreet and Turenne, 2013: 14).

Shetreet, S. and Turenne, S. (2013) *Judges on Trial: the Independence and Accountability of the English Judiciary*. Cambridge: Cambridge University Press.

THE ACCOUNTABILITY OF JUDGES

We have suggested that the personal views of judges and political considerations might influence the way in which the courts operate. If we accept that judges are able to inject personal or political biases into their work, especially when interpreting the law, then we need to examine the sufficiency of mechanisms through which judges can be made to explain and justify their actions and, if necessary, be punished for them. In a liberal democracy members of the legislative and executive branches of government (who in theory are charged with initiating and carrying out legislation) are accountable for their actions. Ultimately, they rely on public support to enter or remain in public office. Judges, however, are usually insulated from any direct form of political accountability for their actions, even when these have a fundamental bearing on political affairs. They are usually unelected (although this method of appointment does apply in some American states) and once appointed enjoy security of tenure.

There are, however, some formal controls over the activities of judges. In the UK, the Lord Chancellor and Lord Chief Justice jointly exercise control over judicial discipline, supported by the Judicial Conduct and Investigations Office, which carries out investigations. The penalties available for judges found guilty of misconduct are that of dismissal, suspension or reprimand.

Other formal controls include the ability of politicians to intervene in the operations of the criminal justice system (which in the UK includes legislation setting out a wide range of mandatory sentences which judges are required to implement).

The use of juries may help to offset judicial biases. The decisions of judges can also be set aside by a successful appeal to a higher court, revision to the law or an amendment to the constitution.

However, judges may be subject to informal pressures. In particular they may be influenced by a consideration of what is acceptable to the public at large and seek to ensure that their judgments accord with what they discern as the prevailing political consensus. It has been argued that the American Supreme Court watches the election returns. This suggests that public and political opinion may play a role in determining judicial decisions.

Dig Deeper

Griffith, J. (2010) *The Politics of the Judiciary*. London: Fontana Press, 1997, 5th ed. reissue.

Hodder-Williams, R, (1996) *Judges and Politics in the Contemporary Age*. London: Bowerdean.

Shetreet, S. and Turenne, S. (2013) *Judges on Trial: the Independence and Accountability of the English Judiciary*. Cambridge: Cambridge University Press.

Stevens, R. (1997) *The Independence of the Judiciary*. Oxford: Clarendon.

Fact-check

1 In England and Wales, which court tries the majority of criminal cases:
   a The Magistrates' Court
   b The Crown Court
   c The High Court
   d The Court of Appeal

2 In the UK, which new court was created by the 2005 Constitutional Reform Act:
   a The Crown Court
   b The Magistrates' Court
   c The Supreme Court
   d The Court of Assize

3 In the UK, the jury for a criminal case consists of:
   a 6 members
   b 12 members
   c 15 members
   d 20 members

4 The term applied to judges who develop the law rather than merely apply it in their judgements is:
   a Judicial flexibility
   b Judicial freedom
   c Judicial activism
   d Judicial rulings

5 In the USA, Justices of the Supreme Court are appointed by whom:
   a Existing justices
   b The Attorney General of the USA
   c The Vice President of the USA
   d The President of the USA

6 In the UK, senior judges can be removed from office by:
   a The Lord Chief Justice
   b The Justice Secretary
   c A joint petition of both Houses of Parliament to the monarch
   d The Prince of Wales

14

Sub-national government

When we think of government, we tend to focus on the operations of national government. However, many of the public services that we use and the key decisions that affect our everyday lives are not the responsibility of central government but are instead performed by lower tier bodies that we refer to in this chapter as 'sub-national government'. This term includes local government, regional government and, in states with federal systems of government, state government. In this chapter we will examine the operations of the various bodies that constitute sub-national government.

Definition of sub-national government

Key idea (1)

The term 'sub-national government' embraces units of government whose jurisdiction is limited to specific geographic areas within a state.

A major role performed by government is to provide services for the benefit of the general public. Many of these are provided by national government. However, others are controlled and administered by bodies covering only part of a particular country. There are a wide variety of these, but in this chapter we will confine our attention to state, regional and local authorities. These constitute important examples of what is meant by 'sub-national government'.

Key idea (2)

Federal political structures entail political power being exercised by both national and sub-national government. The latter are often termed 'states' or 'provinces'.

Sub-national governments are subject to considerable variation. A key distinction concerns the autonomy that such units enjoy. In federal states such as Germany, Australia or America, power is divided between national (or federal) government and the constituent units of government. The division of responsibilities is provided for in a single source, usually a written constitution, which allocates specific functions to each sphere of government. Each enjoys autonomy in its own area of jurisdiction, which means that one may not intrude into the operations of the other. There may also be functions that are exercised jointly by both tiers of government.

The alternative to a federal state is a unitary one. In unitary states, political power is centralized in the hands of the national government. Countries including the United Kingdom, Sweden and France possess such forms of government. However, unitary states often possess a unit of government that is intermediate between national and local government. These are usually regional bodies, which provide services for a relatively wide geographic area where the inhabitants share some form of common identity such as language, culture or race. Regional authorities vary according to the autonomy they possess: some exercise power that is devolved from national government, thus giving them a wide degree of control over such delegated responsibilities, while others merely function as administrative bodies whose role is to provide regional services according to guidelines laid down by national government.

In both federal and unitary states a range of services are provided by subordinate authorities, termed 'local government', whose activities will be discussed later in this chapter.

Federalism

Key idea (3)

Federalism possesses advantages derived from localities being empowered to run their own affairs. But there are also difficulties, especially in connection with the division of powers in federal political structures.

ADVANTAGES

We have identified the division of power between a national government and constituent units such as states or provinces as the essence of a federal form of government. This situation possesses a number of advantages.

▶ Aids the relationship between the government and its citizens

Federalism was historically viewed as a safeguard against the overbearing power of a strong, central government. In large countries, it breaks down the remoteness that would otherwise occur if government were provided by a distant national authority. Government is thus brought closer to the people who additionally are provided with the means to participate in its activities through the process of voting or through their involvement with locally orientated pressure groups.

▶ Facilitates diversity in a country

New Right ideology emphasized the virtues that derive from the diversity with which a federal system of government may be associated. Variations within one country in matters such as taxation or level of services may prove attractive to citizens or to commercial organizations that are encouraged to move from part of the country to another to benefit themselves. Diversity may perhaps encourage competition between states to attract people and industry.

▶ Maintenance of national unity

The autonomy possessed by state governments in a federal system may be of benefit to nations whose existence is threatened by significant internal division. So long as a nation provides recognizable political or economic benefits to all of its citizens, groups with divergent interests may be encouraged to remain within the one state when the power possessed by the national government is limited with most functions being provided by governments controlled by local people. Federalism thus empowers localities to run most aspects of their affairs in accordance with the wishes of the people who reside there with restricted 'interference' by a national government. It may thus contribute towards retaining the existence of states threatened by separatist tendencies.

Belgium granted considerable powers of self-government to its Flemish and Walloon communities within the confines of a federation in order to prevent the break-up of the state along linguistic lines. For similar reasons, a wide degree of autonomy has been granted to the Canadian province of Quebec where, in an attempt to retain national unity, Canada's federal system of government has provided Quebec with considerable powers of self-government, especially in connection with the official use of French.

Federalism in America

Federalism in America is based upon the Tenth Amendment to the Constitution (1791), which stated that powers not expressly ceded to the federal (national) government and that the Constitution did not expressly deny to the states were reserved to the states or to the people.

The Constitution did not, however, provide for a once-and-for-all settlement of the balance to be struck between national and state government, which has subsequently undergone several changes. Terms that include 'dual federalism', 'co-operative federalism' and 'creative federalism' have been used to describe different approaches that have been adopted to the power relationship between federal and state governments in the delivery of public policy. Post-1981 Republican presidents were associated with what is termed 'new federalism', which seeks to restore to the states powers that it is alleged have been taken away from them by the federal government. Other terms (such as 'horizontal federalism', 'marble-cake federalism' and 'picket-fence federalism') have been used to describe the way in which policies and programmes administered out by the states are planned and delivered.

DISADVANTAGES

There are, however, problems associated with federal systems of government. We discuss the main ones below.

▶ Fragmentation of government

Federalism results in government in one country being fragmented. Diverse standards of service provision operating in a single country are not necessarily desirable. Further, the autonomy granted to sub-national units of government may provide a minority with the means to frustrate the will of the majority. The progress of civil rights in America was impeded by the ability of southern state governments to resist or to slow down the implementation of such legislation. Some of these problems may, however, be mitigated. In America, for example, the existence of intergovernmental bureaucracies, composed of paid officials operating at all levels of government, has served to promote common approaches to problems pursued by all tiers of government.

▶ The balance of power between state and national government

One particular difficulty with federalism concerns the distribution of power between the national and constituent governments. This division is provided for in the constitution and disputes between the two tiers of government are arbitrated by a constitutional court. However, a tendency for the power of national governments to be enhanced at the expense of states has been observed in many federal countries. In America, this alteration to the fundamental nature of federalism has partly arisen from the willingness of the Supreme Court to interpret the constitution in a manner that is favourable towards national governments playing an increased role in economic and social policies. A particular consequence has been increased reliance by the states on revenue provided by national government, although what is termed 'new federalism' (one aspect of which in America is Block Grants, which replaced the General Revenue Sharing policy adopted during the 1970s and 1980s) is designed to shift power back to the states.

The states' freedom of action may also be circumscribed by action imposed by the national government designed to enforce conformity and set minimum standards of service provision. In America, pre-emption is an example of this. This imposes a legal requirement on states to meet certain minimum standards of service provision, to achieve standards of quality or to provide stipulated services. Environmental policy is often shaped by a requirement that all states should adopt minimum standards set by the federal government (although they may exceed these if they wish).

Nonetheless, states continue to play an important role in the economic and social life of a federal country. In America, for example, the ability of the states to raise some of their own revenue and their role as implementers of public policy may enhance their image as dynamic institutions even if they are subject to the strong central control exerted by the federal government over many aspects of their operations.

CONFEDERATION

Key idea (4)

A confederation entails independent states establishing a mechanism to secure commonly agreed goals but without ceding power to this central body.

A confederation is a political structure in which a group of nations agree to co-operate to achieve common aims that are frequently of a defensive or economic nature. It bears some relationship to federalism; the key difference concerning the powers of the centralized mechanism that is created.

In a federal structure, a central (or national) government is created that has a wide degree of power, which may (as has been the case in America) be expanded at the expense of the state governments. By contrast, the central body of a confederation has extremely limited powers with most tasks of government being performed by those states or countries that are part of it. These retain their sovereignty and their right to secede. A particular feature of a confederation is that the national government has no direct powers over citizens: functions such as taxation and law enforcement are exercised by the constituent governments.

The main difficulties associated with confederations include the absence of a strong central government able effectively to co-ordinate the actions of its members, which may especially be required in times of crisis. These structures are also often dominated by the larger of its members.

A confederal system of government was established by the American colonies engaged in the War of Independence against Britain. The Articles of Confederation, which were drawn up by the Continental Congress in 1777, provided for a confederacy to be known as the United States of America. The eleven southern states of America that seceded in the Civil War were also subject to this form of government between 1861 and 1865.

The Commonwealth of Independent States (CIS – established in 1991 following the collapse of the Soviet Union) is a more recent creation. This is composed of 11 of the former Soviet Republics (Turkmenistan discontinuing its membership in 2005 when it became an associate member) that agreed to work together on the basis of sovereign equality. The CIS possesses few supranational powers but does have important co-ordinating functions in the areas of trade, finance, law making and security.

Further examples of confederations are also found in organizations which seek to promote social, political or economic matters that are in the mutual interests of those who are members. Membership of such organizations is typically voluntary and includes the North Atlantic Treaty Organization. The European Union also has some elements of a confederal political structure. Confederations may develop into federal structures of government (as happened in Switzerland, which became a federation in the fourteenth century, despite it retaining the title *Confédération Helvétique*).

Governing a divided nation – consociationalism

Consociationalism (which is often referred to as 'power sharing') seeks to provide a stable system of government in a plural society that is characterized by the existence of fundamental divisions (which may be based upon religion, race, language, ideology or culture) and in which other key aspects of civic affairs (such as political parties, pressure groups and the educational system) are organized on the same basis. The groups into which society is divided compete for control of the same territory. This model for governing divided societies was developed by a Dutch political scientist, Arend Lijphart, who wrote *Democracy in Plural Societies* (published in 1977). He subsequently argued that *'in ... deeply divided societies the interests and demands of communal groups can be accommodated only by the establishment of power sharing'* (Lijphart, 2004: 96).

He put forward four key features of consociational democracy. The first feature was government by a grand coalition of the political leaders of all the significant sections into which society was divided. This entailed co-operation by political elites in the formation of an executive branch of government. Lijphart argued that this required leaders to *'feel at least some commitment to the maintenance of the unity of the country as well as a commitment to democratic practices. They must also have a basic willingness to engage in cooperative efforts with the leaders of other segments in a spirit of moderation and compromise'* (Lijphart, 1977: 53). The second feature was the introduction of a veto that the various sections could use to defend their interests against majority decisions and a third was that political representation should be based on proportional principles. The final aspect of consociationalism was that each section of society should be granted a high degree of autonomy to regulate its own affairs.

It has been concluded that *'divided territories, be they regions or states, with historically antagonistic ethnically, religiously or linguistically divided peoples are effectively, prudently, and sometimes optimally governed according to consociational principles'* (McGarry and O'Leary, 2006: 43).

One example of consociationalism in practice affects Northern Ireland. The 1998 Northern Ireland Act provided for an assembly elected under proportional representation and an executive committee composed of ministers drawn from the major parties represented in the assembly. This arrangement was designed to bring together the leaders of Northern Ireland's nationalist and unionist communities.

Lijphart, A. (1977) *Democracy in Divided Societies: A Comparative Exploration*. New Haven, Connecticut: Yale University Press.

Lijphart, A. (2004) Constitutional Designs for Divided Societies. *Journal of Democracy*, 15(2) pp 96–109.

McGarry, J. and O'Leary, B. (2006) Consociational Theory, Northern Ireland's Conflict and Its Agreement. Part One: What Consociationalists Can Learn from Northern Ireland. *Government and Opposition*. 41(1) pp 43–63

Regionalism

Key idea (5)

States with unitary political structures may decentralize some of the tasks of government onto regional machinery. Its control over the activities for which it becomes responsible is subject to considerable variation.

States with unitary political structures are often accused of being centralized: power resides in the capital and citizens living in areas that are geographically distant from this area may feel neglected by a government they regard as remote. Some unitary states, therefore, have utilized regional apparatus to offset the disadvantages which are sometimes perceived in a centralized state. This involves a state being divided into a number of smaller areas within which certain tasks of government can be discharged. The role and composition of regional machinery is variable and many different forms may be used even in one state. We consider the main varieties of regional machinery in the following sections.

ADVISORY

Regional machinery may be purely advisory. It can be utilized as a consultative mechanism to facilitate overall government planning of particular activities (such as the nation's economic development) or it might be established by individual government departments to aid the flow of information between that department and citizens living in each region. This may enable central government to adjust the operations of a policy to suit the particular requirements of a region and its inhabitants, or it may be used to provide advice on government policies to people or public authorities residing there. This machinery is typically staffed by civil servants and possesses no power other than the ability to act as a vehicle that facilitates a two-way process of communication between government and the governed.

ADMINISTRATIVE AND GOVERNMENTAL

A region may alternatively provide the geographic unit around which services are administered. This embraces the decentralized regional apparatus used by national governmental organizations but also includes regional machinery that has been established to provide services. Regional machinery may be established to discharge individual services: in Ireland, for example, health services were administered by area health boards between 1971 and 2005. Alternatively several governmental functions can be co-ordinated at a regional level. Those who administer services in this fashion may possess some discretion to tailor them to address specific regional needs or requirements.

Regional machinery may be given some degree of power. This will often be exercised by representatives who are elected at regional level and who then discharge a range of services over which they possess partial or total control. Italy, for example, is divided into 20 regions, each of which has a directly elected council that exercises control over a wide range of functions. A considerable proportion of the national budget is under the control of Italy's regional councils. France has 27 administrative regions (22 in France and 5 overseas, divided into departments) administered by a *Conseil Régional* whose members are elected for a term of 6 years. In 2014, President Hollande announced plans to reduce the number in France to 14. The regions have no legislative autonomy but possess tax-raising powers. They manage sizeable budgets and possess discretionary powers to spend on education, public transport, and urban housing.

In the UK, the Scottish Parliament and the Welsh and Northern Ireland Assemblies have exercised control over a number of responsibilities allocated to them by the 1998 devolution legislation and subsequent measures.

The terms 'devolution', 'federalism' and 'home rule' are similar, but it is necessary to differentiate between them. These terms have been defined as follows:

Devolution: this involves the transfer of power from a superior to an inferior political authority. The dominance of the former is generally exhibited through its ability to reform or take away the power which it has bestowed.

Federalism: this necessitates a division of power between central and sub-national governments. The existence of the latter and the general range of powers they possess is usually embodied in a codified constitution.

Home rule: this requires the break-up of a nation into a number of sovereign states, each exercising total control over their internal and external affairs. This demand is usually based on the existence of a national identity (Joyce, 1999: 415).

Joyce, P. (1999) *An Introduction to Politics*. London: Hodder and Stoughton.

DEVOLUTION IN SCOTLAND, WALES AND NORTHERN IRELAND

Key idea (6)

Devolution measures designed to bring government and the people closer together were contained in three measures enacted in 1998 dealing with Scotland, Wales and Northern Ireland.

The 1998 Scotland Act provided for the creation of a Scottish Parliament of 129 members serving a fixed term of four years. This body appointed a first minister, who in turn chose other ministers who were responsible to the first minister. This body was initially termed the 'Scottish Executive' but assumed the title of 'Scottish Government' in 2007.

The Scottish Parliament was able to make laws on all domestic matters, including health, education and training, law and home affairs, economic development and transport, local government, environment, agriculture, fisheries and forestry, and sports and the arts. It was financed by the Scottish Block grant (or the 'assigned budget', which in 2009 was around £35 billion) and can be supplemented by the 'tartan tax'. This permitted the Scottish Parliament to vary the standard rate of income tax by up to 3 pence in the pound (3 per cent), thus creating the possibility of supplementing its budget from self-generated revenue imposed on those who live in Scotland for more than half of the year. However, this power was never used.

A wide range of matters (including the UK constitution, foreign affairs, fiscal, economic and monetary policy, defence and national security, medical ethics, social security and employment) were reserved to the Westminster Parliament. Additionally, the Scottish secretary was empowered to overrule the Scottish Parliament and halt legislation believed to be inappropriate and to ensure that the UK's international treaties were implemented in Scotland. The Scotland Act repealed the requirement (provided for in 1986 legislation) regarding the minimum number of Scottish MPs at Westminster.

Following the 1998 Act, additional powers have been transferred to the Scottish government. These included railways in 2005 and planning and nature conservation matters at sea within 200 miles of the Scottish coast in 2008 in the wake of the Calman Commission, which was set up by the Scottish Parliament in 2007 to review the operations of the 1998 Act. Also derived from recommendations made by the Calman Commission, a raft of fiscal powers were transferred to the Scottish government by the 2012 Scotland Act that enabled the Scottish Parliament to raise or lower income tax by 10p in the pound. Any change is applied equally across all tax bands. Other minor tax powers included the control of stamp duty and landfill tax. The Act also provided the Scottish Parliament with borrowing powers for the first time, worth £2.2 billion per year. At the same time, there would be a reduction of some 35 per cent in the Scottish Treasury (or Block) grant, worth about £30 billion a year in 2013, offset by the enhanced revenue gathering powers of the Scottish government.

The Scottish Independence Referendum

At the 2011 elections to the Scottish Parliament, the Scottish National Party won 69 seats, giving it an overall majority. Following this, the Party announced its intention to hold a referendum on Scottish Independence.

On 15 October 2012, the Scottish and UK governments signed the Edinburgh Agreement that set out the terms for the Scottish Independence Referendum. This provided for a single question referendum on the issue of Scottish Independence. Following this Agreement, arrangements for the Referendum were laid down in the Scottish Independence Referendum Act, which was passed by the Scottish Parliament in November 2013. The UK Government stated that if the vote favoured independence, Scotland would become an independent country following a process of negotiation.

Major campaigns were mounted in relation to the referendum. The case for independence was promoted by the group Yes Scotland while opposition was co-ordinated by the organization Better Together, led by former Labour Chancellor of the Exchequer, Alistair Darling.

The Referendum was held on 18 September 2014. The referendum question was: 'Should Scotland be an independent country?' and voters were asked to choose yes or no.

The result was:

Yes	1,617,989 (44.7%)
No	2,001,926 (55.3%)

The total number of votes cast was 3,623,344 and the turnout was 84.59 per cent.

During the campaign, a number of politicians associated with the 'No' campaign called for enhanced powers to the Scottish Parliament as an alternative to full independence and following the referendum, the Scottish Government put forward its own measures to secure this objective entitled *More Powers for the Scottish Parliament: Scottish Government Proposals*. The implementation of measures of this nature is likely to have consequences for the devolution of powers elsewhere in the UK, including to the English regions.

The 1998 Government of Wales Act provided for an assembly of 60 persons. The body chooses a first secretary (*Prif Ysgrifennydd y Cynulliad*) who selects other assembly secretaries. The 2006 Government of Wales Act subsequently separated the National Assembly of Wales from the Welsh Assembly Government. Powers administered by the Welsh Office were transferred to this new body, thereby subjecting them to accountability, and additional administrative functions were transferred in 2010 by Legislative Competence Orders made by the Queen in Privy Council. The assembly possesses no law-making or independent tax-raising powers and remained totally reliant on a block grant (which in 2010 totalled around £15 billion). This system thus primarily provided for a system which democratized existing administrative arrangements as opposed to devolution.

Further changes to devolution were introduced by the 2006 Government of Wales Act. This created an executive body known as the Welsh Assembly government (which in May 2011 was re-named the Welsh Government) that was separate from the legislative body, (the National Assembly for Wales). The constitutional implication of this change was that Welsh Government was altered from being a committee of the National Assembly to being a distinct body. Additionally, the Act created a mechanism whereby powers from the UK Parliament could be delegated to the National Assembly in matters referred to as `Fields', which included agriculture, fisheries, food and agricultural development, local government, public administration and town and country planning. Increased powers could be obtained in one of two ways – through clauses included in legislation passed by an Act of the UK Parliament (in which case the power(s) would be transferred through delegated legislation), or by Legislative Competence Orders granted by Parliament in response to a request from the National Assembly. In 2011, a referendum was held in which voters approved the proposal that the National Assembly for Wales should be able to make laws on all matters related to the 20 subject areas that were specified in the original devolution settlement without having to seek the approval of the UK Parliament. The Assembly assumed the power to enact primary legislation in these areas on 5 May 2011

The 1998 Northern Ireland Act provided for an assembly of 108 members. The executive was composed of 12 ministers. The first minister and deputy minister were elected by the Assembly, and the ministers were chosen by a formula designed to ensure that the Assembly's executive committee reflected the strength of the parties in the assembly. The 2006 Northern Ireland Act introduced reforms to the Northern Ireland Assembly (including the creation of a fixed term Assembly) which helped to create a more durable governmental structure.

The early history of devolved government in Northern Ireland was punctuated by lengthy periods of suspension arising from problems in securing the cooperation of Loyalists and Republicans. The longest of these was from 14 October 2002 until 7 May 2007 when the Assembly's powers reverted to the Northern Ireland Office. Following talks that resulted in the 2006 St Andrews Agreement, an election to the Assembly was held on 7 March 2007 and full power was restored to the devolved institutions on 8 May 2007. Powers in relation to policing and justice were transferred to the Assembly on 12 April 2010. The third assembly was dissolved on 24 March 2011 in preparation for the elections held on Thursday 5 May 2011. This was the first Assembly since the Good Friday Agreement to complete a full term. The fourth Assembly convened on 12 May 2011.

The electoral arrangements for these devolved structures of government also reflected the desire to bring government and the people closer together. The Northern Irish Assembly was elected on the basis of the single transferable vote. In Scotland and Wales, the electoral system was a mixture of the first-past-the-post system topped up by additional members elected by the regional party list system.

The Labour Government also enacted the 1999 Greater London Act. This provided for a new strategic city-wide government for London consisting of an elected assembly of 25 members (14 of whom are elected by the first-past-the-post and 11 are 'top-up' members chosen from party lists drawn up by the political parties) and a mayor who is directly elected by the supplementary vote system.

Local government

Key idea (7)

A wide range of public services are performed by local government which are typically administered by locally elected representatives who are accountable to local people for the nature and quality of the services that are provided.

Local government has responsibility for providing a range of services to people living in part of a country. Many of the functions traditionally associated with local government constitute services that are utilized by large numbers of citizens on a daily basis. These include the provision of housing, social services, environmental services, refuse disposal, and planning. Education is frequently provided by local government, although in France this service has traditionally been subject to a considerable degree of central control. Changes proposed in the late 1990s, however, sought to devolve increased control over this service to local level.

The scope of the activities of local government and the extent of its autonomy is widely varied. In many Western European and Scandinavian countries, local government is created by constitutional enactment, and in America it is provided for in state constitutions. In such countries which include France, Italy, Sweden and Denmark, local government has 'general competence'; that is, the ability to perform any function unless expressly forbidden to do so by law.

In the UK and Ireland, however, local government has no constitutional status. Its existence is derived from legislation, and historically it could only perform those functions that were expressly allocated to it by law passed by parliament. This situation tended vastly to curtail the autonomy that is exercised by local authorities in these two countries, although in the UK discretionary powers provided some degree of operational and innovatory freedom. However, the 2011 Localism Act provided local authorities in England and Wales with a 'general power of competence', which meant that henceforth they could do anything that an individual could do that is not specifically prohibited.

In the following section we will consider the functions that local government may perform in a liberal democratic political system.

PUBLIC INVOLVEMENT IN POLICY MAKING

The existence of local government enhances the ability of citizens to take part in the administration of their own affairs. They may do this by voting in local government elections or by serving as elected members of local authorities. Local government thus increases the number of people in a state able to take decisions related to the administration of its affairs.

LOCAL ACCOUNTABILITY

A major advantage of local government stems from the fact that it is administered by elected officials. In English-speaking liberal democracies these are usually termed 'councillors'. They can be held accountable to the local electorate for the way in which services are provided. In this way, the functions discharged by government can be made compatible with what local people desire. There are alternative ways to provide services (such as through development corporations that have been used selectively in the UK since 1979), but the elected dimension of local government is the key to its responsiveness to local issues and problems.

EFFICIENCY IN SERVICE PROVISION

It has been further suggested that local government is the most efficient way to provide public services. Its size enables local problems (which may be untypical of the nation as a whole) to be addressed, which might be overlooked were all government services administered by larger geographic units such as state or central governments. Local government is also flexible in its approach to problems and has the ability to innovate in an attempt to find solutions to them. In the UK, reforms introduced by the 1997 Labour Government to the management structure of local government were influenced by experiments in local authorities such as Hammersmith and Fulham, which had installed a mayor and small cabinet to speed up decision making.

PURSUIT OF SOCIAL OBJECTIVES

Local government may serve as a vehicle to advance social objectives, such as gender or racial equality, which may have a low priority on the national political agenda. It may do so through its role as an employer, purchaser or provider of services. Since the passage of the 1976 Race Relations Act, local government in the UK has had a statutory duty to eliminate racial discrimination and has been at the forefront of developing equal opportunities policies. A wider range of public authorities were given this responsibility in the 2000 Race Relations (Amendment) Act.

The receptiveness of local government to social concerns may help to overcome the problem of marginalization, whereby particular minority groups perceive that the operations of the conventional political system do not cater for their needs. These may be encouraged to become involved in conventional political activity at local level as it presents a realistic possibility that some of their concerns might be addressed. In both the UK and America, a significant number of councillors derive from ethnic minority backgrounds. This involvement may reduce the likelihood of such minority groups having to resort to more extreme forms of political activity that have a damaging effect on social harmony to be heard.

LINKING CITIZENS WITH NATIONAL GOVERNMENT

In many countries local government is viewed as a training ground for politicians who later occupy high national office. It may also serve as an institutional mechanism linking local people with national government. This is especially apparent in France where leading politicians sometimes hold elected office in municipal government. This situation provides national politicians with powerful localized bases of support.

ACTING AS A PRESSURE GROUP

An important role performed by local government is acting as a pressure group, putting forward local needs or concerns to other tiers of government and seeking remedies, perhaps through the provision of increased funds to the locality or by changes in central government policy. The early 1980s witnessed some Labour-controlled local authorities in the UK providing confrontational opposition to Conservative government policies that they believed were harmful to local people. The ability of local government to act in this manner is enhanced by its elected base, which implies it is acting at the behest of local majority opinion.

BAROMETERS OF PUBLIC OPINION

Although local government elections should be concerned with local issues, their outcome is frequently determined by national considerations. This arises because, in many liberal democracies, local government elections are contested by the same parties that compete for power nationally. This may mean that the outcome of such contests is heavily influenced by voters' opinions on the performance of the parties (including the record of the government) at national level. Local government elections may thus provide evidence of the political mood of the nation and serve as a means whereby the general public can exert influence over the conduct or composition of the national government.

In 2006, the poor performance of the Labour Party in that year's local government elections prompted the Prime Minister to dismiss the Home Secretary and reshuffle his government. Similarly, in 2014, losses suffered by the French Socialist Party in the municipal elections prompted the resignation of the entire government and led to the appointment of a new prime minister.

THE PERFORMANCE OF LOCAL GOVERNMENT

The benefits that are meant to derive from the operations of local government are not always fully realized. Local government may be unable to respond effectively to contemporary issues. Its organizational base may be inappropriate and its revenue-generating capacity inadequate to offer workable solutions to problems such as urban poverty which are manifested at local level, especially in inner city areas. In such places the demand for services is high but the ability of people to pay for them is low. This tends to drive up the level of local taxes and encourage wealthier people to move away. This situation may result in increased reliance on finance supplied by state or national governments, or lead to the delivery of services by purpose-built bodies detached from the organizational structure of local government.

> Although elections to local authorities are a key mechanism through which the public can be involved in decisions regarding the delivery of local services, there is a considerable degree of apathy: in Great Britain *over the past 20 years, turnout in local elections has averaged around 40%. Not only does this put the country at the bottom of the European Union league table for turnout in sub-national elections, it means that it is the only country in the EU where sub-national elections regularly engage the active interest of less than half its citizens*
>
> (Curtice, 1999: 4).
>
> Curtice, J. (1999) Public Opinion and Local Government: the Crisis of Local Democracy in Britain. *Centre for Research into Elections and Social Trends, Working Paper 77.* Available [Online] http://www.crest.ox.ac.uk/papers/p77.pdf [Accessed 25 August 2014].

Local government may not always be adequately responsive to local needs and problems. Its ability to act in this way may be diminished by factors such as the working practices adopted by local government officers or the lack of social representativeness of those elected to local office. Party politics may require elected councillors to put the interests of their party above the concerns of those they represent. Services are administered by full-time officers who may put their professional interests above the requirements of those they view as their 'clients'. In some countries, the political power is centralized within a local authority so that power is wielded by a handful of people. This has the effect of making local government seem remote and unapproachable to ordinary people. The decentralization of locally administered services is one solution to this problem, but it has not been pursued in the UK with the vigour found in other countries such as France and Spain.

Perhaps as a result of these two deficiencies, public interest in local government is low in some countries. In the UK, for example, the turnout in local elections rarely rises above 40 per cent. This suggests that here local government is not particularly effective as a vehicle through which people can take part in government.

Central control and local autonomy

Key idea (8)

Local government lacks autonomy and is subject to various forms of control by higher political authorities such as central government.

There is an important difference between the terms 'government' and 'administration' when applied to local government. The former implies a degree of discretion, usually guaranteed by the fact that local government raises a proportion of its own revenue by taxing its inhabitants. The latter term suggests that local government has no independence of action and exists to provide services whose content is structured by national or state governments. It is effectively an agent of central government.

However, in most liberal democracies, local government is subject to a considerable degree of control by national or state governments. This may be exercised in a number of ways which we consider below.

CONTROL BY THE EXECUTIVE BRANCH

The executive branch may impose a range of controls on the operations of local government. These include specific controls over individual services, limits on local government spending or detailed controls over local government borrowing. In Ireland, central supervision is also exerted over the personnel employed by local authorities.

▶ The prefectoral system

> 'Prefects are officers of the central government responsible for the execution of national programmes at the sub-national level. Each ministry may have its own field service, but these are coordinated and, to some degree, supervised by the prefect. The prefect, in turn, is responsible to the Ministry of the Interior or some other ministry charged with supervising administration. In France ... the prefect has also been responsible for local governments, especially their finances ... there are differences in the exact way in which prefectoral systems operate but the common thread of such systems ... is that one officer should coordinate and be responsible for public services delivered in a sub-national area' (Peters and Falk, 2010: 140).
>
> Peters, B.G. and Falk, M. (2010) *The Politics of Bureaucracy: An Introduction to Comparative Public Administration*. Abingdon, Oxford: Routledge, 6th ed.

The prefectoral system offers a way in which local government can be controlled by higher political authorities. This involves the imposition of an official appointed by central government to act as its eyes and ears in the localities and provide a link between central and local government, effectively fusing the two levels of administration.

The system whereby a representative of central government (usually termed a 'prefect' or 'governor') is appointed alongside an elected regional or provincial assembly is relatively common in Europe. This official is the chief administrative officer of the area whose main purpose is to provide a link between local and national government. He or she is sometimes aided by regional assemblies appointing a board of representatives who meet under the prefect's chairmanship.

Arrangements of this nature exist in Denmark, Sweden, Spain, Greece, and Italy. In France, the prefect (who was termed 'Commissioner of the Republic' between 1982 and 1987) is a civil servant appointed by a decree of the President of France (acting on the recommendation of the Prime Minister and Minister of the Interior) taken in the Council of Ministers. Prefects are placed in each department and, after 1972, in each region. They are responsible for controlling policy within the department by reviewing actions taken by Ministries operating in the locality and also many actions undertaken by the Department and Commune officials.

JUDICIAL CONTROL

In countries in which the powers of local government are rigidly controlled by legislation, judicial control may constitute an important control. In the UK, for example, the courts are able to intervene and prevent local authorities from performing functions that they are not legally empowered to perform, and may also force a council to discharge its mandatory duties if it was ignoring these.

Local government reform in Britain

Key idea (9)

The reform of local government in England and Wales has occupied a prominent position in the political agendas of post-1979 governments, resulting in important changes to its structure, role and powers.

Spotlight

According to the Local Government Information Unit (LGiU), in August 2013 there were 468 local authorities in England and Wales and around 21,000 elected councillors. These councils are financed by grants from central government (around 48 per cent of local government income), business rates charged to local companies (25 per cent) and Council Tax paid by local residents (25 per cent). They spend over £70 billion each year (which is around one-quarter of all public spending in the UK) and employ 2 million people.

Conservative governments between 1979 and 1997 displayed a critical attitude towards local government. They accused it of waste and inefficiency aggravated by poor management and of putting political interests before service to the community. This resulted in increased central control being exerted over local government and a loss of functions with which it has traditionally been associated.

REFORM TO THE STRUCTURE OF LOCAL GOVERNMENT

The structure of local government has undergone a number of changes in recent years. The two-tier system of county and district councils that had been implemented under the provisions of the 1972 Local Government Act was abandoned in the major urban areas in 1986 when the Greater London Council and the metropolitan county councils were abolished.

The 1992 Local Government Act initiated a move towards creating single-tier, or unitary, authorities throughout England and Wales in the belief that it was more efficient and cost effective for services to be administered by one set of hands.

Local government has also been affected by the development of city regions. These seek to provide for strategic planning in areas that include economic development and physical planning that takes place across the boundaries of local authorities. The 2010 Coalition government modified this approach by entailing the creation of combined authorities, the first of which was the Greater Manchester Combined Authority in 2011. It is controlled by ten indirectly elected members, each a councillor from the ten metropolitan Boroughs that comprise Greater Manchester, and derives its powers from the 2000 Local Government Act and the 2009 Local Democracy, Economic Development and Construction Act.

FUNCTIONS

Services were also being taken out of the hands of local government and transferred to a range of alternative authorities including joint boards, quangos and central government. The involvement of central government greatly increased in policy areas such as education, which was traditionally viewed as a local responsibility. Government policy has also served to weaken the role performed by local government in functions that include the provision of public housing. Government policy initiated in the 1980 Housing Act resulted in the sale of vast numbers of council houses, and much of the work previously carried out by local authorities in the area of what became known as 'social housing' became assumed by housing associations.

Additionally, the concept of market forces was introduced into the operations of local government in order to make local government provide enhanced value for money. A large number of services were transferred from direct local government control and made subject to competitive tendering. Legislation, which included the 1980 Local Government, Planning and Land Act, and the 1988 and 1990 Local Government Acts, has moved local government in the direction of an enabling authority rather than one that directly provided services.

However, local government has gained in other areas of responsibility. Post-1997 Labour government has promoted the role of local government in new areas of work that include crime prevention and community safety.

CONTROLS OVER LOCAL GOVERNMENT SPENDING

Key idea (10)

In England and Wales, local government is financed by a Revenue Support Grant, which is paid by central government towards the cost of all local government services, by a number of specific grants also paid by central government that relate to specific services, and by a Council Tax, which is raised by the local authority.

Additional controls were introduced to curtail the level of expenditure by local government. This was justified by the argument that the national government was required to exercise overall control over the level of public spending. Key legislation to achieve this objective included the 1980 Local Government, Planning and Land Act, the 1982 Local Government Finance Act, and the 1984 Rates Act.

Estimates of what each local authority needed to spend were drawn up by central government initially in the form of grant-related expenditure. This determined the level of local government grant paid to local authorities by central government, but it was possible to exceed the government's overall estimate by raising additional funds locally through the rates. Accordingly, 'capping' was introduced in 1984, which allowed the government to enforce a ceiling on the overall expenditure of those authorities that were viewed as particularly spendthrift. In 1990, standard spending assessments were introduced to influence the level of locally raised revenue. Like the previous grant-related expenditure, these limits were also regulated by the sanction of capping.

The key reform introduced by the Conservative Party, which sought to curb local government spending, was the introduction of a new source of finance through which local government would fund its operations. The rates (which was a tax levied on property) was replaced by a tax on individuals. This was the community charge, more infamously known as 'poll tax'. It was designed to enhance the accountability of local government to its residents by forcing all citizens to contribute towards the costs of local government. In this way it was envisaged that high-spending councils would be more readily sanctioned by local electors since exemptions and rebates associated with the rating system resulted in a significant number of local residents having to make no financial contribution to the costs of local services. This new tax became law in 1988 and was first introduced in England and Wales in 1990.

However, the introduction of poll tax was surrounded with controversy. It was an extremely difficult and expensive tax to collect, and its problems were compounded by a campaign seeking to encourage people not to pay. It was argued that the tax was essentially unfair by making all contribute regardless of their means. Eventually, the government was forced to back down. Poll tax was abandoned and replaced by the Council Tax as local government's independent source of finance. This was essentially a tax on property, the level of which was determined by the value of property (which was viewed as suggestive of the financial means of its occupants). In 1990, a uniform business rate was introduced to govern the financial contribution made by business concerns towards the costs of local authorities in which they are situated.

The 2010 Coalition government abolished the capping of Council Tax rises in its 2011 Localism Act and introduced a procedure of referendums whereby local electorates could approve or veto excessive rises in Council Tax.

POLITICAL CONTROL OF LOCAL GOVERNMENT

The 2000 Local Government Act introduced a number of reforms to modernize the operations of local government in England and Wales. A particular aim was to improve the effectiveness of the executive branch of local government. The Act enabled local residents (through the mechanism of a referendum) to decide whether they wanted a directly elected mayor, and also introduced changes to the composition of the executive arm of local government, which could be based upon a directly elected mayor and a cabinet, a cabinet headed by the leader of the council, or a directly elected mayor and a council manager. Additionally, a directly elected mayor for London (in addition to a directly elected assembly) was provided for in the 1999 London Government Act.

However, relatively few local authorities have opted for mayors, and by May 2013 there were only 15 outside of London. Around 50 referendums had taken place since the passage of the 2000 Act and most rejected the introduction of this reform.

THE EMPOWERMENT AGENDA

The desire to secure the empowerment of communities has received considerable attention in the early years of the twenty-first century. The aim of this approach is to give communities more power over local concerns and to ensure that agencies delivering services to localities are aware of and able to act upon local priorities. Empowerment requires effective mechanisms of communication to be established to provide citizens with the ability to raise their concerns and to see what action results from their interventions.

This principle was promoted in the 2000 Local Government Act which – as amended by the 2007 Sustainable Communities Act – extended the role of local authorities to promote or improve the economic, social and environmental well-being of their area through the mechanisms of a sustainable community strategy, and by the 2007 Local Government and Public Involvement in Health Act, which established a 'duty to involve' local people in key decisions and securing the enhanced scrutiny of decision making. This latter role was extended by the 2009 Local Democracy, Economic Development and Construction Act.

The 2010 Coalition Government further promoted the concept of empowerment through the concept of the Big Society and the 2011 Localism Act, which sought to pursue decentralization by measures that included the reduction of bureaucracy, enabling communities to become more involved in measures.

Dig Deeper

Bryne, T. (2000) *Local Government in Britain.* London: Penguin Books, 7th ed.

McKay, D. (2013) *American Politics and Society.* Chichester, West Sussex: John Wiley and Sons, 8th ed.

Panara, C. and Varney, M. (2013) *Local Government in Europe: the Fourth Level in the EU Multi-Layered System.* Abingdon, Oxfordshire: Routledge.

Watts, D. (2006) *Understanding American Government and Politics.* Manchester: Manchester University Press, 2nd ed.

Fact-check

1 A federal political structure is one in which:
   a Political power is centralized in the hands of central government
   b Political power is determined through the process of elections
   c Political power is shared between the national government and sub-national bodies such as states
   d Political power is shared between a president and a prime minister

2 A political structure in which independent nations or states voluntarily set up a mechanism to secure common goals but without giving power to this body is termed:
   a A talking shop
   b Federalism
   c A unitary state
   d A confederation

3 Another term for consociationalism is:
   a A codified constitution
   b Federalism
   c Coalition government
   d Power sharing

4 The transfer of power from a superior to an inferior political authority is termed:
   a Regionalism
   b Federalism
   c Devolution
   d Home rule

5 In England and Wales, an elected member of a local authority is termed:
   a An alderman
   b A councillor
   c A mayor
   d A commissioner

6 In England and Wales, the revenue that local government collects from local residents is known as:
- **a** The Rates
- **b** The Council Tax
- **c** The Poll Tax
- **d** Income Tax

15

The nation state in the modern world

In this chapter we will consider the global environment in which nation states exist within the contemporary world and the extent that this has eroded national sovereignty. In particular, we will examine the institutions and operations of the European Union as an example of the importance now played by supranational bodies and also consider how the informal 'special relationship' between the UK and USA influences foreign policy.

Sovereignty and nationalism

Key idea (1)

The study of politics extends beyond an examination of individual nation states and embraces international relations, focusing on the inter-relationships between them.

In the previous chapters we have considered the political arrangements that exist within individual states. In this chapter we turn our attention to the relationships that exist between nation states. This aspect of the study of politics is referred to as international relations.

SOVEREIGNTY

Key idea (2)

The term 'sovereignty' implies a nation possesses the power to control its own domestic affairs and external relationships, and is not subservient to external forms in these areas of activity.

Sovereignty entails a body possessing unrestricted power. The concept of sovereignty developed from the Peace of Westphalia in 1648. This was the name given to a collection of treaties that ended a series of wars in Europe between 1618 and 1648 (an event referred to as the 'Thirty Years' War'). Sovereignty denoted that rulers of states possess control over their country's internal and external affairs. The concept of the nation state developed from this period. In contemporary politics, sovereignty has two dimensions. These are internal and external sovereignty.

Internal sovereignty refers to the existence of a supreme legal or political authority within a state that has the power to make decisions that are binding on all of its citizens. Internal sovereignty is divided within federal states. In countries which include America, Australia, Canada and Germany, the national government may enact legislation in certain areas of activity while other matters are regulated by the states or provinces into which these countries are divided. In unitary countries such as the UK and France, sovereignty is not divided, but resides in the institutions of national government that have the sole right to regulate these nations' affairs.

External sovereignty refers to a nation's self-determination and suggests that a state has the ability to control its own affairs without interference from outside bodies and countries. External sovereignty has been eroded by the increasing interdependence of nations which has arisen as the result of a number of factors that we will discuss in more detail in the following sections.

Spotlight

The view that sovereign states were the key actors in the international system was associated with realist theories of international relations. These realist theories saw states being motivated by the rational concern of advancing the national interest.

NATIONALISM

Key idea (3)

The desire of a nation (or an area within an existing nation state) to obtain sovereignty is often fuelled by nationalist sentiments based upon factors that include a separate language or distinct cultural identity.

Nationalism is a sentiment underpinning a people's desire to exercise control over their own political affairs. Those who live in a particular locality are united by a desire to be independent of other nations and live under a political system that they control. This unity may be based on a common ethnic identity or cultural heritage (including language and literature), or be grounded upon a sense of shared citizenship which may transcend ethnic or cultural differences. 'Nation state' is the term used to describe the political community that arises when the boundaries of nation and state are the same.

Nationalism may justify attempts by conquered or colonized countries, or those dominated either economically or politically by another country, to shake off the burden of foreign domination and attain self-government. Post-war history contains numerous examples of national identity being the motivating force for movements seeking the establishment of self-governing states. It inspired independence movements in African countries directed against European colonial powers. In Latin America, it was the main force behind anti-American movements in many countries, including Cuba and Nicaragua. The desire to establish a self-governing state has considerable influence on the contemporary politics of Canada and Spain where national minorities (the Quebeckers, Catalans and Basques) desire self-government. In the UK, the demand for Scottish and Welsh home rule resulted in devolution legislation being enacted in 1998.

Nationalism may be a progressive force when it seeks the liberation of subjugated peoples from oppressive, foreign rule. However, it may also be a reactionary movement. The love of one's country (or patriotism) may lead to the hatred of other foreign peoples or races, termed xenophobia. For example, nationalism was the justification for 'ethnic cleansing' (or genocide) carried out in Bosnia- Herzegovina by the Bosnian Serbs against the Bosnian Muslims in 1992 and subsequently by the Serbs against ethnic Albanians in Kosovo in 1999.

Threats to external sovereignty

Key idea (4)

A nation's ability to control its own affairs was eroded by developments that took place in the twentieth century that included the rise of supranational governmental institutions such as the EU and the emergence of a global economy.

It is doubtful whether any state has ever enjoyed total control over the conduct of its affairs. The nineteenth-century nation state perhaps went some way to approximating this ideal, but such countries were often required to pay regard to outside factors when administering their internal or external activities. In the twentieth century, sovereignty is even less of a reality: the ability of any state to function autonomously has been jeopardized by a wide range of factors. These include the development of organizations that seek to secure common approaches by member states to contemporary issues and problems, and the emergence of globalization and the global economy.

SUPRANATIONAL GOVERNMENTAL INSTITUTIONS

Many countries affiliate to governmental organizations that operate across national boundaries. The European Union (which we consider later in this chapter) is an example of such a body. Membership of supranational institutions places limitations on the activities of the member countries whose sovereignty is thus restricted by the expectation that they will adhere to the policies determined by the central decision-making machinery of the organization. The refusal of any member country to do so may result in the deployment of sanctions against it.

ORGANIZATIONS TO SECURE INTERGOVERNMENTAL CO-OPERATION

In addition to supranational organizations that exercise governmental powers across national boundaries, other international bodies primarily serve as forums for co-operation, often in limited areas of state activity. These bodies may operate on a worldwide basis (such as the United Nations or the Commonwealth) or be confined to countries in specific regions of the world (such as the North Atlantic Treaty Organization). These organizations may seek to influence the direction of member (and sometimes non-member) countries through the application of moral pressure, sanctions or force.

Trade embargoes are a potent sanction that international bodies may use to force a government to change the direction of its politics. They may also utilize military intervention to accomplish their aims. The use of ground troops in Bosnia under the auspices of the North Atlantic Treaty Organization (NATO) in 1995 sought to ensure the successful implementation of the Peace Agreement following its endorsement by the presidents of Croatia, Bosnia and Serbia.

▶ The United Nations (UN)

The UN was formally established in 1945 by the leading nations that emerged victorious from World War II. Their main motivation was to prevent future wars by promoting the ideal of collective security. The UN is a global association of governments *facilitating cooperation in international law, international security, economic development and social equity*. In 2014 it consisted of 193 member states.

The key governing bodies of the UN include the UN General Assembly, the UN Security Council, and the International Court of Justice. The organization is headed by the UN Secretary-General who is the chief administrator of the UN Secretariat. Its budget is derived from assessed and voluntary contributions of the member states. The Security Council is charged with maintaining world peace and security. It consists of fifteen members (five of whom – the USA, UK, France, the Russian Federation and China – are permanent members with a veto power over Security Council decisions). It has the ability to ask member states to provide armed forces or other forms of assistance to secure peace and security.

The UN performs a number of important roles. UN peacekeepers have been sent to areas of conflict throughout the world. The organization provides humanitarian aid and seeks to promote human development through a very wide range of specialist agencies that include the World Health Organization, the UN Educational, Scientific and Cultural Organization, the International Labour Organization, the International Monetary Fund, and the World Trade Organization. The UN also helps to negotiate international treaties and agreements and may reconcile disputes between members using the International Court of Justice.

GLOBALIZATION AND THE EMERGENCE OF A GLOBAL ECONOMY

Globalization refers to the increasing integration of nations and the people who live within them. It affects a wide range of issues including economic, social, cultural and political affairs (especially the spread of liberal democratic political values). A particularly important aspect of globalization is the emergence of a global economy.

Globalization is not a new phenomenon and emerged towards the end of the nineteenth century. Its pace then slowed down, but picked up again in the latter decades of the twentieth century in response to neo-liberalism: *'Neoliberal policies include privatizing public industries, opening markets to foreign investment and competition, creating fiscal austerity programs to curtail government spending, removing controls on capital flows, reducing tariffs and other trade barriers, and ending government protections for local industries'* (Engler, 2007: 151). These policies were promoted *'by international institutions such as the Organisation for Economic Cooperation and Development (OECD), the World Bank (WB), the International Monetary Fund (IMF), and the World Trade Organization (WTO)'* (Joyce and Wain, 2014: 6).

Engler, S. (2007) Defining the Anti-globalization Movement in G. Anderson and H. Kerr (eds) *Encyclopedia of Activism and Social Justice*. London: Sage, pp 150–155.

Joyce, P. and Wain, N. (2014) *Palgrave Dictionary of Public Order Policing, Protest and Political Violence*. Basingstoke: Palgrave / Macmillan.

The concept of a global economy rejects the view that the economies of nation states can be seen as independent entities and instead places emphasis on their inter-relationships. This was apparent in connection with the worldwide recession of 2008 onwards when economic difficulties which were partly attributed to reckless borrowing and speculation by banks and other financial institutions had impacts that went beyond the boundaries of individual nations. Globalization emphasizes that the success or failure of the economy of one nation, or bloc of nations, has a major impact on countries throughout the world: the decline of international trade, for example, will cause unemployment in countries that rely on exporting manufactured goods.

Below, we consider forces that have underpinned the development of a global economy to the detriment of national sovereignty.

▶ International trade

The global economy was initially driven by post-World War II attempts to promote trade between nations in which the General Agreement on Tariffs and Trade (GATT) played an influential role. This was a multilateral treaty negotiated in 1947 that sought to reduce trade barriers and promote a common code of conduct in international trade. It led to goods and capital being more easily transferred across national boundaries, resulted in the emergence of world money markets, and aided the development of transnational corporations. It was succeeded by the World Trade Organization, a permanent trade-monitoring body, in 1995.

International trading agreements have placed restraints on the actions of national governments. Membership of regional trading blocs, such as the EU, or wider arrangements, such as GATT and the WTO, limit the ability of member countries to pursue policies such as tariff protection against other participating nations. Broader agreements have also been made to regulate the world's trading system through international actions that included the 1944 Bretton Woods Agreement (which sought to create an international monetary system until its collapse in 1971) and the Group of Seven (G-7) summit meetings consisting of America, the United Kingdom, France, Italy, Canada, Germany and Japan. These initiatives restrict the control that individual nations can exert over economic policies.

It has often been assumed that international trading agreements have a detrimental effect on the poorer nations, for example by enabling industrialized nations to advance rules of trade that are advantageous to themselves. However, global institutions such as the World Trade Organization have the ability to create economic growth for developing countries by insisting on more open trade. This situation may help to reduce the inequalities between rich and poor nations provided that the benefits of increased economic growth are fairly distributed.

▶ Multinational companies

The concentration of large-scale economic activity has resulted in the formation of multinational (or transnational) companies. These have their headquarters in one country but their commercial activities are conducted throughout the world. Incentives for them to do this include access to raw materials and (in the case of firms locating in the third world) the availability of cheap labour. Such multinational companies (many of which are American or Japanese owned) possess considerable influence over the operations of the government of the countries in which they invest, thereby undermining the economic and political independence of such countries. In return for providing jobs and revenue derived from taxing their operations, multinational companies may demand concessions from governments as the price for their investment in that country. They may seek direct or indirect control over a country's political system to ensure that government policy is compatible with the needs of the company.

Dependency

Dependency seeks to explain the unequal relationship that exists between first world countries over those in the third (or developing) world. It suggests that the overt political control formerly exercised by developed nations over their colonies (which were sometimes referred to as 'dependencies') has given way to a new form of dominance exerted over third world countries based on the economic power of the first world. Factors such as the superior market position of first world countries, and the reliance of the third world on foreign aid and development loans from the first world, form the basis for the economic imbalance between countries of the first and third world and from which the latter find escape hard.

Dependency suggests the existence of an economic form of colonialism that seeks to ensure that third world countries serve the economic interests of the industrially advanced nations by supplying raw materials required by the industries of the first world, and latterly by serving as a market for the goods they produce. This tends to distort the pattern of economic development in such countries, which is typically concentrated on agriculture and the mining of minerals to the detriment of the development of domestic manufacturing industry.

Dependency is buttressed by loans made available to third world countries by bodies such as the International Monetary Fund. The interest rates charged and the conditions stipulated by the lending body erode the sovereignty of the receiving country and may result in the pursuance of policies that are to the detriment of many of its inhabitants. The need to export agricultural produce to pay the interest on foreign loans may, for example, result in the local population suffering from hunger and starvation and place the country in a very weak position from which to pursue economic development.

THE END OF SOVEREIGNTY?

In the previous sections of this chapter we have documented some of the restrictions imposed on the freedom of action possessed by national governments. But it would be wrong to assert that nations now have no meaningful control over their internal or external affairs. For although national economies are subject to broad global considerations and restraints, individual governments retain the ability to manage their economies, at least in the short term. In many liberal democracies, incumbent governments will initiate policies such as taxation cuts or reductions in the rates of interest in order to court popularity with the electorate.

Although the economic policy of a nation may be subject to a wide range of external forces, it possesses freedom of action in other policy areas. Individual governments may further pursue actions regardless of the opinions of other countries. Further, sovereignty remains a term that enters into the rhetoric of political debate and influences political behaviour.

The European Union

Key idea (5)

The European Union is an important example of a supranational governmental body whose activities have considerably expanded since 1957.

The European Union (EU) is a supranational governmental body. Countries that join this organization forgo control over their own affairs in areas encompassed by its treaties. Decision making in these areas becomes a collective exercise involving representatives of all the member countries. The UK's voice in the EU, for example, is put forward by its 73 members of the European Parliament, one commissioner (who is nominated by the UK government), and the one vote it possesses in common with every other member in the Council of Ministers.

In the following section we briefly discuss the evolution of the EU and describe how its work is performed.

THE EVOLUTION OF THE EUROPEAN UNION

World War II provided a key motivating force for the movement towards closer co-operation between the countries of Europe. There was a desire by leading politicians from the victorious and defeated nations to establish institutions to avoid a further war in Europe. The first step towards co-operation was the establishment in 1951 of the European Coal and Steel Community. It was envisaged that the sharing of basic raw materials that were essential to the machinery of war would avoid outbreaks of hostilities. This initiative was followed in 1955 by the formation of the European Investment Fund. The body now known as the 'European Union' developed from an organization initially popularly known as the 'Common Market'. The key milestones that have shaped its development are described below.

The creation of what was initially referred to as the European Economic Community derived from experience of the Second World War and a desire to avert a future war of this nature – *'The Second World War was a catalyst for a renewed interest in European unity. It contributed to arguments that nationalism and nationalist rivalries, by culminating in war, had discredited and bankrupted the independent state as the foundation of political organization and international order, and that a replacement to the state had to be found in a comprehensive continental community'* (Urwin, 2010: 12).

Urwin, D. (2010) The European Community: From 1945 to 1985 in Cini, M. and Borragan, N. *European Union Politics.* Oxford: Oxford University Press, 4th ed., pp 11–25

THE TREATY OF ROME (1957)

This treaty established the European Economic Community (EEC) and Euratom (the European Atomic Energy Community). The EEC initially consisted of six countries (France, West Germany, Italy, the Netherlands, Belgium and Luxembourg). The UK, the Irish Republic and Denmark joined in 1973, Greece in 1981, Spain and Portugal in 1986 and Austria, Finland and Sweden in 1995.

THE SINGLE EUROPEAN ACT (1986)

This Act sought to remove obstacles to a frontier-free community by providing the legal framework to achieve a single market by 31 December 1992. This would entail the free movement of goods, services, capital and people between member states.

THE MAASTRICHT TREATY (1993)

This treaty (which is also known as the Treaty on European Union) was drawn up by the heads of member governments at a meeting of the European Council and sought to provide a legal basis for developments concerned with European political union, and economic and monetary union. The treaty laid down the conditions for member countries joining a single currency. These required a high degree of sustainable economic convergence measured by indicators that covered inflation, budget deficits, exchange rate stability (which would be guaranteed by membership of the Exchange Rate Mechanism) and long-term interest rates. Moves towards common foreign and security policies and an extension of responsibilities in areas which included justice, home affairs and social policy were also proposed.

The then Conservative government in the UK objected to the 'Social Chapter' designed to protect workers' rights, and had reservations concerning the terms and timing of monetary union. It thus signed the treaty only when it was agreed to exempt the UK from the former and leave parliament to determine the latter issue. It was further satisfied that the inclusion of the subsidiarity principle in the treaty would limit the scope of the future policy making by the EEC. Subsidiarity was the principle that decisions should be taken at the lowest possible level of the political system. Although this term was subject to diverse interpretations across Europe, it implied that member states remained responsible for areas that they could manage most effectively themselves, and that the EU would only act in those areas where member states were unable to function adequately. Other countries also experienced problems with this treaty. It was rejected in 1992 by a referendum in Denmark, a result that was reversed after this country succeeded in securing four opt-out provisions. In the UK, it was ratified by legislation in the form of the 1993 European Communities (Amendment) Act.

Following ratification of this Treaty in 1993, the term 'European Union' was employed, implying the creation of an organization that went beyond the original aims of the EEC.

THE LISBON TREATY (2009)

The negative views of a number of member states towards an EU constitution that had been agreed at the 2004 Brussels Summit resulted in it being substituted for a Treaty. This, the Treaty of Lisbon, came into force at the end of 2009. Unlike the constitution that would have replaced all earlier treaties, the Lisbon Treaty merely amended the earlier Treaties of Rome and Maastricht. However, the 2009 Treaty incorporated many of the provisions that had been put forward in the aborted constitution.

Its main provisions provided for the following arrangements:

- A president of the European Council who would serve for 2.5 years

- A High Representative who would give the EU more influence on the world stage

- The EU Commission would consist of 27 members (one for each member state); the accession of Croatia increased this number to 28. The Treaty initially mandated a reduction of the number of commissioners to two-thirds of member states from 2014 unless the Council decided otherwise. However, this was a key concern in the Irish referendum in 2008 in which the Treaty was rejected and led to an upwards revision to increase the number of Commissioners that was accepted by Irish voters in a second referendum in 2009

- Between 2014 and 2017, a redistribution of voting weights between member states would be introduced: qualified majority voting would entail a 'double majority' based upon support from 55 per cent of the member states who represented 65 per cent of the total population of the EU

- New powers would be given to the European Parliament and the European Court of Justice affecting justice and home affairs

- The European Parliament would be placed on an equal footing with the Council in connection with most legislation that included the EU budget and agriculture: this was termed 'co-decision'

- National vetoes were removed in a number of areas that included fighting climate change, energy policy, security, and emergency aid. Unanimous support remained required for policies affecting taxation, foreign policy, defence and social security

Although the Treaty was designed to make the EU more democratic, efficient and transparent, critics argued that it sought to advance a federalist agenda that would undermine national sovereignty.

The main institutions of the European Union

THE COMMISSION

The Commission is based in Brussels and currently consists of 28 members appointed by the governments of each member state. Each commissioner serves a five-year term, which may be renewable. On appointment, commissioners take an oath not to promote national interests. This oath then provides the EU with its most obvious supranational dimension. Decisions are taken collectively by what is termed the 'College of Commissioners'. The Commission is headed by a President of the European Commission who is elected by the European Parliament and serves a five-year term of office. The commissioners are allocated specific responsibilities (termed 'portfolios') by the president. They are served by a civil service (around 23,000) organized into departments, termed 'Directorates General'. The Commission provides political leadership to the EU and performs a number of key tasks related to this role. These include:

▶ Initiation of policy: The Commission is the only EU body that has the right of legislative initiative to propose laws to the EU Parliament or the EU Council of Ministers

▶ Implementation of EU policies: Laws passed by the Council of Ministers are passed to the Commission for implementation which thus serves as the EU's executive arm. This role often includes enacting delegated or secondary legislation. Much policy is not directly administered through the Commission's civil service, but is discharged by the member states

▶ Financial: The Commission is responsible for preparing draft budget proposals that àre submitted to the EU Council of Ministers and EU Parliament

- ▸ Supervisory functions: This body also serves as a watchdog and may draw the attention of the Court of Justice when EU law is not being implemented.

- ▸ Representing the EU on an international stage: The Commission may present a unified EU-wide voice on key issues in forums such as the World Trade Organization

THE COUNCIL OF MINISTERS

The Council is also based in Brussels and is composed of ministers of the member states whose membership varies according to the topic under discussion. It is the EU's supreme law-making (legislative) body.

When approved by the Council, legislation becomes part of the national law of member states and it is in this sense that membership of the EU results in a loss of sovereignty. Initially, sovereignty was safeguarded by the practice of unanimity, whereby all members of the Council were required to approve a proposal in order for it to be adopted. This effectively gave individual governments the power to veto proposals and thereby preserve national interests. Since the mid-1980s, however, there has been a movement towards taking decisions on the basis of qualified majority voting, which erodes the single-nation veto. The Single European Act, the Maastricht Treaty, and the Nice Summit extended the areas that could be determined in this manner, and the Treaty of Lisbon provided for a new procedure governing this process.

THE EUROPEAN COUNCIL

The European Council consists of heads of state or government of EU member states and operated informally until formalized in the Treaty of Lisbon. Its meetings are commonly referred to as EU Summits. It has no formal legislative power but acts as a strategic (and crisis-solving) body that provides the union with general political directions and priorities. One example of this was the meeting held on 31 July 2014 to strengthen sanctions against Russia in the wake of the shooting down of Flight MH17 over Ukraine. Any decisions reached at its meetings would require ratification by the Council of Ministers.

THE EUROPEAN PARLIAMENT

The European Parliament meets in Brussels and Strasbourg and consists of representatives who (since 1979) have been directly elected by the citizens of each member country, the number of representatives being determined by population. MEPs serve for a term of five years. For much of its existence the European Parliament was regarded as an advisory body, a 'talking shop' that considered proposals put forward by the Commission but which exercised little power over decisions. However, the Single European Act and particularly the Maastricht Treaty sought to provide it with a more vigorous role. Its new responsibilities included the right to reject the EU budget, to be consulted on the appointment of commissioners, and the ability to play a more significant role in the law-making process. In 1998, it rejected the EU budget in protest against accusations of fraud and mismanagement by the Commission, and in 1999 proposed that individual commissioners alleged to be responsible for this situation should resign. The dispute between the EU Parliament and Commission resulted in the collective resignation of the latter in March 1999.

The EU Parliament makes wide use of committees, whose roles include considering the content of proposed EU laws. A key deficiency in the Parliament's powers concerns its lack of control over the Council of Ministers which the co-decision provisions in the 2009 Lisbon Treaty sought to address.

EUROPEAN ECONOMIC AND SOCIAL COMMITTEE (EESC)

The European Economic and Social Committee was established in 1957 under the Treaty of Rome as a forum to discuss issues regarding the single market. The EESC gives Europe's interest groups – trade unionists, employers, farmers, etc. – a formal mechanism through which they can put their views to the Commission, Council and Parliament regarding draft EU legislation. It has around 350 members drawn from economic and social interest groups across Europe. Members are nominated by national governments and appointed by the Council of the EU for a renewable five-year term. Members of the EESC belong to one of three groups – employers, employees, key interests (such as farmers and professional associations) – and the number of members is related to a nation's population size.

THE EUROPEAN COURT OF JUSTICE

The Court of Justice (not to be confused with the European Court of Human Rights) sits in Luxembourg and is staffed by judges and advocates drawn from member countries. They serve for six years. The main purpose of the Court is to ensure that EU law is adhered to within member countries. Disputes between member states, between the European Union and member states, between individuals and the European Union, or between the institutions of the EU are referred to this court. It has the power to declare unlawful any national law that contravenes European law, and also has the power to fine companies found to be in breach of such legislation. A number of national courts (including those of France and the United Kingdom) have upheld the view that European law has precedence over national law.

Key policies of the EU

Key idea (7)

The EU is responsible for a number of common policies. In this section we will briefly discuss some of the main ones.

THE COMMON AGRICULTURAL POLICY (CAP)

This was introduced in 1960 as a key element in the newly formed Common Market in order to preserve the rural environment. It consists of agricultural subsidies paid from the EU budget, and is designed to guarantee a minimum price to farmers and also to subsidize the production of specific crops (although current developments seek to transfer these latter subsidies to ones based upon the area of land under cultivation). Minimum prices are ensured by a mechanism whereby if the internal market price of an agricultural product falls below a price that has been set in advance, the EU will buy it, which has the effect of causing its price to rise.

COMMON COMMERCIAL POLICY (CCP)

The main aim of the CCP was to establish a common trade policy throughout the EU, effectively creating a customs union between the member states. The CCP covers areas that include the adoption of a common external tariff (which applies to goods entering the EU from non-member countries), the conclusion of trade and tariff agreements with non-member states, and the formation of uniform policies in measures concerned with trade liberalization, export policy and the protection of trade (for example to combat dumping). The community's trade policy is determined by the Article 133 committee, which is composed of representatives from each member state.

ECONOMIC AND MONETARY UNION (EMU)

In 1977, a scheme known as the European Monetary System (EMS) was initiated that sought to produce currency stability in the EU by the introduction of the Exchange Rate Mechanism (ERM) and a quasi-currency known as the ECU (short for European Currency Unit).

The Maastricht Treaty included a commitment to establish an Economic and Monetary Union by 1999. A three-stage process to harmonize the economic policies of EU member states was adopted to achieve this. Stage 1 entailed the abolition of exchange controls and the entry of all currencies into the ERM. Although the UK had negotiated an opt-out of this policy, the UK entered the ERM in 1990, but left (against the background of currency speculation) in 1992 and has never rejoined. Other member states continued with stages 2 and 3 in the creation of the EMU by adopting policies that included replacing national currencies with the Euro in 2002, and enabling the European Central Bank to set interest rates.

UK Sovereignty and the EU

In the UK, allegations that sovereignty is threatened by the policies of the EU are a potent political argument that crosses traditional political divisions.

The United Kingdom Independence Party has recently emerged as a major political force. Its main policy is withdrawal from the EU, coupled with the repeal of the Human Rights Act and withdrawal from the European Convention on Human Rights.

In the 2014 elections to the European Parliament, UKIP received the greatest number of votes (27.49 per cent) of any British party and ended up with 24 MEPs (a net gain of 11 on its performance in the 2009 contests). The Party won seats in every region of Great Britain and won a seat in Scotland. The present Prime Minister, David Cameron, has pledged that if he remained prime minister following the 2015 UK general election, he would negotiate reforms of the EU and then hold a referendum by the end of 2017 on an in–out basis; that is, do we stay in a reformed EU or do we leave it?

EU–USA relationships

Key idea (8)

A key issue affecting international relations in the twenty-first century concerns the relationship between America and the EU.

The Cold War ensured that Europe would exert a considerable influence on American foreign policy decisions since it acted as a buffer against communism. This situation meant that Europe could rely on American involvement to deal with problems that arose there. However, the end of the Cold War has meant that Europe is less strategically important to America. New centres of conflict (in particular in the Middle East) have made it important to develop and consolidate alternative alliances (especially with Israel) and it is unlikely that America can be relied upon to respond to European conflicts in the manner in which it did in the past. Disputes have also surfaced between the EU and USA on matters such as trade, climate change, and the 2003 invasion of Iraq.

It has been alleged that Europe and America have increasingly developed alternative views of the world – an opinion summarized by Robert Kagan's assertion that '*Americans are from Mars and Europeans are from Venus*'. Although this may overstate the dissimilarities existing in the foreign policy stances of the EU and America (for example, the Spanish Government offered America the use of military bases on Spanish soil in order to mount retaliation following terrorist attacks on 11 September 2001, and a number of EU countries supported the Bush administration's stance over Iraq in 2003), it does suggest that the EU will not be able to rely so consistently on American aid to respond to problems that occur in Europe as has been the case since 1945.

THE USA–UK 'SPECIAL RELATIONSHIP'

Key idea (9)

The UK and USA have traditionally enjoyed a close relationship that has been maintained in recent years, especially in connection with the war against terrorism.

An important underpinning to post-war global foreign policy has been the relationship struck between America and the UK. The desire to sustain this relationship may result in UK leaders endorsing actions undertaken by America which are opposed by many of her European neighbours.

The origins of the term 'friendly relationship' date from a speech given by Winston Churchill in Fulton, Missouri, in 1946 in which (in the context of the rise of communism and the descent of the 'iron curtain') he referred to the 'traditional association of the English-speaking people'. The term 'special relationship' was used on that occasion to refer to the friendship that existed between the British Commonwealth and Empire, and the USA, in particular in the area of military co-operation.

The special relationship between the two countries has not consistently led each to embrace a common political approach to world problems. The military invasion of Egypt in 1956 by British and French forces in response to the nationalization of the British-owned Suez Canal provoked American opposition and strained the relationships between the USA and UK. The Argentinian invasion of the Falkland Islands in 1982 (which resulted in a British task force being dispatched to liberate them) placed America in a difficult position which made it impossible for President Reagan to immediately endorse the British position. The administration of President George W.

Bush also proved unresponsive to pressure by the British Prime Minister, Tony Blair, to sign up to the Kyoto Protocol on the emission of greenhouse gases.

In 1946 the British statesman and war-time Prime Minister, Winston Churchill, drew attention to the *growing challenge and peril to Christian civilisation* posed by communist parties. In particular he pointed to the Soviet domination of Eastern Europe, stating that *From Stettin in the Baltic to Trieste in the Adriatic, an iron curtain has descended across the Continent. Behind that line lie all the capitals of the ancient states of Central and Eastern Europe. Warsaw, Berlin, Prague, Vienna, Budapest, Belgrade, Bucharest and Sofia, all these famous cities and the populations around them lie in what I must call the Soviet sphere, and all are subject in one form or another, not only to Soviet influence but to a very high and, in many cases, increasing measure of control from Moscow* (Churchill, 1946). This speech is seen as an important landmark in defining divisions which underpinned what became known as 'the Cold War'.

Churchill, W. (1946) *The Sinews of Peace*. Speech delivered at Westminster College, Fulton, Missouri 5 March. [Online] *http://history1900s.about.com/od/churchillwinston/a/Iron-Curtain.htm* [Accessed 25 August 2014].

In particular, the emergence of the EU has also posed the dilemma as to whether the future direction of British foreign policy should be orientated towards its European neighbours rather than America (or perhaps to suggest that Britain can act as a bridge between the EU and USA). However, the special relationship has been reinvigorated as a response to terrorist actions associated with fundamentalist Islamic groups in the early years of the twenty-first century.

The UK–USA Special Relationship

Following Churchill's 'iron curtain' speech in 1946, the term 'special relationship' has subsequently been used in connection with the cordial relationships that exist between the USA and UK in a number of areas – political, diplomatic, military, intelligence sharing, cultural, and economic – and has been underpinned by the good relationships that have existed between some USA and UK leaders (most notably between Ronald Reagan and Margaret Thatcher, and also between George W. Bush and Tony Blair).

Terrorist attacks in New York and Washington on 11 September 2001 added to the vitality of the USA–UK special relationship. Following these attacks, Tony Blair visited America and the President informed Congress that 'America has no truer friend than Great Britain'. Subsequently, Blair devoted a considerable amount of effort to secure international support for military action to be taken against Iraq. British troops played a significant role in the invasion of that country in 2003 and in the subsequent policing of it, and have also played an active role in Afghanistan. Co-operation has also been evidenced in the 2003 USA–UK Extradition Treaty which was designed to speed up the extradition of terrorist suspects. However, critics of the special relationship assert that British support for American foreign policy is militarily insignificant, that its main purpose is to provide USA actions with a degree of international legitimacy, and that it restricts the development of new UK alliances.

Dig Deeper

Axford, B. (1996) *The Global System – Economics, Politics and Culture*. Cambridge: Polity Press.

Dumbrell, J. (2006) *A Special Relationship: Anglo-American Relations from the Cold War to Iraq*. Basingstoke: Palgrave / Macmillan, 2nd ed.

McCormick, J. (2011) *Understanding the EU: A Concise Introduction*. Basingstoke: Palgrave / Macmillan, 5th ed.

Nugent, N. (2010) *The Government and Politics of the EU*. Basingstoke: Palgrave / Macmillan, 7th ed.

Pinder, J. and Usherwood, S. (2013) *The EU: A Very Short Introduction*. Oxford: Oxford University Press.

Fact-check

1 The concept that the rulers of a country possessed total control over its internal and external political affairs is termed:
   a Federalism
   b Nationalism
   c Sovereignty
   d Home rule

2 The term 'xenophobia' means:
   a Hatred of one's country
   b Hatred or dislike against people from other countries or races
   c A desire for liberation from foreign rule
   d A desire by a ruler to conquer neighbouring countries

3 What body was set up in 1945 to promote collective security and thereby prevent future wars:
   a The International Monetary Fund
   b The Common Market
   c The International Court of Justice
   d The United Nations

4 What organization was created by the 1957 Treaty of Rome:
   a The European Court of Human Rights
   b The European Economic Community
   c The World Trade Organization
   d The North Atlantic Treaty Organization

5 What treaty was responsible for establishing the European Union:
   a the 1993 Maastricht Treaty
   b the 1997 Treaty of Amsterdam
   c the 2003 Treaty of Nice
   d the 2009 Lisbon Treaty

6 The supreme law-making body in the European Union is:
   a The European Parliament
   b The Council of Ministers
   c The European Council
   d The European Court of Justice

16

International terrorism

Events that took place in America in 2001, in Madrid in 2004, and London in 2005 provided all of us with evidence of the role played by terrorism in contemporary world politics and the extent to which terrorism is a key issue affecting the Western World in the twenty-first century. In this chapter we will consider what is understood by the term 'terrorism', how terrorism seeks to achieve a political objective, and the global nature of contemporary terrorism. In particular we will consider changes in the nature of terrorism and discuss the dilemmas that confront Western nations in effectively combating it where a balance has to be struck in balancing the need to provide security to the population with the placing of restrictions on civil and political liberties.

Definition of terrorism

Key idea (1)

Terrorism is a difficult term to define precisely. It is often applied in a negative way by a state against groups whose actions it wishes to condemn. The label of 'terrorist' is designed to legitimize coercive responses to the group.

What is terrorism? The operational definition used by the American Federal Bureau of Investigation in the 1990s defined terrorism as *'The use of serious violence against persons or property, or threat to use such violence, to intimidate or coerce a government, the public or any section of the public, in order to promote political, social or ideological objectives'* (Lloyd 1996, para 5.22).

In the UK, the current definition of terrorism is provided by the 2000 Terrorism Act (which was slightly amended by the 2006 Terrorism Act). This legislation defined terrorism as the use or threat of action which *'involves serious violence against a person, involves serious damage to property, endangers a person's life, other than that of the person committing the action, creates a serious risk to the health or safety of the public or a section of the public, or is designed seriously to interfere*

> *with or seriously to disrupt an electronic system'.* However, in order for actions of this nature to be deemed to constitute terrorism, it is also necessary that the use or threat of action *'is designed to influence the government or an international governmental organisation or to intimidate the public or a section of the public'* and the use or threat of action *'is made for the purpose of advancing a political, religious or ideological cause'* (Terrorism Act 2000: Part 1 Section 1).
>
> Lloyd, Lord (1996) Inquiry into Legislation Against Terrorism. London: TSO, Cmnd 3420.
>
> Terrorism Act 2000 (c11) London TSO.

Terrorism entails the use (or the threat to use) of some form of physical force that is applied by a group against those whose actions are disapproved of. The target of this violence may be governments (where the aim may be to change the direction of public policy or to force the government from office) or organizations that operate in the private sector (where the objective is to alter commercial or operating practices). Terrorism empowers those who engage in it and even if their objectives are not met, the violence with which it is associated may temporarily achieve empowerment by enabling participants to violent actions to feel that they have 'got one over' on their enemies.

Spotlight

The lack of precision concerning the definition of terrorism suggests that the term is often used subjectively, determined by our own political perspective or our own views as to what is right or wrong behaviour. The Civil War that has raged in Syria since 2011 illustrates this dilemma well – the Syrian government regards the rebels as terrorists while much of the outside world views them as legitimate opponents of a tyrannical regime which has killed large numbers of its own people.

One important aspect of terrorism (and often a defining feature when the state is on the receiving end of violence) is that terrorists do not seek a head-on confrontation with the police or army (indeed, they may be too weak to do so). Instead they seek to achieve their aims by conducting a war of attrition (whose conduct is not constrained by the conventions of war) that seeks to wear down the state and its law enforcement agencies.

Terrorist aims and objectives

Key idea (2)

The use of violence has been associated with a wide range of political objectives. It may seek to secure changes in public or commercial policy, to be a mechanism through which to initiate regime change or to rid a country from rule by an occupying power. State-sponsored violence may also constitute terrorism.

Terrorism has been used by groups with a diverse range of objectives. An important factor that links these groups, however, is that terrorism courts publicity, the level of which is influenced by the spectacular nature of the violence that takes place. Let us consider some of the objectives that have been advanced through the use of violent means.

CHANGES IN THE DIRECTION OF PUBLIC POLICY

Terrorism may seek a change in the direction of public policy. For example, the campaign in the UK to secure votes for women that was mounted by the suffragettes in the early twentieth century involved acts of violence, some of which could be labelled as 'terrorism'.

Alternatively, violence may be directed against business enterprises where it seeks to alter the practices performed by commercial organizations or individuals who carry out actions that are disapproved of by those who carry out violence. Examples of this include the freeing of animals from medical research laboratories by animal rights activists or the destruction of genetically modified crops by environmental activists. These examples illustrate the difficulty in precisely distinguishing between terrorism and direct action, and the subjective nature of the definition of terrorism whereby one person's terrorist is another person's freedom fighter.

REGIME CHANGE

Terrorism may alternatively be designed to advance radical political changes that were historically associated with replacing absolutist monarchies with liberal democratic political structures and (during the twentieth century) to overthrow capitalism in favour of socialism. In the twenty-first century, terrorism has been influenced by religious impulses and carried out by Islamist fundamentalist groups, in particular, al-Qaeda. Violence of this nature (which we will consider below in connection with the debate of 'old' versus 'new' terrorism) may seek to alter the direction of the foreign policy of Western nations, or serve as the means to create a new society based on Islamic principles.

TERRORISM INSPIRED BY NATIONALISM

Terrorism is sometimes carried out by groups inspired by nationalist impulses. Their objectives range from seeking a greater degree of autonomy from the central state to the desire to create a self-governing independent state, totally divorced from the rule of the country that currently exercises powers of government over them. Nationalist terrorist groups may also seek to rid their country from the rule of an occupying foreign power that exercises political and economic domination over its citizens.

Violence that seeks to achieve a country's liberation from foreign rule may possess psychological benefits for those who carry out such actions in addition to being practical means to achieve this political objective. It has been argued that such violence may fulfill the purpose of a *'cleansing force'* which *'frees the native from his inferiority complex and from his despair and inaction; it makes him fearless and restores his self-respect'* (Fanon, 1961: 73–4). This heightened sense of self-esteem may provide the basis for future and bolder revolutionary acts.

Fanon, F. (1961) *The Wretched of the Earth.* Harmondsworth: Penguin edition, published in 1982.

Those who engage in acts of nationalist-inspired violence reject the label of terrorism and view themselves as freedom fighters, seeking to replace what they regard as a repressive and illegitimate form of government with one that will enjoy the consent of those who live in the region or country from where the group derives. For this reason, nationalist-inspired terrorist groups frequently enjoy support from populations who share their objectives and approve of their use of violence to attain them. Below we will consider in more detail the activities of the Basque Separatist Group *Euskadi Ta Azkatasuna*, (usually referred to as ETA).

Euskadi Ta Azkatasuna (ETA)

A nationalist group that has used terrorist tactics to achieve the goal of liberation is *Euskadi Ta Azkatasuna*, (ETA, or 'Basque Homeland and Freedom'), which seeks full independence from Spain for the Greater Basque Country. The aims of ETA and the PIRA are similar in nature and the two groups established contact during the 1970s.

ETA was formed in 1959 and originated as a student protest movement whose main concern was to promote Basque language and culture in response to the repressive policies adopted towards the Basque Country by Spain's military dictatorship headed by General Franco, which included banning the Basque language. It subsequently evolved into a paramilitary group seeking independence for the Basque country. Franco's death in 1975 resulted in a transition in Spain to liberal democracy, and in 1979, 17 regions (or autonomous communities) were set up, each with an assembly and a president. However, although these new arrangements resulted in the grant of a considerable degree of autonomy to the Basque region (which includes control over policing, education and the power to collect taxes), they fell short of the full independence to which ETA aspires.

In order to achieve this aim, campaigns of violence have been waged, punctuated by ceasefires (in 1989, 1996, 1998 and 2006) and lengthy cessations of action. The most recent ceasefire was declared on 5 September 2010, and in January 2011 a permanent ceasefire was announced.

The tactics used by ETA have included selective violence directed at members of Spain's national police force, the Guardia Civil, and politicians who are opposed to Basque separatism. Its most notable act of this nature during the period of Franco's dictatorship was the assassination in Madrid of Admiral Luis Carrero Blanco in December 1973 by a bomb planted in a sewer over which his car passed. Blanco was President of the Government and Franco's chosen successor. Other attacks included the bombing of the Plaza Republica Dominicana in July 1986 which killed 12 members of the Guardia Civil and injured 50.

A highly publicized attack was the July 1997 kidnapping in Ermua of Miguel Angel Blanco, a Popular Party councillor in the Basque region. ETA demanded the transmission to prisons in the Basque region of its 460 prisoners held in gaols across Spain as a condition for his release. When this demand was not met, Blanco was shot twice in the head and died from his injuries. It was estimated that over 6 million people across Spain demonstrated to demand an end to ETA violence. This led ETA to call a ceasefire in 1998, which was ended in December 1999 as the government refused to discuss ETA's demands for Basque independence.

Indiscriminate violence has also been used by ETA including an attack on the Hipercor shopping centre of Barcelona in June 1987 which killed 21 persons and injured over 40. A number of random attacks were also launched in 2001, which included a car bomb attack in Madrid in November that injured 65 people. Later attacks of this nature included the bombing of a car park at Madrid airport in December 2006.

This campaign has led to in excess of 820 deaths in the past 40 years, and in the late 1970s an average of 100 people were killed each year.

ETA is banned under anti-terrorist legislation in Spain, France, the UK and America. The success enjoyed by law enforcement agencies against ETA (especially in France in addition to Spain) has led to it changing its structure, becoming a more decentralized organization operating under the umbrella of a small directorial committee known as *Zuzendaritza Batzordea*.

Like the Provisional IRA (PIRA), ETA has a political wing which has operated under the names of Herri Batasuna, Euskal Herritarrok and Batasuna. Unlike the situation in Northern Ireland, however (affecting Sinn Féin), the political wing has been banned in Spain since a 2003 decision by the Supreme Court of Spain relating to the *Ley de Partidos Políticos* which banned political parties which supported violence or were involved with terrorist groups.

STATE-SPONSORED VIOLENCE

Although states are frequently on the receiving end of terrorist campaigns, they may conduct violence of this nature themselves against their external or internal enemies. Death squads that eliminate internal opposition to a regime are an example of state-sponsored violence. These are often associated with authoritarian societies, although liberal democracies have also used such tactics against groups associated with terrorism.

Above, we considered the Spanish separatist group ETA. The campaign against ETA made use of violent methods, including the 'dirty war' waged by death squads supported by Spanish security forces and intelligence services during the 1970s and early 1980s, and later in the 1980s by a paramilitary group, *Grupos Antiterroristas de Liberación* (GAL) (Anti-terrorist Liberation Groups) also connected to the Spanish authorities. Until the end of its activities in 1987, GAL was responsible for kidnappings, torture and assassinations of suspected ETA members.

Terrorist tactics

Key idea (3)

The violence with which terrorism is associated takes various forms. Two major tactics are selective violence and indiscriminate terrorism.

The violence that is associated with terrorism is diverse and includes selective (or targeted) violence, indiscriminate violence, and attacks mounted on economic targets. Tactics that include hostage-taking and hijacking may be used selectively (targeting specific individuals) or indiscriminately (directed at random members of the general public). The main aims of these tactics are to secure funds through ransom demands, or to trade the victims of such activities for terrorists who have been imprisoned.

SELECTIVE VIOLENCE

The target of selective violence carried out by terrorists is typically those whose activities are deemed essential to the functioning of the state: politicians, judges, soldiers, and police officers are frequently targeted through activities ranging from kidnapping to murder. One example of this was the assassination of two senior members of the Royal Ulster Constabulary (Chief Superintendent Harry Breen and Superintendent Bob Buchanan) by the IRA in South Armagh in 1989.

The prime aims of selective violence are to incapacitate the operations of the state (so that it cannot govern) and to undermine a government's resolve to continue with a course of action upon which it was embarked, since, *'the required outlay becomes so great that the political object is no longer equal in value [and] ... must be given up'* (Clausewitz, 1832). This aim has particular relevance to campaigns seeking to liberate a country from foreign occupation. A secondary aim of selective violence is to *'stimulate the political will and resolve of those who perpetrate it by demonstrating the extent to which the state and its key personnel are vulnerable to a concerted campaign of violence'* (Joyce, 2002: 159–160), thus encouraging further acts of violence against its functionaries.

von Clausewitz, C. (1832) *On War.* Translated by J.J. Graham (1873) London: N. Trübner [Online] *http://www.clausewitz.com/readings/ OnWar1873/BK1ch02.html* [Accessed 28 December 2013].

Joyce, P. (2002) *The Politics of Protest. Extra-parliament Politics in Britain since 1970.* Basingstoke: Palgrave / Macmillan.

Selective violence may also be used by groups whose opponents are not associated with the state but who are responsible for performing actions of which they disapprove. One example of this is the violence displayed towards individuals and organizations that provide abortions which has taken place since the latter years of the twentieth century in America, Canada, Australia and New Zealand. This has included arson (directed against abortion clinics), and the kidnap, assault, attempted murder, and murder of those engaged in delivering abortion services. Groups that are involved in committing or advocating violence of this nature, which has been dubbed 'terrorism', include the Army of God in America.

INDISCRIMINATE VIOLENCE

Indiscriminate violence is directed against members of the general public in a random fashion and may take the form of bombs being planted in public places or facilities used by the general public or, more recently, being carried by suicide bombers. Modes of transportation have especially been the subject of this form of random violence, examples of which include the Madrid train bombings in 2004 and the London bombings in 2005, both events being associated with Islamic fundamentalist groups.

The indiscriminate use of violence seeks to cause a state of *'disorientation'* (Bowden, 1977: 284) in which people are unable to lead normal, everyday lives. In this sense it has been argued that *'the purpose of terrorism is not military victory, it is to terrorise, to change your behaviour if you're the victim by making you afraid of today, afraid of tomorrow and in diverse societies ... afraid of each other'* (Clinton, 2001).

This form of violence 'works' if an intimidated public (whose fear is underpinned by the perception that their government is failing in its prime purpose of safeguarding the lives of its citizens) put pressure on the government to concede to the terrorists' demands – *'therefore, by definition, a terror campaign cannot succeed unless we become its accomplices and out of fear, give in'* (Clinton, 2001).

Bowden, T. (1977) *Breakdown of Public Security; the Case of Ireland 1916–1921 and Palestine 1936–1939*. London: Sage.

Clinton, B. (2001) The Struggle for the Soul of the Twenty-first Century. *BBC Television, the Dimbleby Lecture*, screened 14 December. [Online] http:// australianpolitics.com/news/2001/01-12-14.shtml [Accessed 12 July 2009].

Indiscriminate violence may entail tremendous loss of life, as occurred in America on 11 September 2001 when four hijacked aircraft were deliberately crashed into the Twin Tower Buildings of New York's World Trade Center and the Pentagon Building in Washington DC. Almost 3,000 people were killed in these attacks and damage amounting to around $10 billion was caused.

Although weapons such as bombs can be made from material that is readily available (a mix of icing sugar and agricultural fertilizer formed the basic ingredients of some weapons used in Northern Ireland during the 'Troubles'), the ability to cause devastation on a large-scale has been aided through technological advances that includes explosives such as semtex, and through developments in communications such as the internet, enabling terrorists to strike anywhere in the world.

Terrorists are also associated with acts of violence directed at economic targets. Typically violence of this nature has been directed against property seen as essential to the nation's trading, business, or commercial life. One example of this was the 'commercial bombing campaign' waged by the Provisional IRA during the 1970s to discourage investment and destroy jobs in Northern Ireland in order to dissuade moderate nationalists from backing the political *status quo* there on the grounds that it secured good economic prospects.

Similarly, the IRA's bombing campaign on mainland Britain was directed at targets that sought to disrupt the tourist industry (such as the Tower of London bombing in 1976), the commercial life of the City of London (including the bombing of the Baltic Exchange in 1992 and Bishopsgate in 1993), and to cause damage and disruption in shopping centres (such as the IRA's bombing of Manchester City Centre in 1996). Violence of this nature may be designed to undermine the economic basis of approaches pursued by a government to 'buy' support for itself and its policies or (as with indiscriminate violence) to pressurize a government into making concessions to the demands of the terrorists.

Old versus new terrorism

Key idea (4)

In recent years, a distinction has been drawn between what is termed 'old' and 'new' terrorism.

Developments associated with globalization and technological developments affecting means of communication have helped to promote terrorism on the international stage. Thus the grievances of citizens in one country may result in acts of violence in another (perhaps carried out by a third party), especially when the policies pursued by a government or interests with which it is associated are deemed responsible for these problems. This has made terrorism different in character from earlier manifestations of violence of this nature.

The term 'new terrorism' has been utilized since the 1990s to indicate that the face of terrorism has changed. In particular, the 9/11 attacks provoked a more intense debate as to whether terrorism was different in nature to that which had existed before, a debate that identified al-Qaeda as the prototype of new terrorism underpinned by religious fanaticism.

The key features of new terrorism have been identified as *'structured in loose networks rather than organizational hierarchies'*, *'transnational, rather than localized in its reach'*, *'deliberately targeted at innocent civilians'*, *'motivated by religious fanaticism, rather than political ideology'* and *'aimed at causing maximum destruction'* (Gofas, 2012: 18). In particular, it has been argued that new terrorism is *'apocalyptic, catastrophic terrorism'* (Morgan, 2004: 29) in which extreme violence *'is viewed as an end in itself rather than the means to an end'* (Morgan, 2004: 30).

Gofas, A. (2012) 'Old' Versus 'New' Terrorism: What's in a Name? *Uluslararası İlişkiler.* 8 (32), Winter, pp 17–32. [Online] *http://www. academia.edu/3588549/Old_vs._New_Terrorism_Whats_in_a_Name*

Morgan, M. (2004) The Origins of the New terrorism. *Institute of Strategic Studies* [Online] *http://strategicstudiesinstitute.army.mil/pubs/ parameters/articles/04spring/morgan.pdf*

However, the extent to which terrorism is 'new' has been debated. The view that new terrorism is organized differently and is characterized by an international network of loosely connected cells and support networks rather than by a hierarchical command and control structure located in a specific country or region has been countered by assertions that 'traditional' terrorist groups like the Provisional IRA accorded a considerable degree of autonomy to its cells.

Religion is a fundamental feature of contemporary terrorist activity. However, a religious motive underpinning terrorism is not a new phenomenon and can be traced back to the Zealots of the first century. Additionally, indiscriminate mass-casualty attacks have long been a feature of terrorism.

State reaction to terrorism

Key idea (5)

The state response to terrorism commonly takes the form of anti-terrorist legislation which may prejudice civil and political liberties.

States that are faced with terrorist campaigns may adopt a range of responses to counter the problem. These responses are usually contained in anti-terrorist legislation. In the USA this comprised of the 2001 Patriot Act which was made permanent by the 2005 USA Patriot Improvement and Reauthorization Act.

The main legislation in the United Kingdom is the 2000 Terrorism Act, the 2001 Anti-terrorism, Crime and Security Act, the 2006 Terrorism Act, the 2008 Counter-terrorism Act, and the 2011 Terrorism, Prevention and Investigation Measures Act.

Anti-terrorist legislation typically contains a number of features that are designed to limit the capacity of terrorist organizations to operate. Measures of this nature include:

▶ The regulation of travel and movement either to and from a country (such as powers to exclude or deport) or within it (such as surrounding city centres with 'rings of steel' to monitor those who seek entry)

- ► The prohibition of organizations directly associated with terrorism: we refer to this procedure as *proscribing*

- ► Extended police powers (in areas that include stop and search of persons or property, the periods suspects can be held for questioning and to facilitate the gathering of intelligence)

- ► Changes to the judicial process (such as internment or the abandonment of trial by jury)

- ► The imposition of restrictions on the freedom of expression (for example, the UK's 2006 Terrorism Act created the offence of 'glorifying terrorism', which may embrace declarations of support for a political cause associated with terrorism or attempts by academics to explain why groups may resort to violence to advance their political objectives)

- ► Censorship (such as the broadcasting ban imposed in the UK in 1998 designed to prevent members of Sinn Féin from live television broadcasts in order to deny terrorists (in this case the IRA) the 'oxygen of publicity')

- ► The formation of specialist police units (for example, the UK's Bomb Squad, established in 1971 and renamed the Anti-terrorist squad in 1976)

- ► International co-operation (including bi- and multilateral agreements on matters such as extradition, exchanges of information and intelligence between national police and security organizations)

There are, however, problems associated with anti-terrorist legislation. It often entails the use of coercive responses to terrorism rather than addressing the root causes as to why individuals may be tempted to join terrorist groups or condone their activities. This suggests that measures designed to appeal to 'hearts and minds' and to prevent radicalism offer a more productive way to tackle terrorism.

Additionally, measures pursued by liberal democratic political systems against terrorism must balance the requirements of security against the reduction of civil and political liberties that they inevitably involve. As we have already highlighted in this chapter, a particular problem is that legislation designed to outlaw terrorism fails to draw an adequate distinction between this activity and direct action and may enable the state to prohibit the activities of almost any group that uses some form of physical activity to further its cause.

A further example of how anti-terrorist legislation may erode civil and political liberties relates to creating a specific offence of terrorism. The activities associated with terrorism have always been unlawful in all countries, being catered for crimes that include murder and manslaughter. However, serious crimes of this nature are not always easy to prove in court, whereas a more nebulous crime of terrorism is easier to prove. This runs the risk that criminal sanctions may be unfairly applied against citizens whose actions have offended the state but where there is insufficient evidence to secure a conviction for traditional crimes.

In liberal democratic countries, the judiciary is often called upon to act as arbiters to ensure that the balance between security and liberty is struck correctly and to intervene if it is not. In the UK, for example, provisions contained in the 2001 Anti-terrorism, Crime and Security Act that permitted the internment of foreign nationals suspected of connections with terrorism were struck down by the Law Lords in 2004 as incompatible with the European Convention on Human Rights. This led the government to abandon this initiative and enact new legislation (the 2005 Prevention of Terrorism Act) which replaced internment with control orders.

Why are terrorist campaigns hard to counter?

Key idea (6)

The structure of terrorist organizations and the tactics used by terrorists make it hard for states to effectively combat terrorist campaigns.

Terrorist activities pose particular problems for liberal democracies since those who intend to use violence to further their aims are able to take advantage of the freedoms found in such systems of government (such as the freedoms of association, speech and movement) to recruit members and plan their operations.

Additionally, the manner in which terrorist organizations function and the tactics that they pursue also make it difficult for states to counter their activities. The use of, for example, cell structures makes it difficult for states to monitor these organizations and undertake actions to thwart their violence.

A particular problem that states subjected to violence associated with al-Qaeda have had to deal with has been the decentralized nature of the organization. The American bombing of al-Qaeda training camps in Afghanistan in the wake of the 9/11 attacks resulted in the fragmentation of the organization whose members were sent back to their own countries to wage jihad there. Further changes affecting the recruitment of activists hindered states' responses. The Madrid bombings in 2004, for example, were carried out by activists recruited from the local population. These recruits slipped under the scrutiny of the police radar that was focused on persons from abroad suspected of harbouring al-Qaeda sympathies.

In recent years, terrorist organizations have constantly adjusted their tactics. Responses that include the removal of litter bins in airports and train stations in the UK make it harder for terrorists to plant bombs in such receptacles, but the use of suicide bombers renders this initiative redundant.

The 9/11 attacks in America heightened airline security, to which terrorists responded by planting bombs in trains (Madrid 2004, or the London Underground system in 2005). Security measures were then introduced at railway stations (including the deployment of sniffer dogs to detect explosive devices). In 2007, a motor vehicle loaded with liquid gas canisters was driven into the glass doors of Glasgow airport in an attempt to blow up the building. In response, concrete blocks were erected around the perimeters of many UK airports to prevent vehicle access. In all of these examples, it appeared that the state was one step behind the terrorists, reacting to their latest act of violence rather than being able to prevent them from being carried out in the first place.

Dig Deeper

Chaliand, G. and Blin, A. (2007) *A History of Terrorism: From Antiquity to Al Qaeda.* California: University of California Press.

Combs, C. (2009) *Terrorism in the Twenty-first Century.* Harlow: Longman, 5th ed.

Hoffman, B. (2006) *Inside Terrorism.* New York: Columbia University Press.

della Porta, D. (1995) *Social Movements, Political Violence and the State.* Cambridge: Cambridge University Press.

Fact-check

1 The terrorist group blamed for the attacks on New York and Washington (2001), Madrid (2004) and London (2005) was:
   a The Provisional IRA
   b ETA
   c Al-Qaeda
   d The Angry Brigade

2 Which two terms are often seen as the distinguishing features of 'new' terrorism:
   a Inspired by a religious imperative and decentralized
   b Inspired by a nationalist imperative and centralized
   c Inspired by a revolutionary imperative and secretive
   d Inspired by a hatred of politicians and organized over the internet

3 The word that describes violence directed randomly at the general public is termed:
   a Targeted
   b Unlawful
   c Indiscriminate
   d Disorganized

4 In the UK, what innovation to anti-terrorist powers was provided in the 2001 Anti-terrorism, Crime and Security Act:
   a Control orders
   b Internment
   c Deportation
   d Detention without trial

5 The organization Eta seeks independence for:
   a Spain
   b Gibraltar
   c South-West France
   d Catalonia

6 Which event brought to an end the 'Troubles' in Northern Ireland:

   a The Easter Rising

   b The Partition of Ireland

   c The visit of President Clinton

   d The Good Friday Agreement

Glossary

ACCOUNTABILITY: this procedure requires an individual or organization to whom power has been delegated to submit to the scrutiny of another body or bodies to answer for the actions that are intended to be undertaken or which have already taken place. The scrutinizing body possesses sanctions that can be used if those actions are considered to be unacceptable.

ADVERSARIAL POLITICS: a state of political affairs based around conflict between political parties who put forward differing policies underpinned by contrasting political ideologies. It makes for a situation in which one party is automatically inclined to reject the views and opinions put forward by its opponents as a matter of principle.

AFFIRMATIVE ACTION: measures that a state may adopt to give preferential treatment in terms of matters such as employment to social groups who have traditionally experienced discrimination based upon factors such as class, gender or race.

ARAB SPRING: a series of popular uprisings in a number of Arab Nations that commenced in 2010 when a young Tunisian, Mohamed Bouazizi, burned himself to death as a protest against his treatment by the state authorities. This prompted protests in Tunisia that led to the overthrow of the President in 2011. These protests spread to neighbouring countries and resulted in the ousting of the rulers of Libya and Egypt, the resignation of the President of Yemen and the initiation of a civil war in Syria.

ARM'S LENGTH BODIES: a range of organizations and agencies that perform functions of government but which are not government departments. Sometimes referred to as Quasi-autonomous Non-governmental Organizations (QUANGOs), they include executive agencies that were set up in the wake of the 'Next Steps' programme that derived from a report written by Robin Ibbs in 1988.

AUTHORITY: the ability of a body (typically a public official) to secure compliance to its decisions due to general acceptance on the part of those who are instructed to undertake a course of action that the person issuing commands has the right to do so. Obedience to instructions is secured as the result of the moral force possessed by the person that issues them as opposed to the application of coercive sanctions.

BICAMERAL LEGISLATURES: these consist of a law-making body composed of two separate debating chambers (such as the House of Commons and the House of Lords that constitute the UK's parliament). A law-making body that consists of only one debating chamber is referred to as a **unicameral legislature**.

CHECKS AND BALANCES: a system of government whereby the functions performed by one of the three branches of government (see **separation of powers** below) were subject to scrutiny by one or both of the other two branches. This process could result in overturning the actions undertaken by the branch that was subject to scrutiny.

CIVIL DISOBEDIENCE: this method of protest is a form of **direct action** (see entry below) that deliberately rules out the use of violence to further a group's objectives, and is thus sometimes referred to as 'non-violent direct action'. One example of this is the refusal to obey a law that protesters feel to be immoral or unjust.

CIVIL RIGHTS: guarantees (usually contained within a constitution) that govern the relationship between citizens of a particular country and its government. Civil rights protect citizens against arbitrary conduct and typically provide for a range of personal freedoms (such as the freedom of speech, assembly and religion) that all citizens can enjoy.

COHABITATION: a term applied to a situation in which the president of a country is forced to appoint a prime minister not from his own party. This arises when the legislature is dominated by a party that does not support the president.

COLLECTIVE MINISTERIAL RESPONSIBILITY: the relationship between the entire executive branch of government and the legislature, one aspect of which is that if a vote of 'no confidence' in the government is passed by the legislature, all members of the government are required to resign.

COLLECTIVISM: this political doctrine views groups rather than individuals as the key focus of political action. Governments should place objectives that affect the lives of large numbers of people (such as the alleviation of poverty) above promoting the ability of individuals to pursue their self-interests regardless of the plight of others. Collectivism is associated with the ideology of socialism.

CONFEDERATION: a political structure in which a group of nations agree to cooperate to achieve common aims but which do not cede any significant degree of power to the central body responsible for coordinating the activities of the constituent nations.

CONSOCIATIONALISM: this entails the creation of a political structure that enables political power within a nation to be shared between conflicting groups whose divisions may derive from ethnicity, religion, culture or language. The aim of such arrangement (which has been practiced in Northern Ireland since 1998) is to prevent historic divisions tearing a nation apart, which would be likely to occur if one group was able to exercise total power over the other(s).

CONSTITUTION: a constitution (sometimes referred to as 'Basic Law') provides a framework within which a country's system of government is conducted, establishing rules that those who exercise the functions of government have to obey. This framework may be contained within one specific document (in which case the constitution is said to be 'codified') or it may exist within a range of sources, as is the case with the UK's uncodified constitution.

CONSULTATION: procedures whereby citizens can make their views known on particular political issues. However, these opinions are not binding on policy-makers, who merely agree to listen to what is being said.

CORE EXECUTIVE: bodies, agencies and procedures that are responsible for coordinating policy and managing conflict within national government. In the UK, this embraces an array of actors other than the prime minister and cabinet to include the Treasury, Bank of England, Whitehall, government departments, leaders of insider pressure groups and informal meetings organized around the prime minister.

CROSS MEDIA OWNERSHIP: the ownership of a diverse range of media outlets (such as newspapers, radio and television) by a single individual or corporation. This situation may limit the diversity of information received by the public on political issues and also gives the owner considerable political influence.

DEALIGNMENT: a process that describes the loosening of established attachments towards a political party by voters. It may entail partisan dealignment (in which voters detach themselves from the party they have traditionally supported) or class dealignment (in which the historic ties between a social class and a political party are reduced in intensity). Both of these processes may be a prelude to realignment in which social groups form an attachment with a political party with which they were not formerly identified.

DELEGATED LEGISLATION: in the UK this refers to law that is written by civil servants, the authority to do so being derived from an Act of Parliament (which is termed 'primary legislation'). Typically, delegated legislation adds detail and substance to a more general provision contained in primary legislation. Statutory Instruments are one form of delegated legislation.

DEMOCRATIC POLITICAL SYSTEM: a democratic political system is one in which the citizens are the ultimate source of political power. Governments are chosen by the people and the actions they undertake are accountable to the people, who have the right to remove them from office.

DEVOLUTION: this entails the transfer of power from a superior to an inferior political authority. The dominance of the former is maintained through its ability to take back the power that has been ceded to the subordinate authority.

DIRECT ACTION: a method of protest that entails the use of some form of physical action to further the objectives of the protesters. The tactics involved in direct action may be directed against items of public policy or those pursued by business concerns and may entail confrontation. A consumer boycott is an example of direct action that seeks to alter the commercial practices of private companies.

DOMINANT PARTY SYSTEMS: a situation in which one political party regularly wins election contests. It differs from a one-party state (where only one political party is allowed to function) as other parties are free to openly operate but they lack the level of electoral support to enable them to win election contests.

EQUALITY: this term suggests that all citizens should be equal in terms of the **civil rights** (see entry above) and liberties that they possess and also in terms of the opportunities that they possess to achieve their full potential in life. The latter aspect of equality seeks to remove impediments to success based upon various forms of discrimination experienced by disadvantaged social groups.

EXIT POLLS: a form of opinion poll where the voter is asked who he or she has supported as they leave the polling station. Their aim is to enable the media to predict who has won an election contest before the votes are counted.

FACTION: a formally organized group that exists within a political party. It seeks to promote its ideology and policies as the official views of the political party within which it is located.

FEDERAL SYSTEM OF GOVERNMENT: a system of government in which sovereignty (which may be defined as the exclusive right to make and enforce laws) is divided between national and sub-national units of government, each of which have their own spheres of responsibility into which the other may not intrude. The American system divides powers in this manner between the federal government headed by the President of the United States and fifty state governments.

FIRST-PAST-THE-POST ELECTORAL SYSTEM: in order for a candidate to be elected to a public office under this system, all that is required is for him or her to come top of the poll. Successful candidates are not required to obtain an overall majority of the votes that are cast in an election contest.

FOURTH ESTATE: in countries with **liberal democratic political systems** (see entry below), this term is used to describe the role of the media as the guardian of that country's constitution and the values that underpin it. A key role associated with this activity is scrutinizing and making public the actions undertaken by government, and so requires the media to be free and independent and be able to exercise freedom of speech without political interference from the government.

FUNCTIONAL REPRESENTATION: a legislative body whose composition is based on the representation of specific groups that exist within a country, such as culture, commerce, industry and trade unions. The *Seanad* in Ireland is partly constituted on the basis of functional representation.

GLOBALIZATION: this term refers to the increasing integration of nations, which is reflected in a range of activities that include social, cultural, political and economic affairs. An especially important aspect of this trend is the emergence of a global economy in which the economies of separate nations have increasingly become interdependent.

GOVERNMENT: the institutions within a nation that are concerned with making, implementing and enforcing political decisions. Baron Montesquieu (see **separation of powers** below) referred to the existence of three branches of government – the legislative, executive and judicial branches.

HUMAN RIGHTS: entitlements that are designed to safeguard an individual from interference by other citizens or by the government. Unlike **civil rights** (see entry above), human rights consist of privileges that should be available to all human beings, regardless of their country of residence. An important statement of human rights is contained in the European Convention for the Protection of Human Rights and Fundamental Freedoms that was drawn up by the European Council in 1950 and which, in the UK, was incorporated into the 1998 Human Rights Act.

INCUMBENCY: a person who already holds public office and who puts him- or her-self forward for re-election to that office.

INDIVIDUAL MINISTERIAL RESPONSIBILITY: the formal relationship between a minister and the government department of which he or she is the political head. In the UK, the minister is ultimately accountable to parliament for the actions of his or her department and may be forced to resign if an error is made, even though the minister was not personally responsible for it.

INDIVIDUALISM: this political doctrine holds that the role of government should be limited and should not make unnecessarily interventions in the lives of its citizens that prevent them from pursuing their individual interests and achieving their own self-fulfilment. Historically, this principle was associated with the ideology of liberalism.

IRON TRIANGLE: a term used in America to denote the close ties that exist between an interest group, the government department or agency associated with the concerns promoted by that group and the Congressional committee charged with exercising responsibility for that area of activity. The ties that exist between these three parties are those of interdependent self-interest.

JUDICIAL REVIEW: in countries with codified constitutions (see **constitution** above) this process enables the judiciary to determine if an act proposed or being undertaken by an authority exercising the powers of government is compatible with the letter or spirit of the constitution. If the court believes this not to be the case, the action may be set aside and rendered null and void. In countries without codified constitutions (such as the United Kingdom), the process of judicial review is more limited in scope, being confined to assessing whether an action undertaken by a public body has followed the correct procedures as laid down in law.

LEGITIMACY: when applied to **political systems** (see entry below), this term refers to popular acceptance of a ruler's right to govern. In the UK, a government's legitimacy is based upon an election victory, which bestows upon it the right to take political decisions that citizens are expected to obey regardless of whether they support them.

LIBERAL DEMOCRATIC POLITICAL SYSTEM: a political system in which a small group of people take decisions on behalf of all citizens within a particular country. Their right to rule is bestowed on them through the process of elections, which also serve as mechanisms to ensure that they are accountable to the people for the actions they undertake. Rulers exercise power with the consent of a country's citizens and govern in their name until their right to govern is withdrawn as the consequence of a subsequent election contest.

LOBBYING: a process that seeks to influence the content of public policy through a process of communication between citizens and policy-makers with the intention of influencing the latter's decisions. This communication may be performed directly by organized groups or through intermediaries, whom we refer to as lobbyists, who are employed by a group to further its aims.

MANDATE: the claim by a government that it has the right to carry out policies that were put forward during in election campaign in official pronouncements such as election manifestos because the public, by voting the government into office, expressed its support for these policies and wished to see them put into operation.

NEW PUBLIC MANAGEMENT (NPM): this term embraces a number of reforms initiated during the 1980s in the UK and America that sought to provide efficiency and value for money in the delivery of public policy. Specific policies associated with NPM included the decentralization of service delivery to agency heads (who would operate within centrally determined constraints such as cash limited budgets), the introduction of performance indicators (or targets) to measure the attainment of objectives, the privatization or outsourcing of public policy delivery to alternative service providers (including the private sector) and the promotion of consumerism as the mechanism through which the public would exert control over the operations of public services.

NON-GOVERNMENTAL ORGANIZATIONS (NGOs): private bodies that are free from control exerted by governments and who seek to influence the content of national and international policy. They are typically non-profit-making and non-violent, and were recognized in the 1945 United Nations Charter as bodies that were entitled to a voice in the United Nations, thus making them 'official' organizations. They may be based in one country but increasingly operate on the international stage.

OLIGARCHIC POLITICAL SYSTEM: a political system in which power is held by a small group of persons who wield it in their own interests (often of a material nature) rather than seeking to advance a political or religious ideology. The actions of those who exercise power are subject to no meaningful control by the citizens of the country.

PARLIAMENTARY SYSTEM OF GOVERNMENT: this term refers to a political structure in which the executive branch of government is drawn from members of the legislative branch and is collectively accountable to the legislature for its actions.

PARTICIPATION: a situation in which citizens have the opportunity to share the role of decision-taking alongside the personnel who operate within the formal institutions of local, state or national government. Measures that include access to information and the ability to hold decision-makers to account for their actions serve to adjust the power relationship between citizens and government to the advantage of the former.

POLITICAL CULTURE: the values and attitudes that are shared by citizens in any one country regarding political behaviour. A country's political culture establishes the 'rules of the game' that guide the conduct of its political affairs.

POLITICAL IDEOLOGY: a term that refers to the set of principles and core values that underpin the conduct of politicians and political parties. In particular, ideology defines the vision of the society that party leaders and their supporters wish to create.

POLITICAL OBLIGATION: this concept explains why and under what circumstances citizens are required to obey the decisions that are formulated by the government of the state in which they live.

POLITICAL SPECTRUM: a model used to differentiate political ideologies and to identify the differences and similarities that exist between them. The terms 'Right', 'Left' and 'Centre' are used to denote the stances that different ideologies adopt towards political, social and economic change: the Right opposes fundamental changes in these areas, the Centre endorses gradual reform and the Left desires more rapid and fundamental alterations to be made to them.

POLITICAL SYSTEM: the institutions, procedures and relationships that are involved in the processes of setting the political agenda, formulating policy and taking decisions. The word 'system' implies that the component parts of the decision-making process form part of an integrated structure. In the UK, the key components of the political system include the formal institutions of government (the prime minister, cabinet, civil service and parliament) and agencies such as the media that exert influence over political actions.

POLITICAL TOLERATION: this term refers to prohibitions imposed by the state on political behaviour that poses a threat to the state or that is designed to protect its citizens from intimidatory or violent actions

POLITICS: the study of human behaviour within a group context. It is concerned with issues that include inter-group relationships, the management of groups, the operations collective decision-making processes and the implementation and enforcement of decisions (especially those made by governments).

POWER: a body that exercises power has the ability to force another party to obey its instructions regardless of whether it wishes to do so or not. Compliance is secured through the possession of sanctions that can be deployed against a party that refuses to do as it is told by the body that wields power.

PRAGMATISM: this refers to political conduct that responds to issues as and when they arise, arriving at decisions that are not underpinned by any principles derived from **political ideology** (see above).

PRESIDENTIAL SYSTEM OF GOVERNMENT: a political structure in which different personnel compose the executive and legislative branches of government. The executive is not drawn from the legislative branch of government and is elected separately from the legislature.

PROPORTIONAL REPRESENTATION: an objective that seeks to ensure that the composition of a legislative body closely reflects (or is arithmetically proportionate to) the popular vote that was cast in an election contest. In the UK, for example, this means that if a party wins 50% of the votes that were cast in a general election, it should obtain 50% of the membership of the House of Commons.

PSEPHOLOGY: the scientific study of voting behaviour that seeks to explain why an elector supports a particular political party.

REFERENDUM: this procedure places an item of public policy before citizens who are requested to indicate (typically by voting 'yes' or 'no') as to whether they support or oppose the course of action that is the subject of the referendum.

RULE OF LAW: a concept that regulates the conduct of the state towards its citizens whereby any interventions into their lives are based upon clearly laid-down procedures embodied in the law that has universal application -- it applies equally to all citizens, and no person or state official can operate outside of the obligations it imposes on their behaviour. This concept also regulates the conduct of individual citizens towards each other.

SEPARATION OF POWERS: a theory advanced by the eighteenth century French lawyer, Baron Montesquieu, who argued in a work entitled *De l'Esprit des Lois (The Spirit of the Laws)* that tyranny was most effectively avoided if the three branches of government (the legislative, executive and judicial branches) were separate from each from the other and were performed by different bodies.

SLEAZE: the abuse of power by elected holders of a public office who use their position for personal gain (usually financial or sexual) or to advance the fortunes of their political party. The term also embraces attempts to cover up inappropriate behaviour of this kind. In the UK, an example of sleaze was the revelation in 2009 of the expense claims submitted by a number of Members of Parliament, some of which were morally dubious and others of which were illegal.

SOCIAL MEDIA: a method of communication between groups or communities that uses a variety of web-based technologies such as blogs and websites using platforms that include Facebook and Twitter. Information disseminated in this way can reach a mass audience in a relatively short space of time and may be put to political purposes, in particular to mobilize protests.

SOCIAL MOVEMENTS: these bodies seek to influence the content of national and international policy. However, they are more loosely organized than pressure groups and non-governmental organizations, and their concerns are typically broader, bringing together a range of compatible concerns under one umbrella movement and aiming to instil new moral values within society that underpin these concerns. Social movements often utilize methods of protest such as **direct action** (see entry above) to further their objectives.

STATE: a state consists of a wide range of permanent official institutions that are responsible for the organization of communal life within a particular country. In the UK these consist of the civil service, police, courts, military, parliament and local government. The Head of State is the monarch.

TENDENCY: the existence of opinion within a political party that, typically, opposes the leadership's views on key policy issues. Those associated with a tendency share common sentiments regarding policy but (unlike a **faction** – see above) do not have formal organization.

TERRORISM: this is an imprecise term but is applied to groups that utilize violence (or the threat of violence) to achieve a political objective. Violence may be directed against governments or against the practices of commercial organizations and may either be targeted against those who are deemed to be the enemy that the terrorist group wishes to defeat or directed randomly at the general population, hoping to place them in a state of fear and put thus pressure on policymakers to give in to the terrorists' demands.

TOTALITARIAN POLITICAL SYSTEMS: political systems in which the state controls every aspect of the political, social, cultural and economic life of its citizens. Power is wielded by an elite who, typically, govern the state according to an ideology that is rigidly (and often coercively) enforced to the detriment of civil and political liberties and human rights.

TRUSTEE MODEL OF REPRESENTATION: a model that suggests that a person elected to a public office should be able to exercise independent judgement on issues that arise for consideration. A representative is not required to slavishly follow the wishes and opinions of those who elected him or her.

WHISTLEBLOWING: actions undertaken by an employee of an organization in the public or private sectors who leak information they obtain as a consequence of their employment to the general public. They may do this directly or indirectly through sources such as the media. When applied to the activities of government, this action may be justified by the whistleblower's belief that the public have the right to know what the government is doing in the name of the public, but which it would prefer to keep secret.

Index

Answers to fact-check questions

Chapter 1
1 b

2 b

3 a

4 d

5 a

6 b

Chapter 2
1 c

2 b

3 a

4 d

5 c

6 b

Chapter 3
1 c

2 a

3 a

4 b

5 c

6 c

Chapter 4
1 d

2 c

3 c

4 c

5 d

6 b

Chapter 5
1 d

2 b

3 c

4 a

5 b

6 c

Chapter 6
1 a

2 a

3 c

4 d

5 c

6 a

Chapter 7
1 c

2 b

3 d

4 a

5 b

6 c

Chapter 8
1 c

2 b

3 a

4 b

5 b

6 d

Chapter 9
1 b

2 a

3 c

4 b

5 d

6 a

Chapter 10	Chapter 13	Chapter 16
1 c	1 a	1 c
2 b	2 c	2 a
3 b	3 b	3 c
4 b	4 c	4 d
5 c	5 d	5 d
6 d	6 c	6 d

Chapter 11	Chapter 14
1 b	1 c
2 a	2 d
3 d	3 d
4 b	4 c
5 c	5 b
6 b	6 b

Chapter 12	Chapter 15
1 c	1 c
2 a	2 b
3 b	3 d
4 d	4 b
5 a	5 a
6 d	6 b